YOUR FIRST POWERBOAT

YOUR FIRST POWERBOAT

HOW TO FIND, BUY, AND ENJOY THE BEST BOAT FOR YOU

BOB ARMSTRONG

International Marine / McGraw-Hill

Camden, Maine • New York • Chicago • San Francisco • Lisbon • London • Madrid • Mexico City • Milan
New Delhi • San Juan • Seoul • Singapore • Sydney • Toronto

The McGraw·Hill Companies

Library of Congress Cataloging-in-Publication Data

Armstrong, Bob, 1937–
    Your first powerboat : how to find, buy, and enjoy the best boat for you /
Bob Armstrong.
        p.   cm.
    Includes index.
    ISBN 978-0-07-149673-5 (pbk. : alk. paper)
    1. Motorboats.   2. Motorboats—Maintenance and repair.   3. Boats and
boating.   I. Title.

GV835.A79   2008
387.2'31—dc22   2008001946

1 2 3 4 5 6 7 8 9 10 11 12 13 14 15 16 17 18 19 20 21 DOC/DOC 0 9 8

ISBN 978-0-07-149673-5
MHID   0-07-149673-4

Photographs and illustrations courtesy the author unless otherwise indicated.

For questions regarding the content of this book, go to
www.internationalmarine.com.

McGraw-Hill books are available at special quantity discounts to use as premiums
and sales promotions or for use in corporate training programs. To contact a
representative, please visit the Contact Us pages at www.mhprofessional.com.

This book is printed on acid-free paper.

CONTENTS

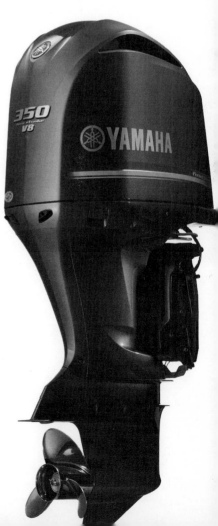

There's an old joke about owning a boat that goes, "The two happiest days in a boatowner's life are the day he buys it and the day he sells it." Okay, so it isn't *that* funny. But, as is often the case with such old chestnuts, it reflects some elemental truths: Having a boat of your own can produce nearly limitless joy, and yet owning a boat can also be such a royal pain at times that only getting rid of it brings relief.

This book is meant to make that first day even happier by helping you find the best deal, helping you avoid "buyer's remorse," and helping you get the most boat for your money. It can also help postpone that second day by guiding you toward a boat that is best suited for your circumstances at the moment—so you shouldn't even think of parting with it until you're ready for a different, probably bigger, boat.

The book is based on practical experiences that span many decades, and it contains lessons that were often painful because I learned them the hard way. But they are important lessons that you can learn for yourself quite painlessly by reading them here.

DECISIONS, DECISIONS, DECISIONS

The basic premise derives from advice my father gave me when I was a teenager—a time in which we humans are about as utterly confused as we can be. I was agonizing over what I thought was an unsolvable problem and had myself tied in mental knots that seemed to be tightening by the second. The pain was becoming unbearable, and I guess it showed. "Relax, son," Dad said calmly, patting me on the shoulder. "This won't be the last time you face such a quandary. You'll encounter many, many more. Believe me."

That wasn't quite what I wanted to hear, so I shot him a look that plainly said, "Thanks for nothing!" as I muttered, "If you think that makes me feel better, think again."

So Dad quickly added, "Don't sweat it, son. Life is really nothing more or less than a constant good news/bad news joke." That left me even more confused, so I asked him what he meant.

He explained that while life can appear to be complicated at times, at nearly every turn we encounter choices that, as confusing as they may seem, are really simple and straightforward, because these choices can usually be resolved by basic "take it or leave it" decisions that he assured me would be obvious if I would only look closely enough to see both the upsides and the downsides to each—the good news and bad news, as it were. He added that recognizing the downsides was not dwelling on the negative but rather accepting reality. He further cautioned me that while unbridled optimism can be an admirable quality, plunging ahead on the basis of seeing only the up-side of any situation is almost always folly. "The real key to success," he explained, "is carefully weighing the inherent good every situation presents against the bad it almost always also entails. And if, in your opinion, the upside outweighs the downside, go for it! Otherwise, you should walk away.

"Remember that, son," he said with a stern look. "No matter how much you may think you want something, if its upside doesn't clearly outweigh its downside, you *have* to walk away!"

But just as I was beginning to believe I had been handed a key to nirvana, my fa-ther brought me quickly back to earth with another brutal truth: "You'll find the whole process amazingly easy," he said. Then, as his stern look turned into a slight grin, he added, "About 80% of the time."

"And what about the other 20%?" I asked, as his grin broadened to a full-blown smile that puzzled me because I couldn't see anything about this discussion that was at all amusing.

"You'll just have to do a little more work," he answered (which explained the growing smile—my father loved to see me work!), quickly adding, "but the results should be worth it."

When I pressed him for details, he said, "Sometimes you'll discover that the good news and the bad news of a situation will balance almost perfectly, so the correct de-cision won't be obvious. In that case, you'll have to do two equally important things: First, make sure you have uncovered *all* the information you need—that you haven't missed a single detail, no matter how in-significant it may appear. Sometimes the discovery of just one more tiny scrap of data can tip the scale. Second, consider your personal preferences and needs. Some

qualities that are generally regarded as bad news might not be so wrong for you. And, the opposite applies as well. Think about it: We all love sweets; sugar is good! But dia-betics have to avoid the stuff. The truth is, son, nothing in this world is equally good for all people all of the time. But if you do your homework without fail, and do it thoroughly in every instance, you'll make the right choices."

Still not sure whether I'd been given an amazing insight or merely another puzzle to solve, I couldn't help but ask one more question: "And what happens if I'm *not* right?"

"You'll be able to live with yourself quite comfortably," Dad explained, "because whatever the result, you'll know in your heart and mind that you did everything you could to make the situation right. If it turns out to be wrong, that won't be your fault. Sometimes things just don't work out. But if you've done everything you should have—if you've applied 'due diligence' as your uncle, the lawyer, likes to call it—there will be no blame attached and no reason to kick yourself. You'll have to accept respon-sibility, of course; the decision was yours. But don't assume *blame*, because it will be something that couldn't be avoided.

"Remember, it's a three-step process: First, get *all* the facts, the good news and the bad. Second, weigh those facts carefully while also considering your personal likes and needs. Then, and *only* then, take the third step, which is to make your decision. Once you've made that decision, stand by it. Don't waffle or try to second-guess yourself. Follow this procedure every time, and you really can't go wrong."

My father's advice has served me well over the years, and I have sorely regretted the consequences every time I concluded that a certain situation was an exception to the rule. The way I see it now (with the amazing clarity of 20/20 hindsight), this rule has *no* exceptions. And so, in this book I've outlined both the potential upsides and also the probable downsides of every aspect involved in buying a powerboat. But the final decisions will still be yours. I can only offer the facts as I know them; the rest is up to you.

K.I.S.S. (I'LL KEEP IT SIMPLE, STRAIGHTFORWARD)

I'm presuming that you are reading this before your very first powerboat purchase, so I have tried to avoid using boating terminology that isn't self-explanatory or fairly common in everyday speech. I don't want to confuse you further by using jargon you don't yet understand. But where using a potentially unfamiliar term was impossible, I've included a definition right then and there [in brackets] to avoid the need for you to look up a word in a glossary. But even if you've bought a boat or two in the past, chances are, given my many years of experience in the marine industry, I've included some points of view that you may have never even thought about before, practical suggestions that will help you do much better this time. None of it is very complicated; "It isn't rocket science!" But

as is so often the case in specialized fields, there are factors to consider in successfully buying a powerboat that probably would never occur to you if you haven't done it much before.

I also acknowledge that my father was so very right: in many cases, weighing the relative balance between the ups and downs of a situation can be quite personal, something that we each have to do for ourselves—it's a practical demonstration of the truth in that old saying about one person's treasure being another's trash. But you can't make a proper call as to whether any particular point may be treasure or trash for you if you don't have all the information, a full disclosure of the potential good and the potential bad in every situation. So here it is: the good news and bad news regarding every potentially confusing boat-buying situation you might ever be involved with. Or, to state it more simply, here are *all* the truths I believe you should always be aware of when buying a powerboat.

Finally, let me assure you that if you heed the advice I share on the following pages, you should be ready to eliminate or at least drastically reduce any confusion that may arise in the process of buying your new powerboat. Who knows, you might even find that it can be fun!

YOUR FIRST
POWERBOAT

CHAPTER 1

DO YOU REALLY NEED TO BUY A BOAT?

Do I Need to Read This Chapter?

You should read this chapter if you want to discover

- ✔ The commitment owning a boat demands.
- ✔ Valid reasons for owning a boat even when it doesn't really make sense.
- ✔ Viable alternatives to ownership that still provide boating fun.
- ✔ How chartering your boat can make owning it more appealing.

OWNING A BOAT CAN BE A BITTERSWEET PLEASURE

Powerboating is enjoyable, no doubt about it. Zipping across the water in a sleek sport cruiser with a group of friends can provide such a high degree of pleasure that you can actually justify the expense involved. This is *living*! So what is it about boats that can also make owning one such a royal pain?

Boats are unbelievably demanding. And not just of money; a boat also demands huge commitments of time, which is equally important. So even if you have deep pockets, you may learn that a boat you don't have time for can become a serious problem because boats don't wear out; rather, they too often rust (or corrode) away from lack of use. The damp salt air that abounds in so many of our favored boating areas can quickly ruin a boat's mechanical systems if they remain idle for too long.

Powerboats need exercise to remain "healthy" fully as much as we humans do. To keep your boat's mechanical systems in proper working order, you need to run them often—at least a couple of times a month and preferably once a week. And while starting the engine(s) and operating other systems at dockside is better than doing nothing, ideally you should cast off the lines, get underway, and let the systems work under normal load for at least an hour, and more if you can swing it.

Use It or Lose It

If you don't give your boat regular "work-outs," you may discover that the boat you intended to use and care for but didn't will rebel by working improperly (or maybe not at all!) when you finally do manage to get some time aboard.

But do you really need to *own* a boat to enjoy the sport to its fullest? In a word, no. There are many other ways to go power-boating, and I'll outline alternatives later in this chapter. But there are also some other aspects of boat ownership that may be important to you, so before we dismiss the idea completely, we'd better consider them. You can always hire someone to care for your boat and keep everything in a ready-to-go state if you don't have the time to do it yourself.

So here are some very good reasons for buying a boat even if you can't really use it that much.

Five Valid Reasons for Owning a Boat (Even When It Really Isn't Practical)

1. **Perceived status.** People who own boats—"yachtsmen," if you will—seem to be a distinguished lot, so it's reasonable that you might wish to join them. (Understand that in calling them yachts*men*, I'm not being sexist. It's a customary term, just as boats are traditionally referred to as "she," though I'm going to be politically correct and use "it" throughout this book. And while we're on the subject, also know that wherever I use "him" or "himself," it is strictly for simplicity and to save space; the words always also mean "her" or "herself" as well. For the same reason, I'll use "s/he" to mean "she or he." But we also have to face the truth:

the majority of boatowners *are* men—we'll just overlook the reality that more than a few of them had to get a wife's permission to make the purchase.)

Yachtsmen are generally friendly enough, but they do often make a distinction between fellow *boatowners* and the rest of the world. If being a part of this seemingly exclusive group is important to you, then yes, you need to buy a boat of your own.

2. **Pride of ownership.** This is different from the previous reason in that it is less about what other people may think and more about what is important to you. If you live in a house or condo you purchased rather than in a rented dwelling, not for its probable appreciation and your growing equity but because you need a place you can call your own, then owning your boat is probably your best bet, too.

3. **Lack of desire to share.** This is not about greed. It is simply accepting that sharing a prized possession involves being able to live with knowing that at least a few of those with whom you share won't give it the care and respect you know it deserves. If you can't do that—if the thought of having others use (or, in your mind, possibly abuse) your precious "baby" bothers you—don't choose any of the nonownership options discussed later in this chapter.

4. **Tax advantages.** If your boat has a *galley* [kitchen], a *head* [toilet], and at least one *berth* [bed], it can qualify as a second home under current IRS rules and whatever interest you pay on your boat loan becomes tax deductible. I'll outline current regulations in Chapter 5. But because the regulations are always subject to change, you

should check with your tax adviser for specifics as to how they may apply to your situation.

5. **You just want it!** I'm sure there are those who would question the validity of this reason. "You can't have everything you want!" is one of our earliest lessons in life. But to quote my father's sage advice again, he once told me, "You know, son, it actually *is* possible to have everything you want; well, almost, anyway. You just have to be willing to pay the price, which is often simply giving up something else you also want—just not as much. That last aspect is so important because you have to remember that the real cost of things can't always be measured in dollars." So I suggest that if you want to own a boat and are both able *and also willing* to meet all of its attendant costs, go ahead and buy one, even if doing so might seem irrational.

Buying Is Just the Beginning

Those "attendant costs" are by no means trivial, so when making the decision to buy a boat, remember that the purchase is only the beginning. You'll also need the funds to enjoy the boat after it's yours. To help you determine what sort of boat fits your budget, I'm including a blank table you can use to work out the figures for yourself. If you are looking at several boats, you should do a table for each to compare the costs. The shaded boxes don't apply and can be left blank. Initial (or down) payments, for example, don't apply to all categories, and only the total cost of a boat needs to be allocated more extensively. The shaded boxes under the "monthly" column are for items that usually don't involve monthly payments; yet they are shaded lightly so

Don't Forget

Buying a boat simply because it can save some on your income taxes can be a huge mistake in that the overall expense will usually more than offset any tax savings you may gain. The tax deduction is nice, but a very weak reason for buying a boat.

that, if you want to analyze your budget on a cost-per-month basis, you can use them to enter one-twelfth of the annual total.

Fixed costs vary depending on the boat. Insurance premiums usually increase with horsepower and also with length. Dockage, off-season stowage, bottom cleaning and painting, and haulouts and other yard expenses (as well as, in some states, registration fees) also increase with length. The best and worst part of fixed expenses is that they *are* fixed; they remain the same regardless of how much you use the boat. Use it a little, and the cost per hour can be ridiculous. But go boating often enough, and these fixed costs become miniscule on a per-hour basis.

Variable expenses, however, depend entirely on how much you use the boat (though more horsepower usually means greater fuel consumption, so even a few hours on a more powerful boat will cost more). Spend more time aboard, and the variables can't help but increase. The good news here is that the more you use your boat, the more fun you have. So the higher costs are usually worth it.

Also remember that whatever the total cost, you will get some of it back when you sell— although, because production boats depreciate rapidly, not as much as you might hope. So many variables are involved in determining depreciation that it's hard to calculate in advance. Just know it will be a part of the total cost, and the newer the boat you buy, the more it will depreciate. You'll get a proportionately greater return when selling a 10-year-old boat you've had for 5 years than you will when selling a 5-year-old boat you bought new.

Projected Budget for _____ **(your boat's name here)**

ITEM	TOTAL COST	INITIAL PAYMENT	TOTAL FIRST-YEAR COSTS	MONTHLY FIRST-YEAR COSTS	ESTIMATED ANNUAL COSTS, YEARS 2 TO 5	TOTAL 5-YEAR COSTS
COST OF BOAT						
Survey						
Base Price						
Accessories						
Extended Warranties						
Sales Tax						
Interest						
Closing Costs						
Total Cost						
FIXED ANNUAL OPERATING COSTS						
Registration						
Insurance						
Dockage, Home						
Off-Season Storage						
Bottom Care						
Haul/Launch, Winterize, etc.						
Total Fixed Costs						
VARIABLE ANNUAL OPERATING COSTS						
Fuel						
Lube Oil						
Pumpouts						
Cleaning, Waxing						
Charts, Cruising Guides, etc.						
Dockage, Away						
Mechanical Maintenance						
Structural Maintenance						
Unexpected						
Miscellaneous						
Total Variable Costs						
GRAND TOTAL						

VIABLE ALTERNATIVES TO OWNERSHIP

If your objective is to have as much boating fun as you can for the lowest possible cost, I'd say don't buy a boat, because you can more easily achieve this goal with any of the following options.

Renting

Renting can be the least expensive way to go powerboating because you pay only as you go. When you rent a boat, you pay for the following: (1) the use of the boat, with a rental fee that's usually by the hour; (2) the fuel you consume (the rental starts with a full tank—you top it off on return and pay for the fuel you've replaced); and possibly (3) a damage waiver fee similar to the collision damage waiver you can get when you rent a car. But that's it. You pay for what you actually use, nothing more.

Renting presents several potential advantages over owning:

• **Availability.** There are usually rental outlets wherever there's good boating,

Renting is the least expensive way to try different boats to see which type suits you best. It can also get you on the water with the minimum cash outlay. When you realize that a boat you own is your responsibility 24/7/365, and that the note payments, insurance premiums, dockage, maintenance, and other expenses go on and on even when you aren't using the boat, the "pay only as you go" aspects of renting can be appealing.

which means you can enjoy the sport on a wide range of waters. Note the plural: usually you have more than one location to choose from in each locale.

Figure 1-1. Rental outlets usually offer a variety of boats, from runabouts to small cruisers.

Rental boats aren't always in the best of shape. Many rental outfits are mom-and-pop operations with limited capital. They may have insufficient cash to keep up with all the requisite repairs and maintenance, and the quality and condition of their boats can reflect this lack of care.

- **Variety.** Rental fleets are usually varied enough that you can choose among several types of boats.
- **Less work.** When you rent, you don't have to clean the boat after you've used it, much less maintain it—another huge difference from owning.

The Downsides of Renting
Here are some other potential drawbacks to renting:

- **Quality issues.** The boats are used by too many people who think, "It's not *my* boat, and we're only using it just this once, so who cares how we treat it?" This cavalier attitude can compound the quality and condition problems found on some rental boats.
- **Location restrictions.** Rental companies usually limit the geographical area in which you are allowed to use their boats—that is, you have to stay close to "home."
- **Time restrictions.** Time limits are often imposed as well, such as daylight

use only or returning by closing time, which may be as early as 5 p.m.
- **Cost.** Paying by the hour can add up to a lot of money if you go boating frequently, although renting can still be the lowest-cost option if you don't rent too often.

If you want to spend a lot of time on the water, there are better ways than renting.

Boat Clubs
Boat clubs also offer the opportunity to enjoy powerboats without the hassles of owning one. You generally pay an initiation fee when you join and then monthly dues that remain the same regardless of how much you use the boats. If you want to go boating often but can't go frequently enough to justify ownership, joining a club could be the answer. Cleaning the boat and other after-trip maintenance concerns are the club's, not yours, which can take a huge load off your mind—and your busy schedule.

If you go boating often, boat-club membership can provide a very cost-effective way of doing it. Dues are generally less than what you might spend either owning or renting, especially when you figure your expenditure on cost-per-hour-of-enjoyment basis.

An attractive bottom line is not the only advantage to joining a boat club. Consider the following:

- **Few restrictions.** Boat clubs usually offer "unlimited" boating. There are rarely any restrictions on when or how often you can use the boats—you can almost always squeeze some boating time into a busy work and social schedule.
- **Variety.** Most club fleets contain several types of boats, so you can usually select the best boat for the kind of outing you have in mind.
- **Availability.** The larger clubs have more than one location, and your membership is usually good at all of them—a nice plus if you want to go boating in different parts of the country as well as close to home.
- **Training.** Most boat clubs provide access to training. There are many things you'll need to learn if you're new to powerboating, and many boat clubs offer education programs—often including hands-on training—as a membership benefit.

Plan Ahead

The need to reserve early can eliminate spur of the moment outings since trying to get a boat at the last minute can end in disappointment if you discover that all of the boats at your club are in use. But this should be a serious problem only at the busiest times, such as on the Fourth of July or Labor Day weekend, when planning ahead is always the best idea. In many areas, however, *every* weekend can be a busy one; if your work schedule permits, weekday boating presents better opportunities. And the waterways are usually less crowded, too.

Don't Forget

"Unlimited" rarely means *totally* unlimited, however. Despite the promises of nearly every boat club, you'll always be somewhat limited by the availability of any particular boat at any particular time. If another member has requested the boat you want before you enter your request, you won't get it. The solution is to plan ahead and reserve early.

The Downsides of Boat Clubs

While boat clubs offer an attractive way to go boating, nothing in life is perfect, and boat clubs are no exception. Here are some other downsides:

- **Quality issues.** Like boats from rental companies, club boats are used by many different people, so they can also fall victim to the "It's not *my* boat" syndrome—though they do tend to suffer less than rental boats. If you plan to join a boat club, carefully examine some older boats in the fleet to see how well they have been treated and maintained.
- **Location restrictions.** Club boats may not be located as close to home as you could keep a boat of your own or even as close as the nearest rental center. Rental outlets still seem to outnumber clubs, though the boat-club concept is growing steadily and you can now find them all over the United States (and elsewhere).

Fractional Ownership

This is similar to time-sharing in real estate, though in many ways it is better. With fractional ownership, you and (typically) three to seven others own a boat together and share its use. Generally, you are guaranteed a minimum number of uses per month; additional uses at no additional cost—subject to availability—are often also a part of the deal. Actual availability, and how you can use it, varies by organization. Realistically, your guaranteed availability will probably be as much as, or perhaps even more than, the amount of time you have for boating; otherwise, you might be a candidate for 100% ownership.

Other benefits to fractional ownership include:

- **Pride of ownership.** The boat is yours, even if only partially, and thus you gain all the benefits, both real and imagined, that ownership entails.
- **Better boats.** Each user recognizes his or her vested interest in the boat and tends to give it better care than renters or club members give the boats they use.
- **Maintenance and upkeep.** Relax; none of this is your concern because the managing company normally takes care of these details.
- **Guaranteed availability.** Most fractional ownership groups use sophisticated computerized reservation systems to practically guarantee that the boat will be available when you want it.
- **Variety.** Fractional ownership organizations usually have multiple locations, and it is often possible to use a fractional ownership boat at a more exotic locale than your home port. And, some fractional ownership plans move the boats to different home ports at different times

Quick   Tips

Fractional ownership lets you partly own a boat for a small percentage of the cost of being a sole owner. In round numbers, fractional ownership generally costs less per month than the insurance and dockage alone would cost if you owned the boat completely.

Typically, you buy shares in the corporation or LLC (limited liability company) that is the owner of record, which means that in buying (or selling) your portion of the boat you avoid all the hassles of sales tax and registration details, which are handled by the corporation or LLC. Admittedly, this isn't a huge benefit, but *anything* that saves you some hassles has to be worth considering.

of the year, so you gain some variety automatically.

The Downsides of Fractional Ownership
Fractional ownership has its downsides, too:

- **You have to share.** Despite the careful scheduling that computerized reservation systems allow, if a boat has eight owners, seven of them cannot possibly use the boat on any given day. This can mean seven disappointed owners on a particular Fourth of July or holiday weekend.

- **Location, location, location.** Given that fractional ownership programs are not that widespread as yet, the nearest available boat may not be as close to home as you could keep a boat you own completely.

Leasing

Some boat-sharing programs involve leasing rather than owning. The result is the same: you have a guaranteed number of uses over the duration of your lease, and you get to go boating at a lower cost—you merely lose the ownership aspect. Full-time leasing as an alternative to buying, an option often exercised when acquiring a new car, has also started to surface in the world of boats, though it is still not as common on the waterways as it is on the highways. And yet, boat leasing is steadily becoming more widespread, and for many people it offers a practical alternative to ownership. The specifics vary from lease to lease, but most arrangements result in a flat monthly fee that covers everything but fuel, dockage, and, if required, the crew (if you lease a very large yacht). At the end of the lease, you have the option of simply turning the boat back to the dealer or buying it outright at its depreciated value. Not all makes are available for lease and not all dealers offer the option, so this may not be a realistic alternative. But if the concept intrigues you, it's worth exploring.

The Upsides of Leasing

- **Cost.** The prime advantage of leasing, whether fractional or 100%, is the lower cost. Either way, what you pay each month will be less than what owning the same vessel would cost you, though not always by as much as you might expect.

- **Easy payments.** One payment covers nearly everything. You'll have to pay extra for fuel; it's an inescapable part of powerboating. And with a full-time lease, you'll probably be responsible for dockage (which is usually included in fractional deals). But most lease programs lump everything else into one monthly payment, which can be a huge convenience for busy people.

- **Less work.** Because the lease usually includes routine scheduled maintenance, one major headache of boat ownership is eliminated completely.

- **Fewer hassles.** Leasing also eliminates unknowns. When you buy a boat, you never know just when you may sell it or for how much. With a lease, you know in advance when the contract will end and exactly how much it will cost you in the meantime.

The Downsides of Leasing

- **You build no equity.** How much of a downer this may be is relative; for many it's irrelevant. But it is a factor. At the end of the lease, you will have nothing but receipts (and great memories!) to show for the money you've spent.

- **Availability.** Leasing is not universally available. You might not be able to lease the boat you want anywhere near to where you live.

- **Depreciation.** Because a production boat depreciates so rapidly (see Chapter 3), its value at the end of the lease will be much less. Leasing a boat costs comparatively more than leasing a car.

Partnership

Partnership is about as close to 100% ownership as you can get without owning a boat entirely by yourself. It is a perfect solution

Get Started

When leasing, first, negotiate the boat's selling price. As with buying, you should bargain for the best deal possible. Then, negotiate the boat's value at the end of the lease, a figure that can be quite shocking to newcomers—the depreciation involved can be considerable! The difference is the basis for the lease. Add the peripheral costs involved, including interest, insurance, and maintenance, and then divide the total by the number of months in the lease: that's your monthly payment. It will probably be higher than you would expect but still much less than what it would cost you to own the same boat.

to the "available time" problem since you and your partner will undoubtedly have more time to use the boat collectively than either of you would have individually. Together, you should be able to use, and maintain, a boat sufficiently to keep it in working order.

The Upsides of a Partnership

There can be several other advantages to a partnership:

- **Affordability.** In dividing every expense by two, you can probably own a better boat than either of you could comfortably afford on your own.

- **Location.** You can likely keep the boat closer to where you both live, at a nearby marina or perhaps even behind your or your partner's home if either of you has waterfront property (see Chapter 6).
- **Ease of use.** You can more easily coordinate use of the boat with your available time than you could through any of the previous options.
- **Availability.** This is simply better, period! There's only one other user.
- **Pride of ownership.** Psychologically, owning half a boat is far greater than the one-fourth to one-eighth of a boat you typically have in fractional ownership.

The Downsides of a Partnership

Partnerships have their disadvantages, too. Friction can develop between you and your partner, even if you've been best buddies since preschool. Consider these potential points of conflict:

- **Cleanliness.** You and your partner may have vastly different ideas about what constitutes a properly cleaned vessel.
- **Maintenance.** Similarly, you and your partner may not agree on a desired level of maintenance. Eventually one of you may become quite disgusted by the lack of maintenance and care given the boat by the other.
- **Availability.** Agreeing on who uses the boat when can become quite contentious. It should be simpler to work out a sharing plan for two than for the possibly eight or so owners you might have in a fractional arrangement, but it isn't necessarily so. Not using your boat on a particular holiday or long weekend is much easier to take when there are several other owners who can't use it either.

It's different when you and your family must remain ashore because your one and only partner has your boat—again!

- **The lack of an intervening third party.** In most of the previously listed options, the management company cares for the boat(s), does the scheduling, and settles disputes when necessary.

Partnerships Can Be Delicate

Partnerships can work well. But such a partnership requires compatible individuals who each have a willingness to work out any problems. Is a partnership right for you? Only you and your potential partner can answer this. If you can work it out, owning half a boat is better than owning none and, in many ways, better than owning an entire one by yourself.

Chartering

Chartering is similar to renting, and yet it's also different. You still pay as you go, but chartering involves larger boats and longer periods of use, so the costs are greater. There are *crewed charters* and *bareboat charters*, either of which can get you a boat for a week or more with the inherent prospect of taking a real cruise.

Crewed Charters

Crewed charters provide not only a boat but also the people to operate it, maintain it, and serve you as well. These charters can involve some very large yachts and are perhaps the most expensive way to go boating—at least in the short term. But they can be the answer if you have a limited amount of time but not as limited an amount of money. They can also be the answer if you have the time for a small boat you can own and care for to meet your basic boating needs but still have a yen for

Get Started

When you establish a partnership, put it in writing! No matter how strong your friendship, or how long you've known each other, you need a formal agreement, drawn up by a competent attorney, to clarify the exact nature of your partnership, including the legal structure under which you own the boat together. Each of the possible options has a different effect on such matters as how you would sell your half should you ever need or want to, or what happens if one of you dies. So be sure your attorney explains all the ramifications of each option before you decide—and remember, you need to have this structure in place *before* you buy the boat. Take the time *at the start* to spell out all the other details, too. This way, if problems ever arise, you avoid the often confusing and generally contradictory "s/he said, s/he said" you're left with if you don't have your agreement in writing.

a real cruise now and then, one that's way beyond your small boat's (and perhaps your own) capabilities.

The major downside is that a week on a large (120 feet or so) crewed charter yacht can easily set you back $100,000 or more. And that doesn't include the cost of fuel, food and beverages, dockage wherever you stop, and gratuities for the crew at the end

A crewed charter may be the ultimate in cruising luxury. The crew usually includes a captain, a mate, an engineer, deckhands, a chef, and one or two stewards to anticipate and care for your every need, from mixing and serving drinks to turning down your bed at night and cleaning your stateroom and head in the morning. Couple this with an elegant, luxurious vessel and visits to some exotic ports (you'll also have to include flying to and from the yacht in your total charter cost), and it's like being on a five-star cruise ship, only much less crowded and with far more personalized attention.

One downside of bareboat chartering is that you must provide a résumé of your boating experience to prove that you are competent to handle a vessel of the size and *displacement* (weight) you want to charter. This requirement can rule out bareboat chartering if you are new to the sport and have yet to acquire much experience, though some charter companies also operate cruising schools to teach you enough to qualify.

of the charter. Smaller vessels with a smaller crew are available for less, though you can still easily spend $20,000 plus expenses for a week on one of these less luxurious charters.

Bareboat Charters

Bareboat charters provide you with a boat only. For the duration of your charter, however, it's like having your own. You can go where you want at the pace you want, and do whatever you choose along the way. And yet, when the charter is over, you walk away with no further commitment and no need to even do so much as wash it down. And unlike crewed charters, which usually require that you book

the yacht for at least a week, you can often arrange a bareboat charter for a cruise as short as three days.

Bareboat charters are also enticing for those cruises that might call for more boat than you currently own—though certainly on a scale far less grand than that provided by crewed charters. You can also charter in locales far removed from where you live (such as in Florida, the Bahamas, or the Caribbean in the winter, when your normal boating area up north is too full of ice and your boat is "on the hard"), which makes booking a bareboat a nice bonus plan even if you have a boat of your own.

Bareboat Charters with a Captain

If you are inexperienced, you can hire a boat and also hire a professional (from the charter company's list of approved captains)

Figure 1-2. Chartering an elegant *megayacht* (a vessel 80 feet and up) can give you most of the advantages of owner-ship with few of the disadvantages—at least for a week or so. And though a crewed charter can be expensive—as of this writing, this 177-foot Trinity goes for $290,000 plus expenses for a week in the Mediterranean—this is still way less than the roughly $39 million price tag this beauty carried when new. *(International Yacht Collection)*

Figure 1-3. Bareboat charters often involve a spacious trawler yacht that is seaworthy, comfortable, and an ideal home on the water for the duration of your cruise. *(Southwest Florida Yachts)*

Quick Tips

Timing is everything. Most cruising areas have an off-season, when there is less demand for boats and, consequently, the charter companies operating there lower their rates to attract more business. Not all companies in all areas will do this, however, and even when they do, the reductions are not always that much. But if you want to charter (bareboat or crewed) at the best possible price, it's worth looking into seasonal discounts.

who will run the boat for you, either for the duration of the charter or until s/he feels you are capable of going it on your own. Bareboating with a captain is also often a viable option for shorter cruises, such as by the day or half day, on a larger boat than you could rent—or perhaps operate comfortably on your own.

Chartering the Boat You Own

There's one more aspect of chartering that you should consider. I've left it until last because it's a perfect transition to the remainder of the book, which is all about buying a boat of your own—a worthwhile undertaking despite the aggravation it can sometimes involve. At the beginning of this chapter, I mentioned that powerboats that don't get used enough may eventually become unusable because salt air can all too soon turn moving parts into parts that *used* to move. If you buy a boat and then discover that you are no longer using it enough to keep its mechanical systems working properly, you might think about putting it into charter service. A yacht-management/charter company will book the clients for you and maintain the boat between charters. You can block out, in advance, the periods (days or weeks) you will want the boat for yourself and, of course, your boat will also be available to you at any other time that it isn't already out on charter.

The Upsides of Chartering Your Boat

There are more advantages to chartering a boat you own when you're not using it:

- **Income.** Though I would doubt you'll actually make a huge profit— maintenance, dockage, and other expenses, as well as the charter company's management/booking fees, will be deducted from the gross—the revenue derived from chartering can often offset the bulk of your boat's expenses, thus making the time you use the boat yourself *nearly* cost free.
- **Tax deductions.** Since your chartered boat will be a business, its expenses may be deductible—though the tax laws are complex enough that you'll want the guidance of an accountant or tax adviser, especially if you still use the boat yourself a lot of the time.
- **Your boat won't just sit.** It will get the use it needs to keep moving parts moving. This will assure you of a boat that's always ready to go when you want to use it yourself.

Quick Tips

A charter company may maintain your boat better than you would yourself. Because reputable companies tend to want the boats they offer to be in the best possible, most presentable condition, your boat will usually receive the proper professional maintenance it needs to keep it in tip-top shape at all times.

The Downsides of Chartering Your Boat
There are also some disadvantages to chartering that you should consider:

- **Increased time on the hour meter(s).** Depending on the aggressiveness and marketing savvy of the charter company you choose (and where it is located), your boat may be used more often than you would ever use it yourself. These added hours can cost you when you decide to sell.
- **Increased wear and tear.** The greater use can also take its toll on other parts of the boat; the carpets, upholstery, galley, and head will all be less pristine than if only you use the boat. This is partly from the greater use itself and partly because there will be people using the boat who won't give it the care it deserves, which brings up the following negative.
- **Others will be using *your* boat.** If lack of desire to share was one of the

motives behind your opting to buy your own boat, you'll probably find chartering distasteful. Even if you restrict it to crewed charter or bareboat with captain, there will still be lots of strangers enjoying your baby. And if you charter it bareboat, they'll be operating it, too!

- **Increased insurance costs.** You'll need a different, and probably more expensive, insurance policy because chartering is "commercial use," which is not covered by most yacht policies (see Chapter 11). On the plus side, some charter companies maintain "blanket" policies that cover every boat in their fleet with far greater limits of liability than you'd probably find affordable for a single boat.
- **Increased registration cost.** If your boat is documented, as most boats larger than 30 feet will be (see Chapter 5), you'll need to have the document endorsed for "coastwise"; yachts documented strictly for pleasure cannot be used for commercial purposes. Endorsements for anything but "recreation" normally carry an added cost.
- **Possible loss of your "second home" tax deduction.** Once you make the boat a business, other factors come into play, including the number of days you use the boat yourself relative to the number of days it is in charter service. Realistically, this may not be a downside. Current tax laws allow only one "vacation home," and if you already have one ashore, you have to decide whether the boat or the real estate should be used for the second home deduction you are allowed. But if your boat is a charter business, many more expenses than just the interest will be deductible, so maybe the loss of "vacation home"

Don't Forget

Chances are that you'll opt for chartering the boat you own if you lack enough time to use or maintain it yourself. If so, be sure to place your boat with a company that will not only handle its charter bookings but also properly care for your boat. Some yacht-management companies are less concerned about the maintenance aspects, and even the best of companies have a variety of contractual arrangements ranging from, "we'll report the details of all necessary maintenance and repairs; you have to arrange and pay for the work yourself," to "we'll take care of everything for you." Your percentage of charter income will be less in the latter arrangement (you have to pay for this total care), so you may be tempted to go with an alternate plan. Because one way or another you're ultimately going to pay for your boat's maintenance anyway (and even more if you neglect it!), in the long run it can be to your advantage to select a company that promises to "take care of everything" and then hold them to it with a binding written contract and a watchful eye on the maintenance your boat receives. You may have a smaller cash flow from your charter business if you take this route, but it can still be the best way to go.

status for your boat is no loss at all. Since the tax status of your boat will depend on many factors, many of them complex, you should discuss this matter with your tax adviser or accountant.

While it's far from being an answer to all of the potential downsides of owning a boat, putting yours into charter service can be a win-win situation if you don't get to use it that much yourself.

So let's assume you've decided to spring for buying a boat of your own and move on to eliminating the potential confusion that may be involved.

It's a Wrap

WRAP

✔ Owning a boat can demand huge commitments of money and time.
✔ There are legitimate psychological reasons for owning a boat even when it doesn't make sense economically.
✔ There are viable alternatives to owning when having your own boat is totally out of the question.
✔ Chartering your boat to others can be a practical solution to many of the problems inherent in ownership.

CHAPTER 2

CHOOSING THE RIGHT BOAT

Do I Need to Read This Chapter?

You should read this chapter if you want to discover

- ✔ How to avoid buying the wrong boat.
- ✔ The importance of buying the proper size of boat to suit your current needs.
- ✔ The relative differences in power options.
- ✔ The specialized needs of different types of boating, such as fishing, cruising, and diving.
- ✔ The importance of a sea trial.

THE WRONG BOAT CAN NEVER BE RIGHT

Although you can conduct almost any on-the-water activity aboard anything that floats, you and your passengers will find more enjoyment in a boat that's properly suited for what you want to do. Buying the wrong boat can be as much of a disappointment as marrying the wrong person—and as costly!

Why would anyone do this? A price that couldn't be refused often tops the list. But a gift boat or one that you won in a raffle will ultimately cost you in dockage, insurance, and maintenance. Even a free boat is never a free lunch.

The Case of an Imperfect Fit

I once had a student who had bought a used powerboat at what he called a price

Don't Forget

The wrong boat is never a bargain. If it isn't the boat you really need for what you want to do, it won't be a good deal no matter how low the price.

he couldn't resist—"an unbelievably great deal," he told me. The boat was a real beauty—a 32-foot center-console speedster rigged for fishing and driven by a pair of 250-horsepower (hp) outboards. The hull was a narrow deep V capable of maintaining speed in fairly rough water, and the motors were mounted on hydraulic *jack plates* (adjustable mounts that raise or lower the engines for optimum performance in varying conditions).

After covering the basics, I started to teach him how to trim the motors and use the jack plates to attain the highest possible speed. But no sooner had I begun this phase of instruction than my student said, "I have no desire to go fast, Captain Bob; I just want to putter around on the Intracoastal Waterway and maybe explore the bays and rivers. I'll rarely go out in the ocean either; it scares me out there." In short, the man had bought the wrong boat for what he wanted to do—as wrong as buying a racehorse to give kiddy rides at a petting zoo! The motors were not meant to run for hours at idle, and the boat handled much better when going fast than at low speeds. Needless to say, the guy quickly became disenchanted with powerboating. Soon, he stopped using the boat, and eventually he sold it at a loss because he was so eager to get rid of it.

If this man had bought a boat better suited to his intended use (something roomier, with less horsepower and more creature comforts), he would have enjoyed it more and not been in such a hurry to sell. He had been unable to avoid taking advantage of the "bargain" he saw in the boat's asking price, but as the facts eventually bore out, it was no bargain at all. It was an expensive mistake because it wasn't the right boat for what he wanted to do.

THINGS TO CONSIDER BEFORE YOU BUY
Size

Size matters, but bigger is not necessarily better. Your objective should be to acquire a boat of the proper size for your current needs, one that would satisfy Goldilocks if she were sampling boats: a boat that's "just right."

You should consider the following:

- **The number of people you'll normally take with you.** A boat of 20 feet or less is required to have a *capacity plate* that indicates the maximum number of people it can safely carry as well as the total weight of people and gear it can hold. If your group is on the heavy side, you must consider the total weight limit as more important than the number of people shown, since the U.S. Coast Guard's "average" person weight may no longer be valid in current U.S. society, which is steadily growing heavier. You'll probably want enough capacity to allow for your normal group plus a guest or two. Boats over 20 feet aren't required to have a capacity plate

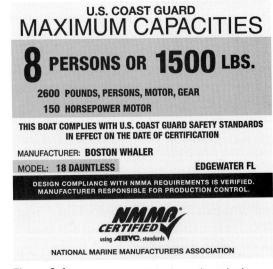

Figure 2-1. A capacity plate shows the maximum load and power a particular hull can handle. This one also shows that the boat is certified by the NMMA (National Marine Manufacturers Association). *(NMMA)*

(though they may anyway), but they will usually state a maximum capacity in the owner's manual or you can use the number of seats as a guide.

• **The waters on which you'll operate.** The larger the boat, the more room it needs around it—and under it, too, because *draft* [the boat's depth below the waterline] usually increases with length. Larger boats cannot go into some waters that smaller boats can. Never buy a boat that's too large to go where you want to.

On the other hand, bigger boats generally can handle the rougher conditions that you're likely to encounter on unprotected waters outside of small bays and lakes. If you're going out on the ocean, you'll need a more solidly built boat with greater *freeboard* [the height of the hull above the waterline] to keep the larger seas at bay. But also consider what I wrote in *Getting Started in Powerboating*: "I feel much more secure taking rough stuff in a 25-foot center-console fishing boat designed to go to sea than I do in a 60-footer that was designed to be a dockside 'cocktail barge.' " I still stand by the principle: A boat's design is critical to its suitability for an intended use.

Bigger Boats Are Bigger in Every Way
Bigger boats also need more care and maintenance, not only because they present more surface area to clean and polish but also because they tend to have more mechanical systems that need attention. These additional systems can greatly enhance your boating pleasure—for example, a pressure water system allows you to have a working shower—but if you don't use the boat often, they can become just added problems.

Quick   Tips

Let your experience be your guide. Traditionally, newcomers to powerboating start small and work their way up, trading for bigger boats as they gain experience. Because of its lighter weight, a smaller boat is less likely to do serious damage if you make a beginner's mistake when maneuvering in tight quarters, such as in a marina. Small boats also respond more quickly to operator input, so you have a better chance of preventing a mistake from doing any damage at all by taking corrective action at the last minute.

Don't   Forget

Perceived status can lead you astray. It's okay to buy a boat so you can become a member of the yacht club set for the social and networking opportunities. But don't get carried away. Larger boats do not necessarily confer greater status. Whatever the size of your boat, your club members have seen bigger.

Don't Forget

Too small is never good either. Although I've cautioned against buying a boat that's too big for your current situation, I can't overemphasize the importance of getting one large enough to carry the total load you'll bring aboard under "normal" circumstances. If you don't, you're setting yourself up for disappointment—and possibly disaster. Overloading is a major cause of boating accidents.

Quick Tips

Don't be underpowered. You might think, "If 80% of the maximum horsepower will save me money, then cutting it to 40% should save twice as much, yes?" No! In fact, installing less than 70% of the maximum allowable horsepower will usually result in an underpowered boat that can't get out of its own way. You'll waste fuel and kill the motor at a very tender age by running it at full throttle too much of the time. Installing 80% to 85% of the maximum is usually the "sweet spot" that should make you and your motors happy. More is okay if you want it (up to the maximum, of course), but less than 70% simply won't work very well.

A Case of the Cramps

A friend invited me for an afternoon aboard his new 23-foot outboard cruiser, and I had to admit the boat was amazing in its layout and design, an impressive example of ingenious naval architecture. This little gem had everything that larger cabin boats have—except the room! The owner had a wife and four kids aboard, plus me. It was a very attractive boat, and it would have been great for a couple or two, but it was cramped and uncomfortable for seven. That boat simply didn't suit the needs of my friend's family, and he didn't keep it long.

Balance Is Everything

Your goal should be to have as much boat as you need—*and* can use and care for—in your present circumstances. Anything smaller will be inadequate and a disappointment (as well as potentially

dangerous); anything larger will just multiply your problems and inevitably disappoint as well.

Power

Power is what defines our sport, so it is an essential element to consider in selecting the best boat for your needs. While it isn't quite true enough to be chiseled in stone, in general the more power a boat has, the faster it can go. If the highest possible speed isn't your goal, you can usually save by buying smaller engines. A boat's weight and the bottom design also influence performance, but total horsepower is so significant that the capacity plates on outboard boats 20 feet and under must display the boat's maximum allowable horsepower (see photo page 18). It is illegal in many states and extremely dangerous anywhere to exceed this limit. And unless top speed is your only objective, you'll usually do quite nicely by installing motors with 80% to 85% of the capacity plate's maximum. This should cost you less to buy and less to operate, since motor prices and fuel consumption both increase dramatically with horsepower.

Be Practical

More power isn't *always* the answer to more speed. If you are almost satisfied with a boat's top speed and it has less horsepower than the capacity plate allows, you may be tempted to upgrade to larger motors. Before you break out your checkbook, however, ask dealers and owners of similar boats whether increased power really means more speed and, if so, how much. Installing larger motors is going to cost you plenty, and if this change will gain you only a couple of *knots* [nautical miles per hour] greater speed, is it worth it? Remember, hull design and the total weight of the boat and gear aboard can influence top speed as much as or more than the engines' power.

Outboard or Inboard?

There are a number of power plant choices to make in addition to total horsepower. One of the first is, outboard or inboard?

Which Is "Better"?

There was a time when I hated outboards and used them only when I had no choice. The first ones I encountered were smelly, cranky, and undependable. "Will it start

Quick Tips

While a full discussion of all the possible means of increasing a boat's speed is beyond the scope of this book, I can't emphasize enough that raising the total horsepower is most often the *least* efficient choice; requisite horsepower tends to increase exponentially when compared to the gain in speed. One easy, low-cost approach is to try different props. The propeller is what converts the engine's torque into thrust that pushes the boat. A slight change in a prop's geometry can often add considerably to its top speed. The same holds for proper trim of a planing boat. By adjusting the angle at which the propeller meets the water on those drive systems that allow it (outboards, sterndrives, and surface-piercing drives) and/or adjusting the boat's trim tabs, you can adjust the angle at which the boat runs through the water, which will greatly influence performance. On outboard-powered boats, you can install jack plates, which can vastly improve performance at a modest cost. Finally, the least expensive and most practical way to increase a boat's speed is to remove unnecessary gear. The less a boat weighs, the faster it should go.

this time?" was a question I constantly lived with, and starting was usually a manual operation that called for a strong arm and a lot of patience. The old outboards were terribly noisy, too, and many people chose inboards simply to have a quieter boat. But outboard technology has improved to the point that I now often prefer them on boats up to about 40 feet. Outboards are inherently safer than gasoline inboards because potential gas leaks are outside the boat. This usually makes them less expensive to insure (see Chapter 11). They are generally lighter than equivalent inboard horsepower. Being out on the *transom* [the squared-off back of the boat], they leave more usable room inside the boat. They're also easier and less expensive to change, an operation measured in hours as opposed to the days it usually takes to remove and replace an inboard. Today's outboards are also much more fuel efficient than the old ones, generating significantly lower levels of air and water pollution. Although some people who loved the outboards of old now say the new models are "too" quiet (a bizarre complaint if ever I've heard one), the numerous improvements have created many converts to outboard power.

On many hulls up to about 40 feet, outboard motors also offer several operational advantages over inboards. Outboards steer by pivoting to redirect their propeller thrust. This is more effective than steering on inboard-powered boats, which keep the prop aligned with the boat and redirect propeller thrust with a rudder. You can also trim, or change the vertical angle of, an outboard while underway in order to adjust the prop's vertical angle of thrust for maximum efficiency. This also makes it possible to change the boat's running angle for improved speed and handling in varying conditions.

Figure 2-2. Although modern four-stroke outboards are heavier than the two-strokes of old, outboards are still lighter than inboard engines of comparable horsepower and offer many other advantages. This Yamaha 350 hp model weighs 800 pounds—less than two-thirds of an equivalent inboard installation. *(Yamaha)*

Quick Tips

Although I've tried to make this book as fact-based and impartial as possible, there are points at which opinion also counts. The matter of outboards versus inboards is one of them. In my opinion, today's outboards are generally far superior to inboards for boats up to 30 feet *LOA* [length overall, the length of a boat on deck] because of their lighter weight, their ability to improve the boat's running angle by adjusting their trim, and the greater room they allow inside the boat. Between 30 and 40 feet, it depends on the boat. For many vessels in this size range, three or four outboards would be a more efficient installation than twin inboards. But this isn't always true. Many boats in this length range have enough overall volume to make them better candidates for inboard power. And for boats over 40 feet LOA, inboards are usually better all around.

Don't Forget

There *are* exceptions, and most of them relate to the boat's primary use. Many builders of dedicated ski boats, which are usually less than 30 feet, use inboards exclusively. It aids operating efficiency to have the point at which the propeller applies its thrust close to where the boat pulls on the towrope, and for both of these spots to be near the boat's pivot point. This balance occurs more easily with inboards. Professional skiers and ski boat operators also like having the prop under the boat, where it's less likely to snag the towrope—or skier—and this applies to many other users who spend a lot of time in the water, including divers and families with kids who like to swim. They also like having a full-*beam* [boat width] swim platform, which is impossible with outboards. And there are some boatowners who merely wish to have the transom clear for a full and unencumbered display of their boat's oh-so-clever name. For many reasons, outboards aren't for everyone.

It's also important to note that outboards are the only power plants that have been designed and manufactured specifically and exclusively for boats. Inboard engines are usually a marinized version of a design that was originally intended to power a car or truck.

Inboard Options

Inboard boats normally come with the power plant(s) already installed, but this doesn't mean that you don't have any choices. New boats are usually available

Don't Forget

You can be underpowered with inboards, too. While the lowest available horsepower will usually propel the boat just fine when new, this engine option is often offered primarily to make that model available at the lowest possible price and represents the minimum power the boat can have and still function adequately. After time, performance will often drop to unacceptable levels due to the growth of slime, algae, grass, and barnacles on the hull, combined with the weight of accumulated "stuff" you bring aboard.

Quick Tips

If you use your boat a lot, diesels are unquestionably better because of their greater durability. You have to put a lot of hours on your boat to make up for diesel engines' higher initial cost, but if you do, diesels can be worth it (which is why diesels are almost always better for commercial vessels). Just remember that diesels are as susceptible to damage from lack of use as are gasoline engines (see Chapter 1), so the power plants in a boat that's just sitting will eventually need the attention of a mechanic regardless of their type. And, diesels are usually more expensive to repair. So unless you plan to use your boat a lot, you may be better off with gas engines in boats up to about 45 feet LOA. Over that length, the scale tips back to diesels, due to their higher torque and greater availability of larger, more powerful engines.

with at least two or three engine options, and even when you're buying a used boat, the marketplace will most often include several differently powered versions of the same model. And even this short distance into the book, it shouldn't surprise you that I suggest going for the middle of the available range.

If you decide on inboards, you'll need to make some choices.

Gas or Diesel?

This one used to be easy. Diesel engines cost more to buy, but they last longer and cost less to run. This is still essentially true, though the differences are no longer as remarkable as they were in the days when diesel fuel cost one-third to one-half as much

as gasoline. Nowadays diesel is usually still less expensive than gasoline, though often by less than 10%. Diesel engines are still more fuel efficient, largely because a gallon of diesel fuel contains more usable energy than a gallon of gasoline but also because diesels burn the fuel more completely. But again, the difference isn't as great as it used to be, because fuel injection and improved

Quick Tips

Recently, there has been great interest in biodiesel fuels for their potential as a renewable and more environmentally friendly fuel alternative to pure petroliates. This is somewhat ironic because Rudolf Diesel's original experiments that resulted in working engines often used fuel derived from vegetable oils. Not only does biodiesel fuel help free us from the bonds of petroleum dependence, it turns out to be easier on engines. Field tests indicate that engine life is increased by using biodiesel; when blended as low as 2% with low-sulfur or ultra-low-sulfur petroleum diesel, lubricity increases to the level of traditional high-sulfur fuel. Exhaust from this lower-sulfur fuel not only smells much better (it's been compared to the aroma of cooking french fries!), it creates less air pollution.

Get Started

The boat business is emulating the auto trade and leaning more toward equipment "packages" (see Chapter 4). When buying a new boat, any power option except the lowest will generally prove satisfactory, whether it is gas or diesel.

electronic ignition have increased gas engine efficiency considerably. Diesel engines are still built tougher and last longer, though today's lightweight, fast-turning diesels are much closer to gas engines than the heavy, slow-turning chunks of cast iron of old. In short, while many of the apparent advantages of diesel power have diminished over time, the cost of buying diesels has not. (Note: All of the preceding applies to pleasure boats only. Workboats operate under very different service conditions and almost always benefit from diesel power.)

Safety Factors

Diesel fuel is inherently safer because diesel engines generate less carbon monoxide (CO), often called the silent killer because it is odorless and colorless. People usually don't know that there's a problem on board until someone begins to show symptoms of CO poisoning, including flushed skin, severe headache, dizziness, tiredness, and nausea. These symptoms may progress to confusion, irritability, and impaired judgment, memory, and coordination—and, ultimately, to death. Gas-powered boats should have a CO detector in the cabin, and though diesels generate less of this deadly gas, CO detectors aboard *all* boats with cabins is a good idea.

Diesel fuel is also safer because its vapors won't explode as gasoline vapors will. But diesel fuel will still burn, and a dirty boat with diesel fuel and lube oil in its bilges is nearly as great a hazard as a dirty gasoline-powered boat. Any boat will be safe if you follow proper maintenance and operational procedures.

Single or Twin Engines?

The answer is—you guessed it—"it all depends." Twin engines usually offer greater maneuverability, and on many boats it is more feasible to install two engines of moderate horsepower than one huge engine that meets the total propulsion needs. In fact, with outboards and gas inboards, installing twin engines is usually your only option—these engines haven't generally been available any larger than 300 hp—though there are a couple of 350 hp outboards and more likely to come in the future. It's not uncommon these days to see three or four outboards behind a sleek center-console fishing boat that needs a lot of horsepower to reach its maximum speed. And yet, in many boats, one good engine is all you really need. Just look at the world's commercial fishing fleets: they are predominantly single screw.

Raw-Water or Freshwater Cooling?

Raw-water cooling involves taking in water from outside the boat and cooling the engine by pumping the water through passages in the engine block and then out the exhaust. Freshwater cooling is a closed system similar to what you have in your car. Coolant circulates though the engine repeatedly, losing the heat it absorbs though a heat exchanger, which is essentially a radiator inside a water jacket. As with raw-water cooling, the water in the heat exchanger is brought in from outside the boat and exits with the exhaust after it has done its job. Freshwater cooling is more efficient both in maintaining a minimum operating temperature and in preventing overheating. Perhaps even more important is that hot salt water is extremely corrosive, and running salt water or brackish water through an engine can shorten its useful life significantly. Freshwater

Don't Forget

The notion that having two engines always guarantees "get home" capability is absolute hogwash. But it's an old-wives' tale you often hear on the waterfront. The truth is that while an engine can sometimes stop unpredictably, the primary keys to dependable operation are adequate use and proper maintenance. Well-maintained engines will usually work when you want them to, whether you have one or more. Neglected engines tend to fail when you need them most. Pleasure boats are designed to maximize living and playing areas, often at the expense of engine access. This can make working on twins a real chore compared to singles, and it may lead to neglected maintenance. The bottom line is that one properly maintained engine will always be more reliable than poorly maintained twins. Another common cause of engine failure is bad fuel, which multiple engines are just as susceptible to as singles.

cooling, therefore, is the solid choice for inboard-powered boats used in salt water, unless top speed is your sole priority, since the extra weight of freshwater cooling systems will naturally slow the boat down. All outboards use raw-water cooling.

Figure 2-3. Two motors can offer improved maneuverability. Three or more will provide greater speed.

Figure 2-4. These engines propel the boat nicely, but access for such simple tasks as checking the lube and gear oil levels and examining the cooling water intake strainers is problematic.

Quick Tips

Engines (and used boat buyers) love fresh water! Freshwater cooling costs more because it has more components, but you should get your money back, and then some, when you decide to sell. Smart buyers are always leery of internal engine corrosion and blocked cooling passages in older raw-water-cooled boats and will pay more for a used boat with freshwater cooling.

Flushing raw-water-cooled engines with fresh water after use will prolong their life and probably pay off when you sell. There are devices that clamp over the water intakes on an outboard's lower unit (often called earmuffs because of their appearance) that connect to a hose so you can run fresh water through them until all the salt is gone. These are a bit of a pain, however, and many newer outboards have a freshwater port on the cowling that's threaded to match a standard garden hose to make the job easier.

Inboard engine compartments can also be rigged with a hose connection and manifold to run fresh water through the engines. Some builders now offer the system as either standard equipment or a low-cost option, so you may find that the boat you're considering already has it. If not, the arrangement is simple enough that any competent marine mechanic can install one. The added weight will be much less than freshwater cooling, and the system makes flushing after use so much easier that you'll be far more apt to do it. This setup goes a long way toward enhancing your credibility when you can tell a prospective buyer that you flushed the engines thoroughly after every use.

What About Drives?

If you decide on inboard power, you have yet another choice to make. Fortunately, there aren't any "bad" drives, and today's hulls are often designed with a particular system in mind, so whatever happens to be installed is probably right for that model.

The choice of drive system can be extremely personal. If most of your experience has been on boats with a certain type of drive, you will be more inclined to favor it when you go shopping for a boat of your own. Try to keep an open mind, however, because there are no bad drive systems. There are differences, however, so let's take a look.

Conventional Shaft-and-Strut Running Gear

In this type, the oldest of all inboard propulsion systems still in common use (only paddle wheels are older), the engine is

Figure 2-5. If you run your boat in salt water, after your trip you just remove the screw-in plug (arrow) and attach a garden hose to the flushing port. Turn on the fresh water, and run your engine at idle speed (in neutral) for at least 5 minutes to flush the salt out of the motor. Not all makes and models of outboards have this feature, however. *(American Suzuki Motor Corporation)*

is supported by a strut or two. Steering is achieved by directing some of the propeller's thrust with a rudder that is mounted immediately behind the prop. All of the essential components—the driveshaft, strut, propeller, and rudder—are located under the boat, where they contribute, often significantly, to its draft. Conventional drives may be used in single- or multiple-engine installations. Pleasure boats with more than two conventional drives are rare.

V-Drives

V-drives are simply conventional drives with a bend. Instead of the shaft leading *aft* [toward the stern] from the engine, the engine is mounted so its power output faces forward into a V-drive unit, which may be part of the transmission or a separate unit. The propeller shaft is connected to the V-drive; it faces aft and exits the hull normally, usually beneath the engine. From the V-drive back, including everything underwater, the

mounted roughly *amidships* [the middle of the boat] and the propeller shaft extends through the bottom of the hull facing the *stern* [the very back of the boat], where it

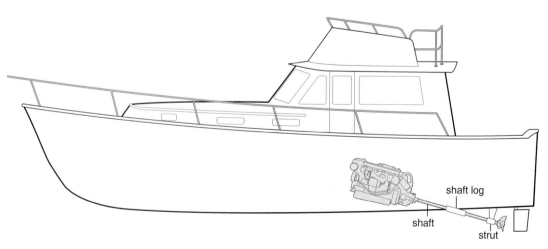

Figure 2-6. The conventional shaft and strut is a simple, straightforward, and time-proven drive system. *(Joseph Comeau)*

Quick Tips

On the plus side, conventional under-water drives are the simplest and usually the least expensive option (though the considerable labor required for proper installation somewhat offsets the lower cost of the parts). They are reliable, with a long-standing record of satisfactory performance on vessels of all sizes. But single-screw installations don't offer the degree of maneuverability you'll find in other drive systems because the rudder controls only a portion of the prop's thrust—the rest of it continues to push the boat straight ahead. Plus, since they require a hole in the bottom for each shaft, they are a potential source of leaks. Conventional drives tend to increase a boat's draft, and the props on conventional drives are most often the boat's deepest point and thus are extremely vulnerable to damage. They are sensitive to shaft alignment, and misalignment (a problem that most often grows as shaft length increases) can cause excessive vibration, rapid bearing wear, and other problems. Long shafts need more support in the form of additional struts or bearings, which also increases friction and decreases efficiency, even if only slightly. Finally, conventional running gear is not "trimmable"—you can't adjust the shaft's vertical angle to optimize performance in different sea states.

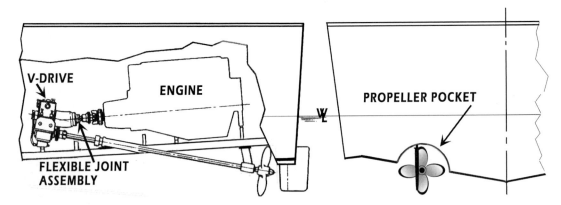

Figure 2-7. A V-drive can be integral to the reduction gear attached to the engine or, as shown here, an independently mounted remote unit with a flexible connection to the engine. *(Walter Machine Company, Inc.)*

Quick Tips

V-drives have advantages and liabilities generally similar to conventional shaft-and-strut systems, but there are a few differences. V-drives allow the engines to be mounted farther aft, which can produce more usable cabin space forward. The shafts are often shorter, reducing potential alignment problems. They often allow the shaft to be mounted at a shallower angle, which increases efficiency and, with the help of propeller pockets in the bottom, helps reduce the boat's draft. On the downside, there is the expense of the additional hardware, and a slight loss of total efficiency because of the increased friction from more gears in the power train. Since the gains mostly outweigh the minor negatives, I would never turn down a boat because it has V-drives, though I would never consider them a particularly strong reason for buying one, either.

components—and their function—are little different from the conventional drive system.

Sterndrives

Also known as an inboard-outboard (I/O) drive (or, occasionally, outdrive), the sterndrive arrangement couples an inboard engine to a transom-mounted drive leg similar to an outboard's lower unit. Introduced in 1959, when outboards were often unreliable and 50 hp was big, sterndrives combine the advantages of outboards and inboards: outboard maneuverability and inboard horsepower and reliability. Sterndrives pivot and tilt like outboards, offering totally directed prop thrust for better turning and propulsion efficiency, and adjustable trim so that the prop's thrust can be set at the most efficient angle. When you also factor in the wider variety of power options available, including diesel, it's easy to see why the sterndrive was considered the best of both worlds throughout most of the 1960s, '70s, and '80s. As outboard technology improved, however, the sterndrive advantage diminished in comparison. It remains totally viable and available on a wide variety of boats. Sterndrives are still the only way to combine the benefits of diesel power with outboard-like maneuverability.

Surface-Piercing Drives

Surface-piercing drives were to the 1980s what sterndrives were to the 1960s: the new kid on the block, the nautical equivalent of a better mousetrap. (Only the execution was really new; the concept goes back to the early 1900s, when Albert Hickman of South Boston, Massachusetts, tried running shafts straight out the transom of his experimental Sea Sleds.) By allowing the propeller to break the surface of the water, surface-piercing drives reduce underwater friction and gain thrust. A constant-velocity joint allows the external portion of the drive to be steered as well as trimmed vertically by hydraulic rams similar to those on sterndrives. The drives are widely accepted by offshore racers and on some high-performance pleasure craft.

Figure 2-8A. This QSB5.9 Cummins diesel engine is coupled with a MerCruiser Bravo Two drive. The QSB5.9 is currently available with up to 480 hp. Despite recent gains in outboard horsepower and reliability, sterndrives remain the only way to combine outdrive functionality with this level of power plus diesel longevity. *(Cummins MerCruiser Diesel)*

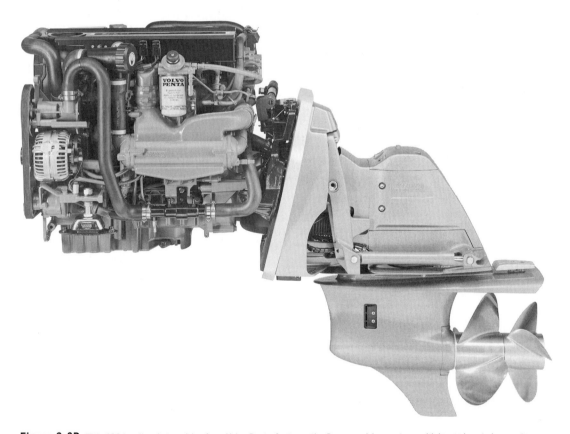

Figure 2-8B. This 130 hp diesel sterndrive from Volvo Penta features the Duoprop drive system, which employs twin counter-rotating props on concentric shafts. The twin props improve drive efficiency and eliminate some unwanted single-screw characteristics, though these drives are more often installed in pairs. MerCruiser offers similar twin prop performance in its Bravo Three drives. *(Volvo Penta)*

Quick Tips

Sterndrives offer a simple "out of the box" installation as a unit with no shaft alignment problems (which tends to somewhat offset the added cost of the equipment itself). They also offer the outboard-like ability to be trimmed way up when running in shallow water. And yet there's a downside too. Having the weight of an inboard engine or two (or three!) just inside the transom can make some boats stern heavy, reducing freeboard (often significantly) when the boat is at rest, making it harder to get on plane and sometimes making it difficult to achieve a good running angle even when on plane. Fortunately, today's inboard engines are often lighter than the power plants of old, so this is less of a problem than it used to be.

Don't Forget

A couple of ongoing problems remain, however. First is the increased friction of the added gears. V-drives have one bend, but outdrives have two: from horizontal out of the engine to vertical down the drive leg, and then to horizontal again to drive the prop. Second is the matter of attaining *and maintaining* a watertight seal around the large hole in the transom that each drive needs for mounting. If you opt for this system, be sure to keep an eye on the transom gasket and have it replaced whenever it appears to be losing its resiliency. Note also that the casings of sterndrives are mostly made of aluminum and are therefore quite susceptible to galvanic corrosion if proper preventive steps are not taken (see Chapter 9).

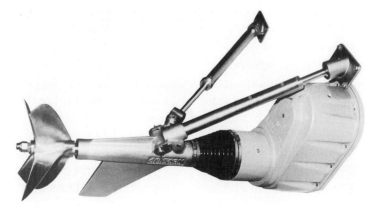

Figure 2-9. Arneson surface-piercing drives are probably the best-known brand, though they are no longer the only one. Note the hydraulic rams used for trim and steering. *(Arneson Marine)*

Surface-piercing drives allow shallower draft and the ability to operate in shallower water. (A boat that would draw 6 feet if equipped with conventional drives may draw only 3 feet with surface-piercing drives.) They also seem to be more efficient at converting engine torque to thrust, leading to higher top speeds. The major downside is cost. The drives themselves are among the more expensive options, and surface-piercing props are also quite dear. And despite the system's inherent steerability, close-quarters maneuvering of a boat with surface-piercing drives is closer to handling a boat with conventional drives than it is to outboards or sterndrives. In fact, their handling properties are unique, so there's a learning curve involved.

A principal advantage of jets is their ability to operate in very shallow water; they have nothing that extends below the bottom. This can be a mixed blessing, however, since running in very shallow water can pick up sea grass and other weeds that plug up the grates, choke off the water supply, and bring the boat to a halt. Jets are not without other drawbacks. They attain their efficiency only at high speeds; at low speeds, jets are less efficient than props. The thrust from a jet lacks the torque-induced aspects of prop thrust (i.e., prop walk), so certain handling techniques are different. And lacking a rudder or another underwater appendage that functions like one (as does an outboard's lower unit), steering control diminishes with decreased thrust and disappears completely when the jet thrust stops.

Jet Drives

Jets generally show up only on very small or very large watercraft. Personal watercraft (PWC, often known by Kawasaki's trade name Jet Ski) use jets to eliminate the danger of a propeller. At the other end of the spectrum, many 100-foot-plus megayachts are powered by large diesel engines turning jet drives, because they are more efficient than propellers at high speeds.

Jet drives use an enclosed impeller to pump water from under the boat and produce a forceful stream behind it. Since the jet's nozzle is steerable, the entire stream pushes the boat in the direction the nozzle is turned, offering considerable maneuverability. Jet pumps cannot themselves be reversed, but a jet-equipped boat can nonetheless be moved *astern* [backward] by dropping a device behind the jet (usually called a bucket) that redirects its stream back under the boat.

Several small jet-driven boats entered the marketplace in the mid- to late 1990s, in

Figure 2-10. Jet drive and engine. *(Cummins MerCruiser Diesel)*

many ways an outgrowth of the popularity of PWC, but few of these stood the test of time. Only a few small boats (as opposed to PWC) are now available with jets, although BRP, the company that makes Evinrude outboards, produces several models under the Sea-Doo brand.

New Systems

In 2005, Volvo Penta introduced the Inboard Performance System (IPS), which places steerable sterndrive-like pods under the boat instead of on the transom. These drives feature counterrotating props on each unit, similar to Duoprop sterndrives.

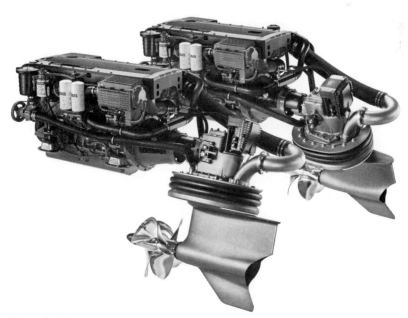

Figure 2-11. Volvo Penta's IPS system is available for two- to four-engine installations in both planing and semidisplacement hulls. *(Volvo Penta)*

Quick Tips

Pods are like sterndrives in that they pivot to redirect 100% of the prop thrust when turning, so boats with pods are highly maneuverable. They are not trimmable, however, being designed so their thrust is always parallel to the bottom, which is usually most efficient all around. The pods also contain the raw-water intakes and exhaust ports, which eliminates the need for additional holes in the hull, while a sophisticated seal keeps water from entering through the one hole each pod requires. And they are efficient, creating much less drag than conventional shaft-and-strut running gear. The main drawback to pods is that they add to a boat's draft and, being the lowest points beneath the hull, are exposed to damage in a grounding or when striking an unseen object. For many people, the increased maneuverability and efficiency of pods outweigh any negatives. They will never totally replace conventional drive systems, but they are definitely a wave of the future.

Figure 2-12. Cummins MerCruiser Zeus drives (shown), Volvo Penta IPS, and MerCruiser Axius sterndrives all offer joystick control for easier and simpler close-quarters maneuvering. *(Cummins MerCruiser Diesel)*

Easier Control

Volvo Penta's IPS drives and MerCruiser's Zeus drives both offer the option of joystick control, which provides a tremendous ease-of-use advantage during docking and similar close-quarters maneuvers, and in *station keeping* [holding a position] despite the effects of wind and current. Given that the younger generations grasp a joystick as naturally as if they'd been born with it, this "video game" approach should make maneuvering easier for beginners in the near and foreseeable future.

My only reservation about this: if you never learn to handle a boat the old-fashioned way, what do you do if the joystick fails? I'm reminded of a conversation with a boating friend who is an airline pilot. He was explaining that 747s are fully capable of landing themselves at any of the world's major airports.

Also different is that the props face forward. Cummins MerCruiser Diesel offers the similar Zeus below-the-hull, steerable drive system, but with conventional rear-facing props.

"How well does the system work?" I asked.

"Okay, I guess," he replied hesitantly. "I've actually never used it."

"Why on earth not?" I asked, somewhat surprised.

His response was enlightening: "Because I never want to forget how to do it myself!"

He made a good point. If joystick control seems better to you, go for it! The ease in handling should make your new toy more enjoyable right from the start. But to cover your assets, I suggest you learn the old way too, just in case you ever need it.

Types of Boats

While you can fish, swim, or dive from any boat, and take any boat cruising, not every boat allows you to conduct these activities with equal ease and comfort. You and your guests will always have more fun aboard a boat that's been designed for the specific activity you have in mind. So let's take a look at a few of the most popular on-the-water activities and examine the features you'll need to enjoy them to the fullest.

Fishing

Stability probably tops the list of desirable fishing boat features. All boats roll in a trough, but good fishing boats have an easy roll that doesn't go far enough or happen quickly enough to throw you off balance. When you check out a boat you'll use primarily for fishing, be sure your sea trial includes seeing how it behaves at trolling speeds and sitting still in a seaway. If it isn't comfortable, keep looking.

Other important fish boat features include:

- Room for anglers to move around as they fight their catch. This means plenty of cockpit space, open deck, or both. If it has a fighting chair, the cockpit must be large enough so that there's still ample space around it. Deck hardware—cleats, chocks, etc.—should be hidden or recessed so that anglers can't snag lines (or shins) while fighting their catch.
- Rod holders, rod and tackle stowage, and a bait prep center.
- Outriggers for trolling, and an aerated well for holding live bait.
- Places to stow your catch and easy means of getting the catch aboard (which means a transom door in larger craft).
- A self-bailing cockpit. The cockpit *sole* [floor] shouldn't be too far off the water, and there should be facilities (pump, hose, etc.) for washdown underway.

Low-speed maneuverability is also important, which generally means you'll want at least twin-screw power. Often it

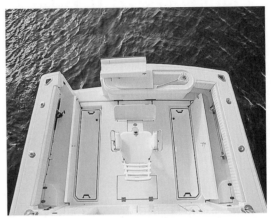

Figure 2-13. Two views of a perfect cockpit arrangement on a well-rigged sportfisherman. It includes a tackle center with large stowage drawers and a fiberglass sink with removable cutting board (left). It also features two large fish boxes (with macerators) under the sole, a live bait well in the transom, a swing-out transom door, and a fighting chair with ample working space around it (right). *(Rampage Sport Fishing Yachts)*

will be needed simply to provide more total horsepower, because the best fishing areas are not always close to the best living areas.

Visibility from the helm is critical—you need to see the signs that indicate the presence of fish, and you need to see your anglers' rod tips when they have a fish on. On larger boats, the console is often elevated with a flying bridge to provide a higher vantage point for better all-around visibility. In many regions, a tower is added to raise the observation point even higher. In large boats, the main station may be so far from the action that a separate console is needed in the cockpit.

Some of these features are options you can add to any boat at any time. But you should really consider them from the start because it may be expensive to make the conversion later.

Center consoles, sportfisherman (aka convertibles), and walkarounds are generally designed primarily for fishing, while bowriders, deck boats, and runabouts are general-purpose recreation boats that also often make good fishing platforms. (See the Gallery of Powerboats for an introduction to these and other boat types.)

Swimming, Snorkeling, and Diving
All you really need for any of these activities is a boarding ladder, which provides an easy way to get back aboard from the water. But given all the bulky gear that scuba diving requires, dive boats need a lot of cockpit space and a clear path over or through the transom. The cockpit sole can be higher off the water than in a fishing boat, as long as there is a good boarding ladder. This is especially true if the boat has a transom platform (aka a swim, or dive, platform).

This feature gives you a place to don or remove gear just inches from the water and is an unbeatable addition to any boat that is used extensively for in-the-water activities. A freshwater shower on or near the platform is a nice plus.

Deck boats can be good for these activities because of the boarding ladder in the *bow* [the very front of the boat]. Their main drawback is size; if the dive/snorkel/swim location is a great distance from home or involves transiting rough water, a bigger boat will be more comfortable. It will also have more stowage space for gear. Convertibles, sedans, and express cruisers are all good because of their relatively large cockpits.

Cruising

Some folks approach cruising simply as travel on water as opposed to travel on land—that is, they consider accommodations as part of the destination package. If you feel this way, just about any boat will work. But many cruising folk don't want to be limited to stopping at marinas with a motel nearby. This means having a boat with a cabin, berths, a galley and dining area, at least one head with a shower, and enough space to prevent cabin fever. Properly divided space is also important to provide a degree of privacy. When you travel this way, your destinations are nearly unlimited.

Speed and range are factors to consider in all boats, but they are particularly important to cruising boats because of how they affect your overall activity. The two are not necessarily mutually exclusive, but either factor can impose severe limitations on the other. If most of your cruising will be done on weekends, speed can become more

Quick Tips

Space to stow scuba gear is extremely important if you plan to do much serious diving. It's amazing how much room this gear can require. Racks for air tanks should be high on the list, because loose tanks on a pitching deck can be dangerous.

Proper *ground tackle* (traditionally pronounced "TAKE • ul"), which includes the anchor(s), the *rode* [the rope and/or chain that connects the anchor to the boat], and the facilities for handling them, is important on every boat, but particularly for swimming and diving. Arrangements that would be acceptable on other boats can prove inadequate when frequent anchoring is routine. A power-driven *windlass* [a device for hauling in rope or chain] is really a must.

A diver-down flag (red with diagonal white stripe) is required in most states whenever you have people in the water who are capable of quickly disappearing beneath the surface, and it's a good idea for people who are merely swimming—it lets other boaters know you have people in the water. A swim/snorkel/dive boat should have a signal mast or some other means of displaying the flag where it can be clearly visible all around.

Don't Forget

Figuring a boat's cruising capacity by just counting berths can be a huge mistake. Since many areas aboard serve double duty—convertible dinettes and sofas that pull out to become beds are perfect examples—the number of berths is usually greater than the number of people a boat can accommodate comfortably. Stowage for clothing, personal belongings, food, and other necessities is also important, and its importance grows with the length of the cruise. A boat that might suit six overnight could become cramped for just one couple after a week if there isn't sufficient storage space.

Figure 2-14A. Displacement boats, like this classic Grand Banks, can be very comfortable if you're not in a hurry. They go *through* the water and usually burn relatively little fuel in the process. (*Grand Banks Yachts*)

important, which means big engines and a planing hull. If getting away from it all for longer periods is more to your liking, you should probably opt for range—that is, smaller engines with a displacement hull. In cruising boats, the ultimate question is often which would you rather spend more of: money or time?

Cuddies, with their small cabins, can be cozy cruisers, while sedans or convertibles (so-called because they easily "convert" from fishing boat to cruising boat), express cruisers, and motoryachts all fit the bill with a lot more privacy and room to stretch out. Houseboats are also ideal—at least for inland waters.

Figure 2-14B. Planing boats, like this Silverton 48, on the other hand, can get you where you want to go quite quickly because they get up and ride on top of the water. Of course, it usually takes more fuel to do this. (*Volvo Penta and Silverton*)

Waterskiing

While you can ski behind any boat with enough power, the best ski boats are small, fast, and highly maneuverable, with a small turning radius and a flat *wake* [the trail of waves boats leave behind when underway]. Ideally, the towrope should attach to a pylon somewhere near the boat's pivot point, though a dedicated transom attachment will also work. Since this combination of features is not always desirable for many other activities, waterskiing is perhaps the one sport that begs a truly dedicated craft.

Wakeboarding

This activity seems so similar to waterskiing, but what it requires from a boat is markedly different. A minimal wake is desirable for skiing, while wakeboarders want the wake as large as possible. Most really good ski boats just can't begin to throw the wake you need for good boarding, though some new designs have ballast tanks that can be filled to add weight to the stern so it will sit lower in the water and increase the boat's wake. If you don't have a dedicated wakeboarding boat, the best alternative is often a sterndrive runabout running not quite on plane.

Partying

Celebrating afloat has a special charm that few parties ashore can match. It's a super way to repay social obligations. As many megayacht owners have discovered, people who might not attend a party at your house will rarely refuse an invitation to your boat. The principle applies even if your boat is considerably smaller than a megayacht.

Of course, available space determines how large a party you can throw—you want your guests to be able to "rub elbows" without actually rubbing elbows! As with cruising, the way space is arranged is often more important than its amount, except that for partying the emphasis is less on places to put things away and more on places to put things out. Likewise, there is less concern for privacy and more for open space and traffic flow. A balance of space is nice, too; the best party setups include both enclosed saloons and open deck areas.

A wet bar, icemaker(s), and liquor and glass storage are nice but not necessary. Their importance varies in proportion to total available space and their compatibility with other uses of the boat.

For pure partying, a cocktail barge doesn't need to be terribly seakindly, since some of the best parties don't require leaving the pier. If you do take a cruise, it will most likely be a short one on protected water in nice weather. Convertibles, sedans, express cruisers, and motoryachts all have the combination of space and layout that good parties demand. Houseboats are excellent for parties on protected waters; they are exceedingly spacious inside.

Other Considerations

Where you do your boating can help determine the best boat for your needs, and this goes far beyond the differences we've already considered between boating on the open ocean and boating on the more protected waters of a bay, lake, or river. For example, where I live in south Florida, the terrain is low and we have a lot of drawbridges. This wouldn't be so bad except that highway traffic is so heavy that very few bridges open on demand, opening instead according to schedules. If your boat can't clear the bridge, you must wait. And while the total size of a boat can have a huge influence in this matter, how it is arranged can be more important. A 60-foot express cruiser that I often run on charters can clear almost all the bridges in the Miami area, but a 45-foot sedan that I also run quite a bit must wait for openings, because of its flying bridge. The flying bridge offers better visibility and is great for fishing, but it would be inappropriate if your plans involved more time on the Intracoastal Waterway and less time fishing offshore. Your own locale may have its own particular considerations and restrictions.

The Value of Buying "Certified"

Most boats have a placard that states: "This Boat Complies with U.S. Coast Guard Safety Standards on the Date of Certification." (On boats 20 feet or less in length, you'll find the compliance statement on the capacity plate.)

This statement would be quite reassuring if it weren't for the fact that U.S. Coast Guard standards for privately owned and operated vessels are very, very low. The sad truth is that you are better protected when you buy a $30 ticket for a trip on a sightseeing boat than when you spend $30,000 for a boat of your own: the Coast Guard

has very strong safeguards for passengers aboard commercial boats. So look for a vessel that it is NMMA certified.

This means that, in addition to meeting USCG requirements, which are ridiculously minimal, the vessel was designed to meet the more stringent standards of the NMMA, which are themselves taken from the American Boat and Yacht Council (ABYC).

Of course, you still may want a Condition and Value Survey (see Chapter 10) before you buy, though it isn't always a necessity. However, a sea trial, or test ride, is a necessity, just to be sure you are happy with the way the boat performs and, perhaps more important, the way it *feels* to you when underway.

Look for the CSI

CSI stands for Customer Satisfaction Index, a program initiated by the NMMA in 2001 to provide boat and engine manufacturers with an independently measured, cost-effective tool to improve customer satisfaction in the boating industry. Since the program's inception, more than half a million surveys have been sent to new boat and engine customers, allowing participating manufacturers to monitor customer satisfaction and benchmark themselves against the industry and competitors. While having a high CSI is no guarantee that a boatbuilder's product will be satisfactory for you, it is a strong indication that it should be as long as that model is suitable to your needs. If I were torn between two similar boats, I would compare the builders' CSIs to help me choose.

LIST YOUR PRIORITIES

Since no single boat can be all things to all people, you're going to have to make

Figure 2-15. This certification placard signifies that the vessel meets NMMA standards. *(NMMA)*

some choices. An excellent way to ensure that you're getting exactly what you want is to write down your needs and desires. A brainstorming session with family and friends who will use the boat with you can be valuable, but if necessary, you can also brainstorm all by yourself. Remember that in brainstorming there are no bad ideas; anything and everything goes on the list. Then go over the list and assign a value to each item you've considered on a scale of 1 to 5. Give the "absolute must-haves" a 5, and assign a 1 to those things you can totally do without. Everything else will fall somewhere in between. You should definitely have some 1s on your list even if you don't literally need them; you're buying a boat because you *want* to, right? Make sure you get what you really want. When you are sure you have a complete list, you are ready to start shopping in earnest.

MAKE THE SEA TRIAL COUNT

Use the sea trial to its best advantage; remember, you're not just going for a boat ride. A sea trial is an opportunity to see what you like and dislike about that boat's performance. It's also a way to determine whether any features that seemed okay at dockside are still okay when the boat is underway. I have to believe that if the man I mentioned at the start of this chapter had used a sea trial properly, he would never have bought the wrong boat.

A sea trial is your last, and often best, opportunity to check the fit between you and the boat. If any part of it seems to pinch a bit, you probably haven't yet found the boat you should buy. Keep looking.

Quick Tips

When you think you have found your dream boat, insist on a sea trial. Whether you're buying a used or new boat, you can't know if it is right for you without seeing how it behaves on the water. For new boats that you plan to order, this may involve a demo ride on a sister ship. Make sure the boat you want to buy and the demo boat are as identical as possible, right down to the propellers. If *any* aspect of the sea trial seems disappointing, speak up and resolve the issue before you commit to purchase. Once you've signed on that dotted line, the boat is yours!

Quick Tips

A proper sea trial is so important that I've devoted an entire section of Chapter 9 to the subject. Be sure to read and heed the suggestions there.

Don't Forget

While finding the right boat for your current situation is essential to fully enjoying the sport, you are never going to find the perfect boat. Every boat is a compromise, and no boat—not even a spare-no-expenses custom-built one—will ever be everything you want. Unless you plan to make your boat-buying expedition a lifetime project, you have to be realistic. When you find a boat that suits your needs better than any other, chances are this is the one. If all other aspects—including the survey (see Chapter 10)—check out, then buy it! Don't let fear of commitment or worries about buying the wrong boat stop you. If it turns out the boat isn't *exactly* right, note what you'd like to be different and apply that knowledge to your next boat-shopping project.

It's a Wrap
WRAP

- ✔ The wrong boat (for you) is never a bargain, no matter how low its cost.
- ✔ The proper size of boat depends on your current needs; it will inevitably change with time.
- ✔ The power option you select can influence your total cost of purchase *and* operation.
- ✔ Different types of boating—fishing, cruising, partying, etc.—call for different features; buy the type of boat best suited to your favored activity.
- ✔ A boat with NMMA certification is built to higher standards than one that merely meets U.S. Coast Guard requirements.
- ✔ You should list your priorities to help narrow your choices.
- ✔ A sea trial is your only chance to determine the total "rightness" of any boat.

CHAPTER 3

NEW OR USED?

Do I Need to Read This Chapter?

You should read this chapter if you want to discover

- ✔ The good news and bad news of buying a new boat.
- ✔ The good news and bad news of buying a used boat.
- ✔ The "secrets" to getting the best value in each.
- ✔ How to determine the value of a used boat.
- ✔ The relative merits of commercial versus private sales.

WHICH IS A BETTER BUY?

The answer can be tricky because each has a number of solid advantages and disadvantages. The choice can be somewhat personal, and what's right for you might be totally wrong for me. And yet the "rightness" of any buying decision can also change over time. The story I'm about to relate doesn't really speak about boats, but it's a perfect example of how changing situations can change your perspective. Our family car when I was growing up was always used, a car my father bought whenever a local banker had traded it in for a new one, which was every 2 years. Dad had an arrangement with the dealer to call him the moment the banker traded. Dad liked buying the banker's trade-in because it was only 2 years old, always had low mileage, and had been maintained immaculately, inside and out, mechanically and cosmetically. It was a very fine car at a very good price. And yet when the dealer called about 4 months before Dad passed away, he came home with a brand-new model instead of the banker's trade-in. He knew his health was failing, and apparently he had decided he wanted to own one truly new car before he died. Whether you buy new or used isn't always a rational decision.

New Boats

The biggest attraction of a new boat is just that: it's brand-new. You get to be the very first to do everything with it and to it. And from the earliest moment we become aware of the nature of new, there's nothing quite as exciting as a brand-new toy that's never been played with.

The Upsides of New

Once you get past the psychological advantage, a new boat also offers several other significant and quite practical upsides:

- **Warranties.** I'll cover these more thoroughly in Chapter 13, but for now just remember that while your new boat is still under warranty, nearly everything that goes wrong with it will be fixed at virtually no cost to you.
- **The latest gear.** New boats usually feature new equipment, and since the rapid evolution of technology can often make even last year's model of just about everything seem akin to dinosaurs, this can be a huge advantage.
- **Better design.** Boatbuilders often make some major design modifications from year to year, so a brand-new 31-foot Express Cruiser may offer a number of very real improvements over last year's similar 30-footer and be quite a bit better than one that's just a few years older.
- **All the owner's manuals.** This may or may not be important to you. But for those of us who are fanatical about such things, it is *very* important. Tracking down lost or discarded manuals for the equipment on an older boat can be a real pain—and all too often, an exercise in futility—for those of us who consider them to be an absolute necessity.

Despite these advantages, new boats are not perfect; nor are they a perfect solution for every boat-buying situation. There are downsides, too.

The Downsides of New

New boats always cost more, and much of the added expense will be lost forever once you've paid it.

You also may have to plan to keep a new boat for a while. That rapid depreciation can quickly put you "upside down" in terms of what you owe versus what your boat would

Quick Tips

Be prepared for the Big D, Depreciation. The harshest downside to buying a new boat is the hit you take the moment that it becomes yours. Production boats depreciate quickly—often down to half their original value in less than 2 years! And the immediate drop in value that occurs when your boat leaves the dealer's inventory to become yours can be quite a shock. You have to decide if the advantages of buying new are worth what you lose in instant depreciation.

bring if you sold it. A trade too soon could find you having to add cash to pay off the note. There are some other downsides, too:

- **The need for a break-in period.** This is no big deal, but it does mean you usually can't just jump aboard and go as you please, especially not at wide-open throttle (WOT). When engines are new, you most often have to follow a precise break-in schedule to prevent voiding their warranty, and to ensure that your engine(s) will perform as expected as they age. A proper break-in is essential to engine longevity because it allows the piston rings to seat as they should, which will ensure proper compression and reduce oil consumption. The exact break-in requirements for your boat's engine(s) will be in the owner's manual (see, I told you manuals were important), and you should follow the instructions precisely until the break-in is complete.

- **The need for a shakedown period.** This is most often quite a bit longer than the break-in. Just because your boat is brand-new doesn't guarantee that everything aboard is going to work as it should. Despite your builder's and dealer's best efforts at quality control (and the good ones usually do try to make everything right), boats these days are complex enough that you're bound to find at least a few items that need further attention. The good news: none of this should cost you a cent; it will all be covered under warranty. The bad news: waiting for it to get taken care of can be frustrating. Considering the price tag your new boat carries, you expect it to be fully functional from day one; discovering that it isn't can be irritating.

- **The intimidation factor.** Knowing that your boat's pretty new *topsides*, the part of the hull from the waterline up to the *gunwale* [pronounced "GUN • ul," the point where the hull meets the deck, or the top edge of the topsides], don't as yet have a single ding or scratch can make you nervous for a while as you worry about when you'll cause the first one and dread its ever happening at all—though you just know it is inevitable. Indeed, the first time you approach a pier with your brand-new beauty can be white-knuckle to the max!

"New" Does Not Equate to "Perfect"

If there are enough hours on the meters, you may discover that the break-in was taken care of by the builder or dealer in the process of delivering, commissioning, and fitting out the boat. Just be sure to ask. But the shakedown period is inevitable. I once took command of a new yacht from a respected builder who had been commissioned by a dealer with an extremely competent staff. Every effort had been made to ensure that all was well; the dealer had spent nearly a month readying the boat. And yet, one morning on our first cruise, I found engine oil in a transmission, a sign of a leaking shaft seal. It was no one's fault, and the repair was covered by warranty; it didn't cost the owner a cent. But we still had to wait for the repairs before we could resume cruising, which cost us over a week in lost time. The engine work also totally disrupted the main *saloon* [the proper name for a boat's living room], because the mechanics needed to open a normally hidden hatch in order to separate the transmission from the engine so they could replace the damaged seal. It was a real mess we had to live with for several days.

And the intimidation factor? Well, the first scratch on that new yacht's hull was made by a friend of the owner when he came alongside in a smaller boat; I didn't cause it, and there was nothing I could do to prevent it. But I must confess that knowing that the first scratch was there took a huge load off my mind—we professionals are human, too.

Used Boats

A used boat can be a very good buy because it will cost less; the asking price will reflect its depreciated value. You get a lot more boat for your money. This is probably why used boats currently account for about 70% of total annual boat sales in the United States. But "used" is a term that covers a wide range of products, from almost new

Figure 3-1. The variety of products you'll see at a boat show makes attending one (or more) an excellent move if you're looking for a new boat. As a bonus, you also often get to see the latest in accessories, too. Besides, boat shows are fun! *(Miami International Boat Show and NMMA)*

to ready for Davy Jones's junkyard. So it covers a wide range of values, too. On the plus side, most used boats will generally be long past both the break-in period and the shakedown period. And that first ding on the topsides will most probably have occurred early on, so you don't have to worry about this aspect, either.

The Case of the Nearly New Bargain

A friend of mine once found a 6-month-old boat with not quite 50 hours on the meters that had an unbelievably low price. Its original owner had traded it on a larger model. Now this is about as good as it gets: a boat still in the current model year with fewer than 50 hours on the meters that he could buy for less than two-thirds of its original price. Of course, he jumped at it! You may

Quick   Tips

The best possible buy is a nearly new boat with low hours on the meters. A nearly new boat with low hours will probably have had all its new boat bugs taken care of. The initial depreciation will be accounted for and the engines should be broken in, and yet the boat itself and most of its systems will most probably still be under warranty (see Chapter 13).

never find a deal quite this good, but it is a perfect example of what you should be looking for if you want a really good buy.

As an aside, I've often wondered why the original owner decided he needed a larger boat when he'd only used that one less than 50 hours in 6 months, which is well below average. The only answer I've been able to think of is that the boat he'd bought wasn't big enough to suit his needs and he was in a financial position to take the depreciation loss and move on. Most of us aren't that fortunate, which makes selecting the right boat from the start so very important.

Begin by Just Looking

As Motown greats Smokey Robinson and the Miracles once told us (and the Captain & Tennille repeated for emphasis several years later), "You Better Shop Around." This is still sound advice, so let me repeat it once more, though in a less melodic fashion: long before you even think of buying any particular boat, you had better—no, let's make that you absolutely *must*—shop around. When you are in the market for a used boat, you need to know the marketplace. Start by reading ads and listings. Look in your local paper, on the Internet, and in such publications as *Soundings* and *Boat Trader* or the back pages of major boating magazines. Used boat ads will cover the gamut. What you're looking for is simply a better knowledge of what's available at what price. Once you have a good grasp of the marketplace as a whole, you can narrow your search and start eyeing some actual boats. Be sure to look at many before you settle on one. Because there are so many variables, you can't begin to appreciate what's most important to you until you've seen a lot of options. Looking at many boats will also help you learn to evaluate quality, so be sure to shop, shop, shop until you develop a concrete idea of exactly what you are looking for and how this relates to price. Whether you shop close to home or all over the place is up to you, but buying close to home will usually cost less in the long run, even if the price is higher.

Do the Math

Experts say that the average operating time for a pleasure boat is around 150 to 200 hours a year (though some estimates are much lower). If you think this isn't enough, consider that 200 hours equals 25 8-hour

Quick Tips

When you're looking for a boat, the Internet is the perfect place to start. At the outset you want variety with a capital V; you need to look at a lot of boats just to learn what's out there. Just remember: the Internet is a great place to *start*. It's superb for looking and may even result in your finding a place to buy a boat. But at some point you'll have to stop viewing images and go examine some actual boats. Virtual reality has its limits. And though you wouldn't be the first to do so, you should *never* buy a boat sight unseen and without having a survey first. This was unwise pre-Internet and is equally foolish today. *Always* make any purchase agreement "subject to successful survey."

Don't forget delivery costs. Even if you find the greatest buy on a boat you love, if it isn't already within your normal boating area, you're going to have to add to your bottom line the cost of traveling to where it is so you can check it out personally and then, if you buy it, the cost of bringing it home. Unless you're getting a *very* good buy, it could be less expensive in the long run to pay a little more for a boat that's closer to home.

You can also get value information online. BUC International (the BUC Book's publisher) also maintains a website, www.bucvalue.com. This is really a two-tier site, which includes BUCValu Professional, which is a subscription-based service for marine industry professionals, and BUCValu Consumer, a free service "for current or prospective boatowners who want to learn the market value of one particular boat." You have to sign up for either. But the consumer service won't cost you a cent, and it can help you get closer to the actual value of a boat that has piqued your interest. Boat U.S. also offers an online valuation service (see the Resources section).

days, just shy of 4 weeks of actual use. Many pleasure boat owners discover that they have years when they use their boats considerably less than this. The majority of even very active boatowners go boating mostly on weekends and then only on one of the days. At this rate, 25 8-hour days means using your boat about every other weekend for the entire year if you live in a 12-month boating area. And if your boating season is only 6 months long, 200 hours means running your engines for a total of 8 hours on nearly every weekend you have available. This is why 150 hours may actually be on the high side, though we often use it as average.

I'll talk more about the ramifications of engine hours in Chapter 9, but my purpose here is to help you figure whether a particular boat should be average priced. Divide the total hours you see on the meter(s) by

the age of the boat. A boat with higher- (or lower-) than-average hours on the meters should be priced below average, especially if the boat is more than a year old. If the asking price isn't below average, negotiate until the selling price is—or keep on looking.

LET THE BUC STOP HERE
When you start to determine the value of boats you are interested in, the ads and listings you researched so thoroughly at the beginning of your quest can come into play. This will help you know current asking prices. But wouldn't it be nice if you could

know what similar models are going for in the real world? There is a way. It's called the BUC Book. Officially entitled *BUC Used Boat Price Guide*, this publication has been the boating industry's used boat pricing bible since 1961. Your lender should have a current copy, and s/he should be able to show you the numbers for the boat you want to buy.

Condition Is Critical!

A used boat can be anything from still virtually new and "used" only in the strictest technical sense to a rotting hulk that's well beyond useful service. And some are not only beyond useful service, they're even beyond repair or restoration. A boatyard owner I worked with years ago in Maine once had a potential customer who wanted an opinion on the restorability of an old wooden hull. After a careful examination of the hulk, the yard owner could only say, "I hope you have a fireplace!" So remember, the value of any used boat depends on not only its age but also its condition. Condition can be even more important than age; a well-cared-for 10-year-old boat can be worth more than a 5-year-old similar model that has been neglected or abused.

In the BUC Book as well as the online service, the value shown is for "average" condition. BUC International suggests adding 15% to 20% for boats in Bristol condition and subtracting 50% to 80% for boats that are merely "restorable." All in all, the company suggests six levels of current condition:

1. Excellent (Bristol)
2. Above average
3. Average (or "BUC" condition, which their listed market value refers to)
4. Fair
5. Poor
6. Restorable

In Chapter 9, I'll offer some suggestions for how to determine which condition level applies to the boat you're considering by using a thorough inspection of your own.

Other Books

The BUC Book is not the only source of used boat pricing. There are also a couple of "Blue Books." One of them, the *Marine Appraisal Guide*, is published by the National Automobile Dealers Association, the same people who put out the automobile industry's book of used vehicle prices. In my opinion, the BUC Book, being based in the marine industry, is the most accurate. It's what I've always used to determine value when doing surveys—or buying used boats. It's also the only one that prices boats by region, which is important because where a boat is located also influences its worth. I've listed other books in the Resources section. What counts most is the book (or books) your surveyor uses, because when you apply for a loan, a professional's estimate of the boat's current value will help determine how much you'll be able to borrow against it (see Chapter 5).

DEALER OR PRIVATE SALE?

Nearly every new boat dealership used to take trade-ins; accepting your old boat was considered a part of your buying a new one—an incentive to the sale. So a new boat dealership was a good place to look for used boats, too. And then some dealerships decided that used boats were more trouble than they were worth. Salespeople would often tell prospective new boat customers who had an old boat to get rid of, "You know, you can get more from a private sale than we can possibly offer you in trade. So sell your current boat yourself. In the meantime, let's talk about its replacement."

These days the pendulum seems to be swinging back. Although more used boats are still probably sold in driveways than at dealerships, many dealers now look at their used boat lot as another profit center. It's quite possible to buy a certified used boat that has a limited warranty attached even if all its original factory warranties have long since expired (see Chapter 13). The dealer's service department will have gone over the boat and corrected any minor problems, so in many ways it's even better than new—no shakedown required. A boat you buy this way will usually cost more than a private sale because the dealer's service costs (and profit) are included in the price. But the limited warranty you'll get, along with access to a service department that knows the boat, can be well worth the difference. In a private sale, you buy the boat as is regardless of what the seller may offer in personal assurances.

Playing by the Rules

Bargaining involves some basic rules. Here are some of the more important ones:

- Always make your counteroffer a little lower than what you expect to pay. You're asking the seller to come down in price, so leave yourself room to come up. If you've done your homework, you'll know the value of the boat sufficiently well that your counteroffer can be about as far below the true value as the seller's asking price is above.
- Never counter with an offer so low that it either insults the seller or indicates a lack of seriousness on your part, either of which can often bring negotiations to an abrupt halt.

Get Started

Larger vessels are most often bought and sold through a yacht broker. A good broker knows the marketplace and can often lead you to some good buys, although brokers make their money from a percentage of the sale price, so it's not in their own best interests to bring it down. A boat you buy through brokerage is still a private sale with no warranties attached and is usually sold as is. If you don't know a broker, look in the back of any major boating magazine; you'll see lots of ads. Having a good broker on your side can be so critical that it's worth cultivating a relationship with a broker you feel comfortable with early in your boat search. Since a good broker-client relationship is often as much about compatible personalities as it is about pure business, keep looking until you find a broker you feel is right for you.

- Continued negotiation is your goal. Ideally, the seller would set an asking price slightly above true value, you'd counter with an offer below it by a similar amount, and then you'd immediately have a meeting of minds at the true value there the middle. In real life it rarely works this way. Most often, each of you will have to counter several times until you finally reach the middle

Quick Tips

Whether you're buying from a dealer or an owner, never accept the asking price; it will always be higher than what the seller expects to get. How much maneuvering room you have in negotiating a lower price will depend on many factors, including the seller's motivation to sell the boat now. While this degree of motivation more often exists in private sales, a dealer can also be strongly driven to sell a boat "today" at the end of a model year or when it is overstocked for any reason, and especially if that particular boat has been in his inventory for a long time. Never think a sticker price is final.

ground. But if you continue to show both an active interest in the boat and an unwillingness to buy until your negotiations result in the right price, you should be able to get it.

REPOSSESSIONS

As I'll explain in Chapter 5, defaults on boat loans are relatively rare and repossessed boats are not all that common. But repos do exist, and their numbers have been increasing slightly—at least regionally, if not overall. Since lenders want money and not boats, when repos are available you'll usually find that they carry a very good price. The lender will often settle for less than the balance due simply to gain something

positive from the repossession and prevent incurring a total loss—even a modest sum from a definite sale is often considered better than holding out for a higher offer that may or may not develop. Every repo deal is different, and you won't know what a particular boat may cost until you ask.

The principal drawback to buying a repo is the probability of getting a boat in poor condition regardless of its age or price. Human nature being what it is, most people who are in financial trouble will have neglected proper maintenance for lack of funds long before their loan reaches the default stage. And once they realize that the boat is gone for sure, maintenance usually ceases completely. Yet the price can often be low enough to offset any added expense you may face in restoration. Heed the opinions of your surveyor in terms of both the boat's present value and the anticipated cost of restoration. If the total represents a reasonable buy and you are willing to wait for the needed work to be done before you can enjoy your new toy, go for it. Otherwise, walk away and keep looking.

"UGLY DUCKLINGS"

Every once in a while, you'll run across a potential purchase that looks absolutely horrible and yet carries such an unbelievably low price that it's attractive nonetheless. The boat will often be larger and basically nicer (if it were in better condition) than you could afford if it weren't priced so ridiculously low, and you can't help but wonder, "Should I?"

The only answer I can give is "maybe." Note I didn't say, "No way!" Surprised? Well, what you have in a fixer-upper is possibly a lot of potential, and if the price is truly right, it can be a very good deal. But before you commit to buying one, ask a lot of questions. The most important ones are those you must ask yourself:

- **When the boat is fully restored, will I be able to afford to use it?** The purchase is just the beginning. Once the boat is operable and beautiful again, you'll need the money to insure it, store it, dock it, put fuel in it, maintain it . . . the list goes on. The larger the boat, the more costly is every item on the list. If you can't comfortably answer yes to this question, say no to the purchase.

- **Am I ready to undertake a *major* renovation project?** If you have ever been involved with a renovation project ashore, you have an idea of what's involved. But that idea may be only a vague one because the complications involved in refurbishing a boat can be both more numerous and more difficult and frustrating than anything that might crop up in renovating a house or an apartment. If you can't comfortably answer yes to this question also, you have to say no to the purchase.

- **Am I prepared to walk away if the survey reports are bad?** You'll need a thorough prepurchase survey, of course, including an engine survey (see Chapter 10). You can live with a report that the engines are shot—you can always repower. And even a small amount of structural damage shouldn't stop you either, as long as it is repairable. But the fiberglass equivalent of "I hope you have a fireplace!" should make you walk away. Quickly! If you can't answer yes to *this* question, you are in deep trouble.

The Realities of Restoration

It's easy to look at an old wreck and think, "All it needs is a thorough cleaning. Some paint, varnish, maybe a new carpet, a bit of reupholstering . . . and then it will be better than new." Well, you could be right. But more often the problems go deeper. And when you sit down to digest the survey reports and start to budget the renovation, make sure you have your priorities straight. When you plan your restoration project, consider the following and in this order:

- **The soundness and structural integrity of the hull, deck, and superstructure, particularly the bottom.** As I noted above, a bit of needed repair will be okay, but if the boat is not structurally sound, walk away. If any structural work is necessary, complete it before you think of doing *anything* else.

- **The integrity of the power plants and related systems.** New engines are always a possibility, but before you commit to purchasing the hulk, be sure you know what repowering will cost. You need to also know all other details of repowering, including whether new versions of the original engines are available or whether the engine compartment will have to be restructured to adapt to new engines. Repowering is a major job in itself, often involving all new stringers, mounts, and *running gear* [shafts and props, etc.], especially if you need to use different engines. If you have to consider repowering in addition to many other tasks, the whole project may be totally impractical even if it remains possible. Think before you act.

- **Electronics.** Yes, many of these are in the "nice but not necessary" category, but very few people want to operate a boat without at least the minimum of depth sounder, VHF radio, and GPS. If these aren't aboard and in full working order, add the cost of buying and installing new ones to your restoration budget.

- **Cosmetics.** You want your boat to look good, and a thorough refurbishing can make all the difference in the world. But unless you take care of the above matters before you do anything else, you'll be shortchanging yourself two ways. First, no matter how good your new boat looks, if it doesn't run properly you won't enjoy it. Second, when it comes time to sell (and there will always be a time to sell), your potential buyer's surveyor won't give a hoot about the boat's new upholstery but will care very much about hull integrity and systems installations. If they aren't up to snuff, you'll have to settle for a lower price—or maybe even lose the sale entirely.

Start with a Plan

Abe Lincoln was once quoted: "If I have 6 hours to chop down a tree, I'm going to spend the first 4 sharpening the ax." The U.S. Navy has a similar thought, stated in the Rule of Ps: Proper Preparation Prevents Poor Performance. Both ideas mean that it is imperative to always get ready before you get going, to know what you're going to do *before* you actually do a thing. In a restoration project, this means carefully planning the work and then working the plan.

A good plan will also help you with budgeting; when you know precisely what must be done, you have a better chance of accurately estimating what the work will cost. Your surveyor can help you with this because s/he will know what tasks are involved and what the cost should be. But even before you reach this stage, you can ballpark the project by figuring that renovation will amount to least half as much as what you

pay for the boat, and even more if the boat is in very sad shape and/or you are able to buy it for a ridiculously low price. Again, the surveyor's estimate will be very close, so always use it when figuring the bottom line—and then add at least 15% to cover the unexpected.

And Be Prepared to Wait

Whether you do all the work yourself (which can be a lot of fun but also time consuming and perhaps beyond your abilities), do some work and hire out the rest (a plausible approach), or hire out all of it, be patient! Restoration projects of every type have one thing in common: they always take longer than anyone thinks they will at the outset.

Restoring a fixer-upper to its original glory can be very rewarding, financially and otherwise. Even if the financial rewards turn out to be less than you initially expected (these projects have a way of always running over budget no matter how carefully you plan), the satisfaction of seeing an ugly duckling

Quick Tips

The waiting involved, along with the inevitable frustrations you'll encounter, means that a renovation project isn't for everyone. If the whole idea is even the least bit daunting, perhaps you shouldn't take this route. Remember, too, that once you start a renovation project, you are committed to finishing it. So again I say, "Think before you act!"

Don't Forget

You should never blow your entire wad on the purchase; always keep a reserve to cover additional outlays that may arise. Whether you buy a brand-new boat or one with more miles under the keel than you want to acknowledge, you're going to have some after-the-purchase expenses. If you've spent all you have on the down payments for the boat, insurance, a place to keep it, and any other inevitable prepurchase and postpurchase expenses, you're going to be one sad puppy. There will always be other matters that crop up only after the boat is yours. If you have a brand-new boat, there shouldn't be many, and if you've shopped carefully and negotiated well for a used boat, the same should apply. But it's almost impossible to avoid them completely. Always keep at least 10% of the total purchase price in reserve—and more if you can.

WRAP

✔ A new boat costs more than a used boat, and much of the added cost is lost to depreciation.

✔ Buying a used boat eliminates depreciation loss, but the boat's condition is critical to determining its value.

✔ The best buy is often a nearly new "used" boat with low hours on the meters.

✔ The value of any used boat can be found in the BUC Book.

✔ Private sales can often save you money, but you get the boat as is, whereas a used boat purchased from a dealer may carry a limited warranty.

✔ Buying a repossessed boat (if you can find one) can often be a very good deal, but also possibly a lot of work.

✔ Ultimately, whether to buy new or used is a personal decision that only you can make.

✔ Never spend all of your funds on buying the boat; always keep some cash in reserve for after-the-purchase expenses.

become a beautiful swan again can make the project worthwhile. Even when the restoration project runs over budget and you add its total cost to your purchase price, the odds are that you will still get a very good boat at a very attractive bottom line.

CHAPTER 4

PACKAGE DEALS

Do I Need to Read This Chapter?

You should read this chapter if you want to discover

- ✔ The nature of packaging.
- ✔ The limitations inherent in package deals.
- ✔ The advantages these deals can offer.
- ✔ Details to watch for when buying a package deal.

WHAT DOES THE DEAL INCLUDE?

There was a time when buying a boat meant simply that: you got a boat and little else. If it was outboard powered, it came minus the motor(s), which you had to buy separately and then pay to have mounted (though you would usually purchase the boat and propulsion from the same dealer). The steering system was usually factory installed, though this could sometimes be a separately purchased aftermarket item as well. If you planned to keep the boat on a trailer, that was also additional. If the boat was inboard powered, the purchase included the engine(s) as well as the controls and steering system—but little more. New boats of any type usually came with almost none of the Coast Guard–mandated safety gear aboard, which meant you had to buy still more accessories before a boat was even marginally usable.

Times have changed. These days, boats are usually delivered ready to go—"Just add water!" is a common sales slogan. It's not unusual for outboard models to arrive at the dealership with engine(s) already mounted; the builder has already done the rigging and, often, the boat will even be sitting on a suitable trailer. The days of buying every item separately are fading quickly.

On the whole, this is good. Economies of scale allow builders to buy everything at the lowest wholesale price, which means they can include all the requisite accessories you would have to buy anyway and still sell a boat profitably for a lower total cost than you would face if you had to acquire all the extras on your own at standard retail—or even at the lower discount outlet price. The builder and dealer save while making and selling the boat, and you save while buying it: a win-win situation for everyone involved.

But there are still some details to consider, not the least of which is that packages are most often inflexible; the boat comes equipped with certain items and that's it. No personal selection is allowed. You may face the same sort of eye-opener I did many years ago when buying my first new car. I really liked the steering wheel on one of the demo vehicles I drove and decided I wanted it in the car I would buy. "Then you want Interior Package C," the salesman told me. "Not necessarily," I replied while looking at a brochure that explained all the details on options, including the additional cost. "I don't care even the slightest whether I have wood panels on the dash or leather map pockets on the doors. But I really do want that steering wheel. I like its look; I like its feel."

"Well, sir," the salesman replied, "it's only available as a part of Package C. If you really want that wheel, you have to take everything that comes with it. There's no other way."

Boats Are Similar These Days

Let me remind you that we're talking new boats here. Used boats are basically WYSIWYG—What You See Is What You Get. Any installed equipment will probably become yours whether it works properly or not, and you have no options regarding changes. This is not necessarily true for equipment that isn't "installed"—for things that are not attached and thus have not become part of the boat.

Beyond the Cosmetic

As the packaging principle applies to powerboats, it often means that certain styling features are grouped—that a particular color and pattern of carpet will be available only as a part of one of several optional interior

Get Started

Whether you're buying a new or used boat, make sure your purchase agreement contains a detailed description of everything included in the sale. If you don't have every detail in writing, you may discover after closing that some of those charming extras that prompted you to choose this boat over all others are no longer on board. Even when buying a new boat, you may discover that some of the little things that you admired—such as throw pillows on a sofa or berth, a lamp on an end table, or folding chairs that provide seating on an otherwise clear aft deck—were put aboard the demo boat to make it appear more like a boat in use, to help you picture yourself using it. If any item isn't specifically mentioned in the agreement you and the seller sign, there's a good chance it won't be on the boat you end up buying. Be particularly careful if your sea trial is actually a demo ride on a sister ship. Dealers will often equip demo boats with every possible option just to show the possibilities (and to make the boat look its best), but any option you don't specifically order will rarely be included. Negotiate well, and then have your oral agreement confirmed with a written one.

decors that also have certain predetermined upholstery and color schemes. But since these choices are of relatively low priority when compared to such things as the boat's seakeeping qualities or maximum cruising speed and range, let's look at some other packaging details that relate more to what really counts: the safe and enjoyable use of your new boat.

Trailer

This common accessory was one of the very first items to be packaged with the boat, motor, and other most-needed extras, which is why I list it first. But since we have a whole chapter on trailer boating (see Chapter 7), and because not every boat buyer will need a trailer, I'm going to leave those details for later discussion and move on to other things you will definitely need whether or not they are part of a package. The more of them you can arrange to have included in your basic purchase, the better off you'll be.

Coast Guard–Required Safety Gear

The Federal Boat Safety Act of 1971 demands that we carry certain safety gear aboard. Actually, the demands began with the original Motorboat Act of 1940. This law was the first to classify boats by their length and was primarily concerned with having sufficient fire extinguishers; one personal flotation device (PFD), or life jacket, for each person on board; and a backfire flame Arrester on all inboard gasoline engine carburetors. The 1971 act added more requirements that have since become more stringent over time.

Coast Guard–approved extinguishers may be either portable or *fixed* [permanently installed] in an engine compartment. Portable extinguishers will carry an A (wood, paper, etc.), B (flammable liquid), or C

Fire Extinguisher Requirements

CLASS (BASED ON LOA)	A (< 16 FEET)	I (16 TO < 26 FEET)	II (26 TO < 40 FEET)	III (40 TO 65 FEET)
no fixed system	1 B-I		2 B-Is or 1 B-II	3 B-Is or 1 B-II and 1 B-I
with approved fixed system	0		1 B-I	2 B-Is or 1 B-II

This table should make it easy to remember three things: 1. The number of B-I extinguishers required is the same as the boat's class—I, II, or III. 2. You can subtract one extinguisher if you have a built-in fixed system in the engine compartment. 3. While this number is the minimum needed to be legal, it is also inadequate in the real world. Three B-I extinguishers are simply not enough for a boat of 40 feet or more! Cabin boats should have one for each cabin, plus one in the galley, one by each helm, one in the cockpit, and at least one *plus* a fixed system in the engine compartment.

Fire Extinguisher Sizes

EXTINGUISHER TYPE	FOAM (GALLONS)	CO_2 (POUNDS)	DRY CHEMICAL (POUNDS)	HALON* (POUNDS)
B-I	1.25	4	2	2.5
B-II	2.5	15	10	10

*The production of new Halon has been banned since January 1, 1994, by edict of the U.S. Environmental Protection Agency. However, fixed systems employing Halon are still around because they were either charged with recycled Halon or were installed prior to the ban; but they are becoming rarer with the passage of time. New agents have been certified, and so far they are proving to be almost as efficient as Halon but not quite. Thus they require a slightly larger container than Halon for equivalent firefighting capabilities, though these systems still tend to be smaller than CO_2. A fixed system of any type offers the advantage of instantaneous response. It can often detect and extinguish a fire in the engine compartment before you even know one exists.

One B-II extinguisher most often holds much more agent than two B-Is, so B-IIs are better if you have the space, though they are not quite as portable because they weigh more and are bigger.

(electrical) classification—usually, more than one, such as BC or, less frequently, ABC—to indicate what type of fire they are suited for. Along with each classification is a size rating—I or II. The Coast Guard is most interested in your extinguishers' ability to handle Class B fires, as the requirements suggest.

Extinguishers Are Included

These days, portable extinguishers are generally a part of the total package, and boats are often built with molded-in recesses in consoles, seats, or bulkheads so that the extinguishers can be conveniently accessible (the regulations require that fire extinguishers be "permanently and conspicuously mounted") yet out of the way. The downside is that there is often only a sufficient number to make the boat "legal"; you may still want to add more. With inboard boats, a fixed system in the engine compartment is often a part of the deal also, though not necessarily. Even when a fixed system isn't included in the boat's base price, it *is* often a standard option and may have been built into the boat you are seriously considering. If it is already there, how much (and even, perhaps, *if*) you'll pay extra for the system can be a bargaining point. A built-in fixed system is so desirable that it is worth paying full retail if you must.

Other Federal Requirements

The table on page 62 lists everything required by law, items that must be either aboard your boat or built into it. One system not on this list, however, and yet that is absolutely necessary if you ever go out (or get caught out) after dark, is running, or navigation, lights—the red, green, and white lights that help other vessels to see you and determine which way you're

Figure 4-1. Boats these days usually come equipped with the required number of fire extinguishers, and the builder will often provide convenient niches in which to mount them.

headed when they may not be able to see the boat as a whole. The good news here is that with just about anything larger than a dinghy, running lights are usually standard equipment. The bad news is that while the installed lights will meet the minimum legal requirements, as with the number of fire extinguishers required, what is legal isn't necessarily safe. Most boats built in the United States will have light fixtures sized proportionately to the size of the boat rather than to their visibility. A leading cause of nighttime collisions is that the operator of the larger boat couldn't see the tiny lights on the smaller one it ran into until it was way too late to stop or turn away. Converting to larger lights with better visibility may be a worthy after-the-purchase consideration with any new boat.

Noisemakers

A signaling device, a horn of some type, will also usually be included among a boat's standard equipment, as will a bell if the boat is large enough to require it. But here's another of those peculiar boat problems: the marine environment, which can wreak havoc with mechanical systems, can ruin electrical components even faster. The horn is often one of the first to quit. Having a handheld, canister-type horn for backup is always a good idea.

Ventilation

Ventilation will also be a part of the boat "as constructed," even including the powered bilge blower(s) required in gasoline inboard engine compartments. Diesel-powered boats will usually have blowers also, because a good flow of air is so important to their operation.

PFDs

One PFD for each person on board would seem a rather simple concept. Ah, if it were only so. In the first place, you have a choice of types. Do you want Type I PFDs, or will Type IIs or Type IIIs suffice? Any of them is okay from a legal point of view.

Type I PFDs are theoretically the best and are required on boats that carry passengers for hire. They provide the greatest flotation (22 pounds minimum for adults) and *must* turn the wearer faceup even if s/he is unconscious. But they are not always the answer. For one thing, they tend to be bulky and can present a stowage problem on small boats. For another, they usually come in only two sizes: adult and child. And since we humans, especially children, tend to come in such a wide variety of sizes, they are not always a perfect fit. Type IIs are most often included in the Coast Guard package that builders

Quick Tips

There has been a push in recent years to require the wearing of PFDs by all people on all boats at all times; they want it to become law. While many of us consider this to be as foolish as requiring all airline passengers to wear parachutes at all times, the truth is that a PFD does you no good unless you are wearing it when you accidentally end up in the water. So when to don one? You should wear a PFD whenever the size of the boat relative to prevailing sea conditions suggests there's even the slightest possibility of your going overboard without warning—and you should always err on the side of caution. It's far better to be wearing a PFD and not need it than to need it and not be wearing it!

and dealers offer with their boats. Given the realities, they are generally an ideal solution: they provide sufficient flotation (a minimum of 15.5 pounds), and though the approval standards do not *require* Type IIs to turn the wearer faceup, most of them will—they have support behind the head. Type II PFDs are available in many sizes, even for very small children, and, if well made (and properly cared for), will serve you well for a number of years. Type IIIs, which are meant for waterskiing or playing on a water toy such as a PWC, are legal but they offer no assistance in turning the wearer faceup.

As long as you enter the water fully conscious, a Type III is okay. In fact, in northern climes where the water (and, often, the air) can be chilly even in midsummer, a Type III "float coat" not only will keep you on the surface but also can offer a degree of comfort the others cannot. This can be true even if you don't go in the water—float coats make perfect windbreakers.

Your main concern in a package deal is the *quality* of the PFDs supplied. All USCG-approved PFDs must meet certain minimum standards. But the minimums are often just that. The more expensive PFDs are usually well worth their added cost because they are better quality. If you take care of them properly, they will last much longer. Even if your boat comes completely equipped, you may still want to invest in better PFDs. The lives of you and your loved ones could depend on them.

The Type IV throwable provided (if one is provided) will often be a cushion, but it could also be a ring buoy or a horseshoe shape, though these are more often seen on sailboats. As long as it is an approved Type IV PFD, the style really doesn't matter; each has its own advantages and disadvantages. Keep in mind that while one Type IV throwable PFD will make a boat legal, you need to be able to grab it and throw it quickly if someone falls overboard. On larger boats, this can mean having more than one, stowing each on a different part of the boat.

Visual Distress Signals

You will be legal with three handheld flares rated day/night. But since each flare has a burn time of only a few minutes and visibility is strictly line of sight, having just three handheld flares can leave you literally in the dark all too quickly. Also, all pyrotechnics—handheld flares, smoke signals, and rockets—have a 42-month life. They are stamped with a manufacture date and an expiration date, after which they may work but can no longer count toward your federally mandated minimum. If you buy a new boat and visual distress signals (VDS) are part of the package, they should be current—perhaps newer than the boat. If you buy an older boat, check the dates on every pyrotechnic device aboard. If they're out of date, there's no harm in keeping

Federally Mandated Safety Requirements

REQUIREMENT	CLASS (BASED ON LOA)			
	A (< 16 FEET)	I (16 TO < 26 FEET)	II (26 TO < 40 FEET)	III (40 TO 65 FEET)
Fire extinguishers	See table on page 59; all extinguishers must be USCG approved.			
PFDs	One Type I, II, III, or V for each person on board; Type V hybrid PFDs must be worn to count.			
		One Type IV throwable.		
Visual distress signals	Three night signals if operating at night.	A minimum of three day and three night signals or three day/night signals.		
Bell and whistle	Vessels less than 12 meters (39.4 feet) need a signaling device capable of producing a 4- to 6-second blast audible for 0.5 mile (as required per Inland Rules). A mouth whistle or horn is legal if loud enough.			Vessels over 12 meters must have a mechanical whistle or horn, and a bell.
Backfire flame arrester	Required on all gasoline engines installed after April 25, 1940, except outboard motors.			
Ventilation	Required on all vessels with enclosed engines or fuel tanks, with the size of vents and duct work based on the total volume enclosed. Since 1980, powered ventilation (a bilge blower) is also required for each compartment that has a permanently installed gasoline engine with a cranking motor for remote starting.			

them aboard as spares, but you'll have to buy some new ones before you can use the boat legally.

Requirements Not Mandated by Law

There are also other things you'll definitely need that may or may not be offered as part of the deal. None of them is required everywhere (though some are in some jurisdictions), but everything listed below is something you *will* need at some time. The more of them you can get in the basic new boat package, the better off you'll be. Used boats will usually have most of them aboard, but their condition and prospects for continued utility could be questionable; this is something you want to check carefully and discuss with the seller.

- **Anchor and rode.** An anchor is useful for mooring in remote locales where there are no facilities. Perhaps more important, an anchor is a boat's only "emergency brake," the one thing that can stop you from drifting into trouble (such as rocks or shallows) if your motive power fails. One anchor is a must; having a backup is a definite plus.

- **Magnetic compass.** This is the only nonelectronic device you have to show which way you are headed; it is the only thing you can count on for directional information if your batteries die and visibility vanishes along with your electronics. A reliable magnetic compass is a must! (And yet a compass is not a requirement of either the U.S. Coast Guard regulations or the laws of a majority of states. Go figure.) Because the magnetic compass is prone to an error known as *deviation*, which is caused by onboard magnetic influences, the steering compass often has to be *adjusted* or

Quick Tips

If your boat's steering compass needs to be compensated, don't let the statement "this service is not included in the package" stop you from having it done. An accurate compass will be worth whatever it costs, so pay extra if you must—but always negotiate to try to have it included.

compensated to eliminate (or reduce) this error. Try to have this service included in the package also, if it's needed—though with fiberglass boats it often is not needed.

- **VHF radio.** This is your connection to the marine "party line" to which other boats, marinas, yacht clubs, the Coast Guard, tow services, and just about everyone else on and around the water will be listening. Cell phones work well in some areas (although cellular service was designed primarily for coverage on land, so it isn't always reliable on the water), and they can be quite useful for calling ahead to a marina, reaching a friend on another boat, or calling someone ashore—the "marine operators" we used for so many years to connect to land lines have been done in by the widespread use of cell phones. A cellular conversation is also considerably more private than a VHF call (though not totally so), which can make it even better than the marine radio under normal circumstances. But a cell phone is a poor substitute for a VHF radio in an emergency when you want to reach as many people as possible with just one call for help; in this case, the lack of privacy is an advantage!

- **Depth sounder.** The bottom is often your closest land, and it can be helpful to know just how close it is. A depth sounder will show you the depth continuously. There are other ways to determine water depth, but none is as quick and easy as using an electronic sounder, which shows you the depth instantly and continuously at nearly any speed.
- **Docklines.** Whenever you tie up to a pier or float, you'll need at least a couple of *lines* [they're "rope" in the store, but "lines" once they come aboard], more often three to six. Docklines aren't a part of the boat as built, but because they're absolutely necessary, a few of them are almost always included by the dealer even when they aren't provided by the builder.
- **Fenders.** These soft items go between your boat and any hard parts of a pier or seawall (or another boat) to prevent scratches or other dings on your topsides. Four is good for most boats, though more is generally better, especially for larger boats; many small boats can get by with fewer, which is good because small boats have less room to stow them.
- **Trim tabs.** These flaps mounted under or behind the transom can be important enough to a planing hull's performance that many builders now provide them as standard equipment and design their boats so that fully retracted tabs are flush with the bottom to minimize

drag. Other builders vehemently deny that their hulls could possibly ever need tabs and will install them only as an extra and then only reluctantly. Tabs are rarely necessary 100% of the time, but they are also rarely *un*necessary 100% of the time. When they are needed, their contribution to performance is sufficient that having them there for "when you need them" justifies their cost.

The Nice but Not Necessary

There are some other things you'll want to have aboard. No federal or state laws require them, and you can operate without them, but the larger your boat and the greater your cruising range, the more desirable they become. And once you get used to using any of these devices, you'll probably feel "lost" if you have to operate without them. The more of these you can get at a "package" price, the better.

- **GPS.** Not a necessity but way more than merely welcome, this navigation system is becoming more and more accepted as standard equipment on even the smallest boats. The satellite-based global positioning system is the most accurate navigation process yet devised by mankind, able to show you your *position* [location] within 36 feet under ideal conditions.
- **Electronic chart/course plotter.** Many small display units can fit just about any boat, even a small center-console fishing boat or outboard runabout. Most will have either an integrated GPS receiver or the means to be interfaced with one. Seeing your position constantly updated on the image of a chart can be quite reassuring, though I'd suggest you also learn to navigate without

the electronics, just in case you ever have to.

- **Radar.** Extremely useful in both navigation and collision avoidance, there are now many sets that are small (and also inexpensive) enough to be installed on some fairly small boats. Incidentally, many radar sets are now an integrated display that also includes GPS and chartplotter. And while these sets tend to cost more, they are less expensive than buying two or three stand-alone devices. More important, given the space restrictions aboard any vessel, having several functions in one device can be a huge advantage.

Quick Tips

The Navigation Rules require that every vessel ". . . shall at all times maintain a proper lookout by sight and hearing as well as by all available means appropriate . . ." Courts have determined that if you have radar and don't use it, you are *not* using all available means; that is, you are not maintaining a proper lookout. Courts have also determined that having radar aboard and not knowing how to use it properly can also be considered a failure to maintain a proper lookout. So take heed: if your new boat is radar equipped, it is imperative that you learn how it works and always use it when underway, in foul weather and fair.

- **Anchor windlass.** The larger the boat, the more important this will be because the anchor and its rode will be larger and heavier and thus more difficult to handle without mechanical help. An electric windlass is best, but even a manual model you have to crank (or ratchet with a lever) is better than having to grasp the rode and pull it directly. Many boats are built with a windlass in mind, and more than a few offer one as a standard option. The price to you is often negotiable, so bargain for the very best value you can get.

- **Autopilot.** This will steer a much straighter course than you or any other human, no matter how experienced. In addition, the electronic compass used with most modern autopilots can be made to be totally free of deviation error through the use of the unit's internal computer, so its display can be more accurate than your magnetic compass (even a fully compensated compass can still have error). A modern autopilot can also usually be interfaced with a GPS to steer along predetermined routes, greatly simplifying normal operations when cruising. The only reason for still having a magnetic compass is that it will continue to work if your battery power fails, which your autopilot's compass will not.

And the Fun Stuff We Often Also Need

The following items are not necessary for powerboating, but most people seem to want them. That's why many are also offered as standard options on new boats and their number and variety seem limited only by the size of the boat.

- **Stereo.** Even little runabouts and bowriders often come with an AM/FM/CD player built into the dash and with weather-resistant speakers installed somewhere in the sides of the cockpit. Larger vessels often have more than one. These days, satellite and HD radio receivers are becoming more and more common.

- **TV.** If the boat has a cabin, at least one *bulkhead* [wall] will undoubtedly feature a built-in TV. Plasma or other flat-screen thin displays are common despite their higher cost because space is at such a premium aboard boats that the value of whatever amount can be gained by not needing the depth for a picture tube behind the screen often outweighs the added expense. A connection for a shoreside cable feed is usually provided also, along with a marine TV antenna mounted outside somewhere as high as possible. If the boat is large enough, the video system in the saloon will usually include 5.1 Dolby Surround Sound.

- **DVD player.** If there isn't one already built into the TV, you can be sure there will be one near it, probably built into a bulkhead or perhaps in a nearby cabinet.

- **Satellite TV.** Once an option even for megayachts, cruisers in the mid-30s now often have a telltale dome on the radar arch or hardtop. You don't really "need" it, but when you're out there where cable can't reach and reception by antenna is marginal (which can include not only when you're out at sea but also at anchor or even when docked at a marina in many remote locales), it surely is good to have.

- **Icemaker(s).** When I began boating, ice was something we bought—always— because it was our only way of cooling things; most small pleasure boats didn't have mechanical refrigeration. Marinas still sell bags of ice cubes because portable coolers remain an effective way to chill drinks and because even vessels with built-in refrigerators often need the added cooling capacity. But boats don't have to be very large to have a built-in dual-voltage (120-volt AC and 12-volt DC) refrigerator in the galley, and I've seen icemakers in the cockpit of boats less than 40 feet long (and their operators still often have to buy ice in order to have enough!).

Bargaining Points

Many of the items listed above will be a part of a good package deal. Sometimes they will be grouped, perhaps with a Coast Guard package that includes such items as fire extinguishers, PFDs, and VDS, and a docking package that includes the lines and fenders. Boats today are also quite often sold with an electronics package that includes the VHF and depth sounder and, commonly, even the GPS and radar.

Most other items, such as TVs, stereos, icemakers, and other such creature comforts, may be standard options, and you may find them already built into many of the new models you look at. At the very least, the boat will often have been designed, built, and prewired (as well as preplumbed, where necessary) for easier installation of these goodies after you've bought it.

The biggest upside to the packaging concept is that the builders can buy so many units that they pay the lowest possible wholesale price. When they pass that saving on to the ultimate consumer, the cost difference can be significant. There is simply no way in the world you could buy the stuff for less—or, in most cases, even as inexpensively. But there is also a downside: the so-called standard options are what they are, and you don't have a take it or leave it decision about anything but the entire package. The brand and model of each accessory have been decided for you, and if you'd prefer something else, you are out of luck. The purchasing scale that allows the better package pricing normally precludes such changes. The boats are built with the accessories for which the builder can pay the lowest price, and while they will all most certainly be acceptable at the very least (and, usually, more than), they are not always either the best or what you might prefer.

FINAL THOUGHTS

Watch out for too low a price, a package with barely adequate components. While it is true that boating is no longer strictly for the rich and there are both new and used boats available in just about every price range, some builders will try to attract new and inexperienced customers by putting together packages that contain the bare minimums (read: very lowest cost) of everything. By including items that are each just barely okay, the builder keeps the total cost of the boat to an absolute minimum, hoping to attract even more newcomers to the sport with an especially appealing low price. My feeling is that this is ultimately counterproductive. A boat that is barely adequate will soon disappoint and, possibly, turn its new owner away from the sport for lack of real enjoyment. My advice: in most cases, you should avoid the lowest-priced model. Instead of buying the least-expensive 21-footer, buy the better-equipped 18-footer that's similarly priced. And so on.

There's most certainly a boat for everyone, whatever one's specific desires may be. Just remember what they say about things that seem too good to be true: they usually are. And even in the best package deal, you

Don't Forget

If you aren't able to negotiate a decent package and thus have to buy each desired component separately, apply the same approach to the purchase of individual accessories that you did to the purchase of the boat itself. Always negotiate for the best possible value and never merely for the lowest possible price. But since price can be important nonetheless, I'm including information on some discount outlets in the Resources section. Just remember the value of time. Sometimes you need things right now, and the only realistic solution is to shop close to home where you can receive your purchases immediately. Keep in mind that if you don't shop locally on occasion when time isn't of the essence, that local store may no longer be there for you when it is. Sometimes it's worth spending an extra buck or two just to help make sure your local supplier will remain in business. Convenience has value, too!

are not apt to find a free lunch. Always shop for the best *value*, not merely the best price. Sometimes it can be worth deviating from a package and paying a little more in order to acquire the precise accessories you wish to have.

WRAP

- ✔ Packaging is here to stay.
- ✔ The concept can make boat buying easier by including all the extras you'll need in one basic deal.
- ✔ Packages tend to be inflexible; they are what they are, and you can't change the individual components.
- ✔ Packages are most often good deals, but beware of buying barely adequate components for the sake of a lower price.
- ✔ Packaging can save you money, but always shop for the best *value*, not merely the best price.
- ✔ You should decline a package if the individual components are too far from being the items you really want.

CHAPTER 5

FINANCING

Do I Need to Read This Chapter?

You should read this chapter if you want to discover

- ✔ Why you should finance your boat even if you have the cash.
- ✔ That interest on a boat loan is often tax deductible.
- ✔ The possible need for a separate corporation or LLC to buy and own the boat.
- ✔ Good sources of boat loans.
- ✔ The types of loans available.
- ✔ How much of a down payment you'll need.
- ✔ The length of loans available.
- ✔ The details of state registration as compared to federal documentation.

WHO NEEDS FINANCING?

Everybody! No matter how much cash you may have, don't use it for more than a down payment. Some say that since a boat is a luxury you really don't need, you shouldn't commit yourself to making payments. That's fine if the boat is small enough to have a very modest price tag. But if a significant sum is involved, you'll be better off financing the purchase even if you don't need to. Chances are that if you invest it wisely, the amount you would have spent in buying a boat can actually provide considerable gain. If you put it all into the boat, it's gone! Add to this that the interest you pay on the loan is usually tax deductible, and not paying cash makes more sense.

The Simpler Life

Because many readers of this book won't need to do a thing but buy the boat and enjoy it (from a financial perspective, anyway), and also because the details of any corporate entities or alternate financing arrangements will be complex and varied, I won't even begin to describe the many possible options. But if your income derives from sources other than a basic salary and/or you have assets you don't want associated with your boat, the Get Started tip on the next page is intended for you. Heed it, please.

Welcome to the Real World

Most of us don't have the available cash that would allow us to even think of not

Get Started

Depending on the complexity of your assets and income situation, your best move might be to first discuss your purchase with your accountant or tax adviser. While most boat loans are made to an individual using the boat as collateral, this isn't the only way, nor is it always best. Sometimes it's better to use other assets as collateral, and borrowing against them is usually wiser than liquidating them to have the cash. This way you continue to benefit from any future appreciation and avoid the capital gains taxes that might impact you when you sell them. There can also be tax (and other) advantages to having a Delaware corporation, an LLC, or another arm's-length, independent entity (such as an offshore company) as the boat's legal owner of record, especially if you plan to put the boat in charter service when you're not using it yourself (see Chapter 1). Since you must have the legal entity that will actually own the boat fully established before the purchase and, most likely, well before any financing can be arranged, you need to get started on this aspect soon after you decide you want to buy a boat.

Quick Tips

You may be able to deduct the interest on your boat loan. Under Internal Revenue code 163(h) (2), you can deduct the interest on the loan for a qualified residence you own. Under Internal Revenue Code section 163(h) (4), a boat will be considered a qualified residence if it is one of the two residences chosen by the taxpayer and the boat provides basic living accommodations, such as sleeping space (berths) under permanent cover, a toilet (head), and cooking facilities (galley). If the boat is chartered, you will have to use the boat for personal purposes either for more than 14 days or for 10% of the number of days during the year the boat was actually in charter, in accordance with Internal Revenue Code section 280A(d) (1). If the amount of charter service rules out using your boat as a "qualified residence," its total of allowable business deductions (Schedule C) may make the loss of this one deduction worthwhile by having even greater scope. Be sure to consult with your accountant or tax adviser for up-to-date info on the current IRS code and how it relates to your tax situation.

financing a purchase on the scale of a new or used powerboat, even a small one. So let's look at the reasonable options. There are really only two: you can deal directly with a lender, or you can get everything, including financing and insurance, through the dealer. The latter, of course applies only when you buy a new or used boat through an established dealership. Private sales usually require that you obtain financing (as well as handle all other aspects of the purchase) on your own or with the help of a broker. If you buy a large yacht through a brokerage house, you'll generally find that most of them now offer all-in-one sales-related services as well (including arrangements for financing), if you wish to take advantage of the convenience. And speaking of convenience, many lenders specializing in boat loans can also help you with the details of registering and insuring your boat.

BOAT LOAN BASICS

By virtue of the amount involved, buying a boat will often be the second most serious financial transaction of your life, following only the purchase of your home. Though each boat-buying situation is unique, there are enough commonalities to discuss them here.

National Marine Bankers Association

Members of the National Marine Bankers Association (NMBA) specialize in boat and yacht loans, so you could do best by dealing with one of them. It's not that other lenders can't or won't make a boat loan but, rather, that members of this organization are better acquainted with the special aspects of boat loans and thus are both more knowledgeable of the requirements and more receptive to the idea. I've discovered that money people rarely lend for projects they aren't familiar with, so it helps to deal with people who know boats.

A knowledgeable marine lender can also help you with more than just the money you need, and it makes sense to establish a working relationship with one long before you've found the boat of your dreams. You don't have to do things this way; it is definitely possible to first find your boat and then find the money. But having an experienced finance person in your corner while you search for the boat you want can be enough of an advantage that it is certainly the better way.

A Knowledgeable Lender = Fewer Hassles

A lender who knows boats can also help you avoid some potential pitfalls that you and unknowing lenders might not be aware of when it comes to buying the boat of your dreams, particularly if it's used. For example, whenever anyone works on a boat and doesn't get paid, that person can file a mechanic's lien against the boat. Of course, the boat can't pay a cent. But when it is sold, its new owner can, and usually *must*, often before or soon after taking possession! If you aren't familiar with this potential snag and the lender doesn't know to search for these liens and see that they are cleared before the closing (as lenders inexperienced in boat dealings may not), you could acquire a bunch of unpaid, overdue bills along with your new pride and joy. And these liens will cling to your boat until they're satisfied, which can often hinder the transfer of ownership or, at the very least, your ability to actually use your boat until these surprising old debts are cleared—a lien holder can have the boat impounded until the debt is paid. A savvy lender will make sure this doesn't happen.

Qualifying

Potential lenders will be interested in three things: your ability to pay, your willingness to pay, and the collateral that will secure the loan. Some lenders will want the information in a full written application, while others will take the details over the phone or via the Internet. Generally, the more you want to borrow, the more details you'll have to supply and the more imperative it will be for them to get everything in writing. Whether by written, oral, or Internet application, it's critical that you provide information that is as complete and detailed as you can make it.

Don't Forget

Identity theft is always a concern. If you apply online, be sure the address bar of your browser shows "http**s**://," not merely "http://." The "s" indicates a secure site. Never provide personal or financial information to a site you didn't choose to go to. That is, though the secure page may result from clicking on a link, that link should be on a page you went to by choice and, preferably, not even via search engine. If you type in the site's URL or choose it through a "favorites" or "bookmark" you initiated, you should be safe. Unfortunately, all other sites may be suspect.

The Application

You'll have to provide all the details regarding the boat, including its make, model year, power, optional equipment, and any upgrades. If you're buying a used boat, include a copy of your survey report also (see Chapter 10); they'll want to see one eventually, so you might as well provide it up front. The lender will compare your application info with the BUC Book (or other source of current worth) to make sure that the amount you want to borrow is compatible with the boat's actual value—the loan-to-value ratio is important with any lender.

You must disclose the total cost, which will include:

- the purchase price
- the additional cost of any equipment upgrades or accessories you may require (or even just want), including extended warranties, if applicable
- sales taxes that must be paid at the time of purchase (if applicable)
- registration, title, or documentation expenses (see the end of this chapter)

In addition to complete information on the boat, all lenders will want your full name, Social Security number, address, phone numbers, employment details (if applicable), a revelation of income sources, details on home ownership (if applicable), and a listing of all your monthly debts. Some may ask for more.

When you sign your application, you confirm that all of the information on it is true to the best of your knowledge. Your signature is also your authorization to have the lender examine your credit. If you make the application over the phone, you will have to authorize the credit review orally. Internet applications usually require some sort of electronic signature, though the particulars vary by lender.

Ability to Pay

Most lenders will need to see proof of income. How much proof will depend on the size of the loan. Some lenders won't ask for proof of income at all if the loan is less than a certain amount. Typically, lenders will want to see pay stubs or copies of your federal tax returns for the past 2 years. If you are self-employed, they will probably also want to see corporate returns for the same period. You may also be asked to prepare a personal financial statement, which is simply a listing and summation of your current assets and liabilities that also shows your *net worth*—the value of your assets minus your liabilities. If your personal financial statement claims any liquidity, most lenders will also want current bank/brokerage statements to verify those claims.

Willingness to Pay

Lenders will examine your credit history for continuity and satisfactory repayment of present and past obligations. They will usually look for loan amounts comparable to your request for the boat loan. They will also be particularly interested in the level of any revolving debt you have (credit cards, gas cards, store charge cards, other installment loans, etc.) as well as the limits on your credit cards, expressed as available credit.

Their primary source of this information will be credit reports from the three major consumer credit reporting companies: Equifax, Experian, and TransUnion. Since the data they provide is so important to securing a loan, you should review your credit reports from all three agencies at least once a year and especially before making a large purchase, such as a boat. You have the right to one free copy of your credit report per year (once every 12 months) from each of the three agencies. See the Resources section for contact information.

This service was mandated by Congress and is provided as a convenience to consumers by the three major credit reporting agencies themselves. The best news is that using it does not enroll you in a credit monitoring service, as does getting your "free" credit reports from a similar website often advertised on TV (www.freecreditreport.com). This service requires joining an "opt out" program (Triple Advantage) that automatically charges a monthly fee against your credit card until you specifically tell them to stop. If you need or want monthly updates on your credit report information, then perhaps the $12.95 per month they charge (as of this writing) could be worth it. I'm not suggesting that you don't use the service; I am, however, informing you that your credit reports are available for free without this ongoing monthly commitment, which means they are really free—once a year, at least.

You can also get your reports by contacting the credit reporting agencies directly (see the Resources section for contact information), and if you wish to dispute any errors you *must* contact them directly.

You are entitled to one free report per agency every 12 months; beyond that, you'll have to buy your reports at a current cost of about $15 each or just under $45 for all three.

If you find an error on any of your reports, the credit reporting agency must investigate and respond to you within 30 days. If you are in the process of applying for a loan, you should immediately notify your lender of any incorrect information in your report.

You Have to Know the Score

One of the most important elements lenders look at will be your *credit score*, primarily the FICO score developed by Fair Isaac Corporation (hence the acronym). Scores range from 300 to 850, with most people scoring in the 600s and 700s. To get the best rate and terms on a boat loan, you'll probably need a FICO score of 680 or higher, though you can usually secure a boat loan of some sort with a score as low as 630. But if you score any lower than that, most lenders will tell you that you might as well forget about a boat loan—it's not going to happen. Even those lenders will admit that the scoring system isn't really fair, but it's what they have and it is what counts. So if your credit score is below 630, you should work to raise it before you apply for a boat loan.

Not Just One Score

Actually, many types of credit scores have been developed by different independent companies, credit reporting agencies, and even lenders themselves.

Be aware that each reporting agency may show a different score for the same person at the same time because they are basing it on different information. And while a lender may examine only one of the reports for a smaller loan, chances are that with the amount involved in a boat loan a lender may look at reports from all three agencies.

If you want to learn more about credit reports and FICO scores, detailed information is available online at Fair Isaac Corporation's website (www.myfico.com).

Debt Ratio

Lenders will compare the total debt stated on your credit report with your annual income to produce a ratio of installment debt to income. Typically, lenders require that your debt-to-income ratio, including your boat payment, fall within the 30% to 40% range based on your gross income. Lenders realize that life is full of uncertainties, and if you were to lose your job, become seriously ill, or have any other calamity that either drops your income or increases your expenses, this would require a shift in your expenditures and could put the loan in jeopardy. Lenders feel that a debt-to-income ratio above the 30% to 40% range would increase the risk of default and could cause you financial harm.

And the Loan Goes To . . .

It doesn't take long to find out if you've qualified; most sophisticated marine lenders can process loan applications with remarkable speed. In many cases, you can be notified of the results within a matter of hours if your creditworthiness (and FICO score) is high enough.

Prequalifying

Prequalifying is always a good idea when you're buying any big-ticket item, whether it's a house, boat, airplane, or vehicle. Knowing in advance exactly what you can and can't afford helps you narrow the search. Some marine lenders will accommodate you in this matter, but many will not. Because the boat itself, the collateral, is such an important part of the loan equation, many lenders simply will not commit to a loan amount, even hypothetically, until they know precisely what boat will be involved. Just know that an unwillingness to prequalify borrowers is not a sign of an uncooperative lender but, rather, indicates one who probably knows the marine marketplace very well. Don't be turned away from a lender simply because they won't prequalify you.

Quick Tips

Shopping for a loan can often be more complicated than shopping for the boat itself. Dealers, brokers, and even private sellers won't hesitate to state an asking price for a boat even as they realize that what you actually pay will probably be less. But it can be difficult to get so much as a ballpark estimate on a loan simply because each is unique, based on such variables as the value of the boat, the creditworthiness of the buyer, and even where you live. For this reason, many lenders won't offer you anything more than broad generalities until you actually apply for a loan and thus supply the requisite information (though some lenders will lowball you with some very attractive hypothetical interest rates and terms that, unfortunately, you'll never really see!). But having too many new credit applications isn't a good idea, either; it can hurt your credit score. So you may hesitate to make multiple applications. The good news is that FICO scores distinguish between a search for a single loan over several possible sources and a search for many new lines of credit, largely by noting when the requests are made as well as what type of requests they are. Do all of your loan shopping within a short period (say, 30 days), and avoid applying for any other credit around the time you apply for a boat loan; multiple requests for different types of credit will definitely hurt your score.

Down Payment

You'll need to make one, of course. Or maybe not! Traditionally, lenders have required 20%, but this is no longer true. Many lenders will now accept 10% down and sometimes even less; buyers with very good credit can often buy a boat with zero down. But while 100% loans are available, I can't recommend them, especially if you're buying a new boat. Remember the Big D? Given the rate at which production boats depreciate, you can find yourself "upside down" after a couple of years even if you've put 20% down. If you start with zero equity, you can be even further behind the eight ball. Although, if you plan to keep the boat long enough, this won't matter; your balance due can start to match book value in 5 to 7 years or so, depending on the total length of the loan because the depreciation curve will flatten. So while I can't recommend a 100% loan, neither can I say you should never do it. Just be aware of what you may be getting yourself into if you do. And while you can have a down payment of 20% or less, it can sometimes be to your advantage to pay more up front. Your objective should be to balance the cash benefits of a low or zero down payment against the increased loan costs and other disadvantages you incur by having to borrow a greater percentage of the boat's total price. Another factor in this equation is the length of time involved in repaying the loan; the longer terms generally require more payment up front.

Terms

Boat loans can now run for at least 15 years and, in some cases, as long as 30. But 25- and 30-year terms also usually require 25% or 30% down, respectively (75% and 70% loan-to-value ratios). The longer the term, the lower the individual payments, especially if you opt for a basic fixed-rate, fixed-term, simple interest collateral loan with a monthly payment plan. And even with the interest being potentially tax deductible, the longer it takes you to repay the loan, the more it costs you overall. More important is that the longer it takes to repay the loan, the slower you gain equity and the greater your chances of being upside down, at least for a few years. A shorter term has many incentives. There are, however, several individual issues to consider, such as your ability to handle the higher monthly payments with a reasonable degree of comfort. Keep in mind that the shorter the term of the loan, the faster you build your equity. The greater your equity, the more money you get to keep when it's time to sell—and there's always a time to sell.

Since everyone is unique, the down payment versus amount financed is another aspect you should probably discuss thoroughly with your accountant or tax adviser before you make any hard decisions.

Despite the length of the loan's repayment period as written, chances are you'll pay it off in full much sooner—for example, if you decide to trade for another boat. Statistically, the average boat loan currently has an actual life of just 42 months. So always make sure that regardless of the loan's full term there is no penalty for repaying it sooner.

Rates

These also vary, not only over time but also from lender to lender, by the exact nature of the loan, and with the creditworthiness of the applicant. The good news currently is that while boat loan rates have in the past been set several points above those of home mortgages, this spread has narrowed over the last few years and you can now get money for a boat for nearly the same rate you'd pay for a real estate loan. A variety of factors have influenced this change, including that default and delinquency rates for boat loans have been very low in recent years—well below those on car or home loans and significantly lower than for credit cards. NMBA statistics show that the delinquency rate on loans of over $25,000 has been less than 1% in the past few years. It was 0.69% in 2004, 0.8% in 2005, and 0.63% in 2006 (the latest figures available as of this writing). Despite an overall economic downturn in some areas, lenders still like to issue boat loans and current rates continue to reflect this. Most financial experts agree that boat buyers prescreen themselves more thoroughly than do home or car buyers, so the slight increase in delinquencies on some real estate and other loans has yet to sour the boat loan market. As for the future . . . well, the crystal ball tends to cloud up when looking at interest rates, so it's hard to say. But the consensus seems to be that regardless of what happens to interest rates in general, boat loan rates should remain closer to real estate rates than they have historically—barring drastic changes in default and delinquency rates for boat loans, of course. Just remember, while the interest rate you can get is important, you should never shop for a lender by rate alone.

Types of Loans

Several types of loans are available when you want to finance a boat. Lenders are required to explain the complete details of any type of loan they may provide. Be sure to ask about the different types available, and choose the one that best suits your financial situation.

Among the currently available loans, you'll find:

- **Fixed rate, fixed term, simple interest.** This is the most common, the simplest, and generally considered the most advantageous type of loan. It carries the same monthly payment for its entire life. At the end of the loan period, you will have paid off all interest and principal, at which point the boat is 100% yours. While regular monthly payments are the norm for this type of loan, there can be other options. You may be more comfortable with a seasonal payment plan that allows you to skip up to three consecutive monthly payments a year and continue to skip the same months each year for the life of the loan. This option can be especially attractive for people with seasonal fluctuations in income. Or, if you receive a large bonus or other once-a-year lump sum remuneration, an annual payment plan may be best. With this option, you make just one payment a year and can usually delay the first one from 90 days to 6 months after the loan is initiated, which gives you some breathing room between the time you buy the boat and the time of your first payment. If your income and lifestyle work best with smaller, more frequent loan payments, a biweekly payment may be what you want—you'll pay less total interest and gain equity faster. Not all lenders will offer all of these options, but if any of the options appeals to you, don't hesitate to ask. The availability of your most desirable payment plan can be one of the many factors you use in determining which lender to work with.

- **Variable rate.** Unlike fixed-rate loans, a variable (aka adjustable) rate loan usually begins with a fixed-rate period, typically a year or two, and then the rate fluctuates—often within a predetermined range—over the remainder of the loan's life. These fluctuations are typically based on a particular interest rate index, such as the prime rate, or the LIBOR (London inter-bank offer rate), the rate at which banks offer to lend money to one another in the wholesale money markets in London. It is a standard financial index used in U.S. capital markets. These loans often offer a low introductory rate over the initial, fixed-rate period. Variable-rate loans are particularly desirable when interest rates appear to be headed downward, but they can also be advantageous at other times because of their overall terms, particularly those low introductory rates. You should look at the adjustable period and other details to clearly understand how payments could change and to anticipate how to manage them. It's always possible for the payments to increase considerably. Variable-rate interest loans rarely have a prepayment penalty other than perhaps during the low-rate introductory period.

- **Balloon payment.** This can be an excellent option for many powerboat buyers, especially for larger motoryachts. A balloon loan is usually for a rather short term, often just 3 years, but the payments are based on amortizing the loan over a term of 15 years or more. Balloon loans often have a lower interest rate and can be (though aren't necessarily) easier to qualify for than a traditional fixed loan. There is, however, a huge downside to consider. At the end of the loan term, you will need to pay off your entire outstanding balance. For this reason, people most often choose a balloon loan when they know they will own a boat for only a few years and expect to pay off the loan when they sell it (most often, to buy a larger boat). This option becomes especially attractive for very large yachts because, quite probably as a result of their overall opulence and comparative rarity, they tend to depreciate far less, and less rapidly, than smaller production vessels.

- **Interest only.** This option is available for most types of boat loans, as it is in real estate. In this case, your payments over an initial period are interest only, which results in lower monthly payments. The drawback is that the principal doesn't diminish during this period but remains the same until your payments start applying to both interest *and principal*, which they will for the remainder of the loan's term once the interest-only period has expired. The result is that during this initial period you build no equity. People usually choose this option in real estate when they plan to flip the property soon after buying it. Since real estate has traditionally appreciated in value, often quite rapidly, these folks expect to sell the property for way more than they paid and thus gain a profit even as they pay the principal in

full after such a short period. Because boats are almost always a depreciating asset, it doesn't work this way very often in the marine marketplace. In most cases, paying interest only will find you upside down when it's time to sell, so I can't recommend this option either.

An experienced marine lender will be able to help you determine which type of loan is best suited to your particular needs.

Minimums

Most marine lenders have a set minimum and won't make a loan for any less. The exact amount varies by lender, but the current range is from $15,000 to $25,000, though a few lenders will go lower. Given the price tags on today's powerboats, this is not at all out of line, but at the low end it may mean buying just a bit better boat than you had originally intended. One thing is for sure: unless you are buying a complete package where one price covers everything (see Chapter 4), you'll need to borrow enough to cover not only the cost of the boat but also the cost of all the extras you'll need before you can use it. So the minimum is often no problem at all. Just be sure to discuss these details with your lender and borrow enough to cover all your immediate needs.

The Closing

As with real estate loans, this session deals with the paperwork and signatures and is the final step in acquiring the loan—and the boat. The dealer, broker, lender, or financial service company will undoubtedly guide you through the process smoothly and professionally. Typically, it only takes 20 or 30 minutes. There are usually some loan-related fees associated with a closing, though there are fewer for a boat loan than in a real estate closing. Very rarely are any *points* involved (a point is 1% of the total loan amount; real estate loans often cost a borrower several points up front). Credit report fees and application processing fees are also rare in boat loans. If you're buying a preowned boat, there will probably be a fee for a search for outstanding maritime liens and other aspects of ensuring a clear title. Other related fees, though they will not necessarily be a direct part of the closing process, include the cost of registering and/or documenting the vessel (see the end of this chapter), which will probably develop somewhat concurrently, and, particularly if you are buying a used boat, the cost of your survey, which will undoubtedly have already been paid since you'll want the survey report before you make your final purchase decision (see Chapter 10).

The one constant in all closings is that any associated fees are both necessary but also often negotiable. They are necessary in that business still seems to thrive on paperwork, and every form or report has its cost. But they're usually negotiable on two counts. First is the specific cost of each report or form; only a few of them have absolute, fixed costs, and more often they carry fees based on what the market will bear. A quiet protest may reduce, and sometimes even eliminate, the fee. The second area of negotiability is who pays. No one wants unnecessary expenses, and lenders will often ask the borrower to pay for items that are necessary only because the lender requires them. You can't blame the lender for trying. But again, a quiet protest will often get the lender to accept the inevitable charges itself rather than risk losing the deal. Always ask about closing costs when you first inquire about a loan and definitely when you submit an application. Lenders must tell you up front exactly what charges will await you at closing. Many times, lenders will throw in many closing costs to get you as a customer. But they usually won't do this unless you ask and maybe not even then. When you are negotiating, you shouldn't leave anything uncovered; the worst the other party can say is no, and it can't hurt to try.

MONEY SOURCES
Banks
Time was when your local bank was the best place to start when looking for a loan of any type. But local banks have become an endangered species. They still exist, but not in great numbers and those numbers seem to be dwindling. These days the chances are that the office where you do most of your banking (if you use an office at all—many people now rely heavily on ATMs, direct deposits, and online services) is merely a branch of a large national or regional bank.

This is not necessarily bad; these large banks have huge reserves and are not scared

Quick Tips

Whether you regularly deal with a truly local bank or a branch of a larger organization, it can still be a good idea to make this the first place you ask. When seeking a boat loan, you should explore a variety of sources. Only when you've investigated all the various possibilities can you decide which is best for you.

in the least by the (often very) large sums that can be involved in the purchase of a boat—though the vast majority of boats are less than 20 feet in length and cost no more than a decent car. Further, several of the large banking organizations now have departments that specialize in boat and yacht loans, which makes them equally as valuable to a potential boat buyer as one of the nonbank lending institutions that specialize in boat loans. They can offer appropriate advice as well as money.

Credit Unions

If you're a member of a credit union that makes boat loans, be sure to include it as a potential money source. Credit unions usually have very attractive rates for their members, and many make boat loans. If they have marine lending specialists on staff, they should be able to offer a competitive deal.

Two potential drawbacks to using a credit union are seen in the first sentence of the previous paragraph: (1) you need to be a member to obtain a loan from a credit union; and (2) if the credit union you belong to isn't familiar with boat loans, it might not be interested in granting one to you.

The first element should be easy to take care of. Membership is generally based on a commonality, such as working for the same company or being members of the same trade union or professional organization. But sometimes it is as broad as residing in the same community. Usually, all you have to do is qualify on the commonality aspect and then open a savings account with a small deposit. The second aspect may not be so easy. If your credit union doesn't offer boat loans, you may be out of luck; it may hesitate to underwrite a loan if it has no experience in determining a loan to (actual) value ratio for the money you want. And even if you can get

Quick Tips

At least one sort of "national" credit union is accessible via the Internet. It's the Digital Federal Credit Union (see the Resources section). Even if you don't qualify for membership (though it has an association with many organizations over a wide geographic area, so you may be able to), it is active in boat loans and its website has several pages devoted to things you should know about securing one, which can make logging onto the site worthwhile even if you eventually turn elsewhere for the money. There are other credit unions that also have a Web presence and offer boat loans. The only question would be whether you can qualify for membership in any of them.

a loan, you will still miss out on the ancillary advice and counsel you could get from an experienced, knowledgeable marine lender.

Dealers

Conventional wisdom often suggests that you are better off to finance a vehicle with anyone *but* the dealer from whom you buy it. The rationale is that the dealer will inevitably get a commission from the lender and that you can avoid this added cost by dealing with a lender directly. Many people hold that the same is true when buying a boat. And yet the truth is there may be advantages to financing your boat through a dealer. Among them are:

- The dealership will usually have established relationships with several finance sources, saving you the time and trouble of searching for the best loan—the dealer can present you with the options or narrow them for you and show you the best one.
- A number of qualified lenders will work only with and through established dealerships—their programs (and any resulting advantages or benefits) are not directly available to the consumer.
- A dealer will have access to extended warranty programs that can be included in your financing if you decide to use one (see Chapter 13).
- There may be special finance programs on certain brands or models based on the dealer's relationship with manufacturers. These programs can be advantageous to you, such as a delayed first payment, no interest for several months, lower rates for a limited time or, perhaps, even a builder-sponsored rebate, similar to what's often given for cars.
- Most dealers are concerned primarily with their bottom line; which particular departments happen to deliver the profit isn't terribly important. Thus, if they can make some money on the sale of the loan, they'll often settle for making a bit less on the sale of the boat itself. This can be especially true at such times as the end of the model year, when clearing inventory becomes especially critical.

Your own bottom line should be the best possible deal all around, regardless of how you achieve it. This is not to say that financing through your dealer will always be best, but rather that you should never let conventional wisdom keep you from finding out. Always include dealer financing among your options whenever it's possible. If it isn't the best deal, don't take it. But you won't know until you ask.

Financial Service Companies

Marine finance organizations are plentiful (see the Resources section) and an excellent source of not only the money to buy your boat but also considerable guidance and practical assistance. Most of these organizations are on par with the large banks when it comes to knowing about boats and boat loans, and I'd be hard-pressed to say which is better, a large bank or a large financial service company. It probably comes down to whom you feel more comfortable with. So start looking well before you need the money, and develop that important working relationship before you actually apply for a loan.

REGISTRATION: MORE THAN FIFTY WAYS TO PAY THE PIPER

This is another requirement of the Federal Boat Safety Act of 1971: Within 30 days of completing your purchase, you must formally register the boat in its "state of principal use." This is not always the state in which you live but, rather, the state in which you primarily use the boat—though they are often the same. And if you think this is confusing, keep in mind that, like many federal laws, the specifics of registration, including which state agency handles the paperwork, the fees to be paid, the length of registration periods, the renewal date (which can range from the anniversary of initial registration to the owner's birthday to a fixed date, such as June 30, every year), and other such details are left to the individual states. Since American Samoa, the Commonwealth of Puerto Rico, the District of Columbia, Guam, the Northern Marianas, and the U.S. Virgin Islands are also bound by the Act, there are considerably more than fifty sets of laws that may apply. While all of them are quite similar, each set of laws is different enough that you usually can't just do what you did in one jurisdiction when you move to another.

Start with Your DMV

Your state's Department of Motor Vehicles is always a good place to start the process; many states saddle this agency with boat registration because it has a registration system already in the works. And just as vehicle registration costs often vary by gross weight, many—but not all—states base a boat's registration fee on its overall length. Some states have a different rate for new boats as opposed to used, yet in others it doesn't matter; instead, there's a flat fee for all boats. As you'll discover, boat registration laws are a fifty-plus-segment patchwork quilt. Some states also issue titles as proof of ownership, but not all do, which can add to the confusion when a boat is sold across state lines. This "some do, some don't" aspect of issuing titles also affects the lending process in that lenders obviously want to be listed on a title as lien holder and yet this is problematic in states that don't issue them. For this reason, most lenders will demand that you document your boat with the federal government, if possible, rather than register it with a state.

Certificate of Number

A boat registration is often called a certificate of number because one thread that persists through all jurisdictions is that it carries a registration number for your boat. This is similar to an auto registration tag or license plate, but it's also different: there's no plate; you have to purchase and apply the numbers individually. When you do this, affix them to both sides of the forward half of the bow so that they read from left to right on each side. They must be bold block letters, not less than 3 inches high, of contrasting color to the hull or background, and they must be placed as high above the waterline as practical. Letters must be separated from numbers by spaces or hyphens: NJ 1234 XX and NJ-1234-XX are okay, but NJ1234XX is not. Also, no number other than that assigned by your certificate of number may be displayed on the forward half of the vessel.

Many states also issue validation decals, which offer visual proof that your registration is current. These decals usually must be displayed close to the boat's registration numbers, though exactly where and how close also varies by state.

Hull Identification Number

All boats manufactured or imported on or after November 1, 1972, must have a hull identification number (HIN). It's another federal requirement. The HIN is a 12-character number that uniquely identifies a particular boat (like the vehicle identification number for your car), and you'll need it to get a registration and/or title in most states. When you buy a boat, you should record the HIN and keep it in a safe place.

On the boat itself, the HIN has been located in two places since 1984. One HIN is permanently attached to (or molded into) the transom on the *starboard* [right] side, as high as possible above the waterline. The second is hidden inside the boat somewhere out of sight, usually beneath some piece of hardware. The location of the second HIN is generally known only to the manufacturer and is used to identify the boat if it is stolen and the thieves change the number on the transom. Some crooks have become quite adept at doing this so well that the change is not easy to detect; having the second HIN helps to foil them.

Federal Documentation

This is an option for recreational vessels of 5 net tons or more. Note that in this case the ton is a measurement of volume (100 cubic feet) not weight. Generally, 5 net tons means a cabin boat of about 28 to 30 feet of length overall. Net tons result when we subtract any space dedicated to essential mechanical equipment, such as the engine compartment, from the total interior space, which is the vessel's gross tonnage.

Documentation exempts a boat from the need to be numbered, and is fairly easy to obtain, though there are some strings attached. First, the owner must be a U.S. citizen or a U.S. corporation. (Foreign flag registration is the norm for vessels owned by offshore entities.) A certificate of documentation may be endorsed for fishery, coastwise (trade), registry (foreign trade), or recreation. But here's the second string: while any documented vessel may be used for recreation regardless of its endorsement, a vessel with only a recreational endorsement may *not* be used for any other purpose. This means a yacht that is documented solely for recreation must not be chartered (see Chapter 1). Chartering is a commercial venture, and if the yacht is so involved, it is not being used for recreation even if the people aboard hired the boat so they could go out and play.

One solution is to document your boat initially with endorsements for the activities you may someday decide to engage in, even if not until a later date. The downside of this is that it will cost more than documenting a recreational vessel; plus, many insurance companies issue policies based on severest possible use, so having a coastwise endorsement on your document could make for more costly insurance than when you document the boat strictly for recreation. Yet the ability to enter your yacht into charter service at any time without having to wait for a new endorsement could be worth it—processing paperwork can take a while these days.

The Upsides of Documentation

Documenting your boat has several advantages. Among them is that no state numbers need to be displayed on the boat's exterior. There is an *official number*, however, which remains with the vessel forever, regardless of changes in ownership, and which must be permanently affixed inside the boat in a place where it can easily be seen. In the days of mostly wooden vessels, the official number was required to be "carved into the main beam." Outlining the numbers with weld beads does the equivalent on metal hulls even today. On fiberglass, a common practice is to use an engraved plaque, which is attached with epoxy so it cannot be removed without taking some substrate along with it. Another solution is to paint the number on an interior bulkhead in the engine compartment and then cover it with a layer of fiberglass cloth and clear resin. This makes it visible but totally secure—you simply cannot remove it cleanly. Times change, and techniques along with them. But the principle remains: The official number is intended to become a permanent part of the hull and now "must be affixed in a manner which would make alteration, removal, or replacement obvious."

Quick Tips

Perhaps the biggest advantage of federal documentation is that it allows issuance of a preferred ship's mortgage, a maritime lien that's recorded with the Coast Guard and has priority over all others, should there be a default. As you'd expect, lenders love the preferred ship's mortgage, and many require one as a condition of financing, which means if your desired boat is 5 net tons or more, you'll have to document it to get a loan.

Paper Trail   Documentation also provides a solid paper trail of ownership, from the builder to the current owner and all in between. Every time a documented vessel changes hands, a bill of sale for documented vessels (Coast Guard form CG-1340) must be recorded with the U.S. Coast Guard, and the vessel's file will always reflect all details of past and present ownership. This can be beneficial, and the lack of such a clear record of prior ownership can be an impediment to documenting an older vessel that was previously only numbered.

Whose Boat Is This, Anyway?   Documented yachts are officially "vessels of the United States," which can help cut the red tape when cruising out of the country. In some countries, the lack of a national document precludes getting a cruising permit, and visitors with state-numbered boats must check in and clear customs in every port they enter, which soon gets expensive. Having the federal government behind you also offers a degree of protection in foreign waters that state registration can't begin to match. This advice may be premature for someone who may be just thinking of buying a boat, but it's good to know. Besides, it pays to plan ahead.

The Downsides of Documentation
Documentation has some disadvantages, too. We've already discussed one: that legal use of the vessel is limited to the activities covered by the document's endorsements. Another is the higher cost. As of this writing, the initial documentation fee for a recreational vessel is $100. And though registration fees vary from state to state and often by size of boat, on average they cost much less than that. Also, while documentation exempts a boat from displaying state numbers, it still may have to be registered, which means twice the paperwork and having to pay both fees: federal documentation *and* state registration. About half the states require resident boats (those that are on the state's waters for 6 months or more) to be registered in the state even if they're federally documented. Although documented yachts that are also registered don't have to display numbers on the bow, they must show a current validation decal.

Other Requirements
Documented yachts must display as their hailing port either the owner's city of residence or the boat's port of registry, which is probably different from the boat's actual homeport. If the owner is a Delaware corporation (and many are—there can be some tax advantages to having a corporation or

LLC own the boat, and Delaware is a corporate-friendly state), it may be officially headquartered in Dover, Delaware, which is why you see that hailing port on so many large yachts. This regulation also explains the strange hailing ports you sometimes see, including some totally landlocked cities that could never be a real home to any boat too big to fit on a trailer, such as Denver, Colorado—or even Dover, Delaware, for that matter, though at least Delaware is a coastal state!

Another minor limitation is that you can't change the name of a documented vessel without involving the Coast Guard and some red tape that includes filing more forms and paying more fees. It's no big deal, but it does involve extra work, time, and expense.

WRAP

✔ You should probably finance your boat even if you have the cash.

✔ Interest payments are often deductible on federal tax returns.

✔ You may want a separate corporation or LLC to buy and own your boat rather than owning it as an individual.

✔ Various good sources of boat loans exist, and you should never choose a loan on the basis of interest rate alone.

✔ Several types of loans are also available, often with a wide range of repayment options.

✔ You need a credit score of at least 680 to obtain the best loan.

✔ Boat loans can run for as long as 30 years, though the average boat loan is paid off in 42 months.

✔ The shorter the term of the loan, the faster you build your equity in the boat, which means more money in your pocket when you sell.

✔ Lenders may require federal documentation of your boat rather than state registration so they can issue a preferred ship's mortgage.

CHAPTER 6

WHERE WILL YOU KEEP IT?

Do I Need to Read This Chapter?

You should read this chapter if you want to discover

✔ That water access is becoming a serious (and growing) problem in many areas.

✔ The need for separate off-season storage in many areas.

✔ The advantages of using a wet-slip marina.

✔ The benefits of dry-stack stowage.

✔ Other boat storage options.

✔ The advantages and disadvantages of each option.

WHERE WILL YOUR BOAT SIT WHEN IT ISN'T IN USE?

This might seem like a ridiculous question, but it isn't. You'll have to answer it before you take possession of your new toy. And coming up with a suitable solution may not be easy! Don't get me wrong; I'm not trying to scare you or talk you out of buying a powerboat. But since the purpose of this book is to make you aware of potential problems as well as potential benefits, I would be less than candid if I didn't include this one. Finding a good place to keep your boat when you're not using it can be a far bigger problem than finding good places to cruise to when you are underway.

This problem is not yet huge in all areas; many prime boating locations (particularly large inland lakes) still have adequate access to the water and marinas abound. But in some of the best boating locales, such as along the Atlantic seaboard, waterfront property is being gobbled up rapidly by real estate developers who build condos and other projects that too often squeeze out the boatyards and marinas that had previously occupied the sites. You can't blame the developers; from a financial standpoint, a marina or boatyard is probably the least desirable use of waterfront property because it provides the lowest return on investment. And yet, without reasonable access to the water, boating becomes a challenge that can range from the merely difficult to down-right impossible.

The Good News on Access

Lest I leave you with gloomy thoughts on this issue, I must also reveal the bright side. As I was working on this chapter, I received news of progress on two levels, federal and state. On the federal level, there is the BIG program, which stands for Boating Infrastructure Grants. This program takes money from the Sport Fish Restoration and Boating Trust Fund (formerly the Aquatic Resources Trust Fund), which is supported by excise taxes on certain fishing and boating equipment and on boat fuels, and distributes it to state agencies involved in building and maintaining sites for recreational boaters.

On the same day I heard about the most recent BIG program grants, I saw a report that in the state of North Carolina, the Waterfront Access Study Committee presented several state agencies with recommendations on ways to improve waterfront access. I also read that the state general assembly in Maryland has approved funding for waterways projects, including the improvement of public access, and shortly thereafter I read reports of some similar new programs in New England. So there are valid reasons to be optimistic. My objective here is to acknowledge the problem and also report that it is being recognized and addressed, at least at some levels, and hope that this action will be impetus for all of us who love boats to get involved also and agitate for better access where we live, because the most important action will always occur locally—wherever there's water and people who want to go boating on it. But no matter how much progress we make, the overall trend is still a bit scary and we can never

again be complacent. Just because easy water access has "always" been available where you live is no assurance it will continue to be. All signs seem to indicate that if we don't fight for easy and plentiful access to our waterways, we'll lose it. So let's keep up the fight. Okay, I'll climb down off the soapbox and get back to the subject of boat storage.

Off-Season Storage

In many parts of the world, off-season storage is as much of a concern as where to keep the boat when you're using it. During the time of year when cold weather makes pleasure boating either totally impossible or, at the very least, so uncomfortable that "pleasure" is out of the question, you have to have a place to keep your boat where this adverse weather can do it no harm. Though many northern marinas have off-season storage, many do not. If you put your boat in a marina that doesn't, you'll have to find *two* places to keep it!

The problem of where to keep your boat is serious enough that you need to give it plenty of thought *before* you actually have a boat. Many marinas and storage facilities have waiting lists, and the wait can be as much as 3 years or more in some locations.

Yacht Clubs

Many yacht clubs have slips for members' boats. But there are several downsides of this plan. First, most yacht clubs have a limited number of slips, far fewer than their membership roster would suggest. So waiting lists are a given, and the wait is often longer than at any commercial marina. Yacht clubs also often cater more to the sailing set and have many more moorings than slips. And since powerboats often need to be plugged in to shore power when they're going to "sit" for a while, you'll probably prefer a slip. There's also the matter of membership. In most clubs you have to be invited to join and also be recommended by a member or two in good standing, so getting into a yacht club before you actually own a boat can be somewhat difficult (it's not always that easy after you're an owner!). Since this potential option probably isn't all that practical at the outset, let's look at some that are.

Wet-Slip Public Marinas

Marinas have been around for about as long as pleasure boating itself. And though the concept is ancient, the implementation has changed over the years and a modern marina offers a lot more than simply a place to tie up your boat. Rare indeed is the marina that doesn't have a variety of electrical connections (30 amp, 50 amp, possibly 100 amp and, if large yachts abound, even 100 amp, three phase) as well as a steady supply of city water. All you have to do once your lines are secure is plug in and hook up the hose. Many modern marinas also have pumpout facilities where you can legally and conveniently empty your boat's sewage (aka holding) tanks.

Marina amenities often vary with the length of the boating season, and in year-round boating areas such as Florida and Southern California, nearly every marina offers all the comforts of home: heads with showers, laundry facilities, cable or satellite TV, telephone connections, daily newspaper delivery, wireless Internet access, and more. At many of these marinas, there are people who actually live aboard and use their boat as their home. The best news is that since these marinas tend to set the industry standard, you'll often find similar convenience these days even where the boating season is shorter.

Other Marina Pluses

Another nice feature of many marinas is a restaurant or two ashore. Though these are usually built to provide a nautical setting for patrons who arrive by land, having a restaurant available when you come back from a long day's outing on the water can be most welcome. It means being able to stop and have dinner without first having to drive home and then cook, clean up, and do all the other chores a meal at home demands.

If there's any tidal range or other fluctuating water level, many modern marinas offer floating piers, too, though in regions where the tidal range is slight, fixed piers still outnumber the floating ones. The main advantage to floating piers is that your mooring lines can be short and tight because the boat and pier rise and fall together. Fixed piers call for longer lines and some slack to allow for changes in water level. Getting the correct length can take some playing around until you figure out just what's needed to do the job—especially where tidal range is great. Too long and the boat moves around too much, maybe even banging into the pier when the lines are slack. Too short and the lines can come under excessive strain at the extreme stages of tide, perhaps even then breaking, which allows the boat to really move around. Floating piers are much better. Probably the biggest advantage to having your boat in a slip in the water is that you can go to your boat and use it at any time, whether the marina is actually open or not. Want to take a midnight cruise? Go ahead. Your boat is there waiting for you.

The Downsides of Wet-Slip Marinas

Marinas can be the most convenient way to moor your powerboat. But they aren't perfect:

Figure 6-1. Bahia Mar Resort and Yachting Center, in Fort Lauderdale, Florida, is, and has been since its earliest days, a prime example of a modern wet-slip marina. *(Bahia Mar Beach Resort and Yachting Center)*

• **They are often busy and crowded.** The biggest drawback to marinas is that there aren't always enough of them for the boating activity in the geographic area they serve. At the worst this means waiting lists, but even when a marina is not quite so jammed as to require a several-year wait for a slip, you still may find there's "no room at the inn" if you don't book early. Marinas in seasonal boating regions where people don't do much boating until late spring or early summer can often have all their slips reserved by the middle of February.

• **They are often busy and crowded.** During the active season, you'll find that you'll have a lot of company in every corner of the marina, in the parking lot, at the fuel dock, and in and around the marina's waterways in general. And all of this congestion can mean patience will often be in greater demand than human nature can supply.

• **They are often busy and crowded.** While most modern marinas have been designed for ample maneuvering room between piers, some have been built to squeeze as many boats as possible into a given area. While this offers the "good news" of a greater number of available slips, the "bad news" is that using the slips can be more difficult because they are so close together.

Dry-Stack Marinas

Many years ago, people figured out that more of them could live on the same small piece of land by stacking their houses atop one another in the form of an apartment building. A similar thing has happened in marinas. First, some forward thinkers realized that many boats don't have to be in

Be early. This applies not only to the boating season as a whole, where reserving a slip well in advance usually assures you of getting one, but also to every day you go boating. Going out early will put you ahead of the crowds (except for the die-hard anglers, who often start their quest for fish even *before* the crack of dawn), not only around the marina but also on the water in general. There's a bonus, too—winds and seas are usually calmer in the morning, which can make the whole trip more pleasant. And if you start your day early, you can wrap it up earlier and get your boat back in its slip well before the late afternoon traffic jam that often occurs at busy marina fuel docks just before closing time.

the water all the time. Soon, others concluded that if the boats were going to be stored high and dry and only put in the water when their owners wanted to use them, it made even more sense to emphasize the "high" and put more than one boat on each patch of land. Thus the dry-stack marina was born.

Figure 6-2. Just as the high-rise buildings in the background allow a greater number of people to occupy the same footprint, dry-stack marinas allow more boats to be stored on a given parcel of land.

A large forklift or other device takes the boat out of the water, moves it to the storage area, and then raises it to the required level, where it sets the boat onto padded longitudinal supports. The process works in reverse when it's time to launch. The usual practice is for the owner to call before leaving home and the marina crew will put the boat in the water so it's ready to go by the time s/he arrives. It is a very practical system.

The cost is usually less than for a wet slip of similar size, which is only fair since it is less convenient. And though the inconvenience is relatively slight during normal boating hours, once the marina closes for the night your boat is totally inaccessible. You can't decide to go boating on the spur of the moment if that moment doesn't happen to coincide with the marina's operating hours.

The dry-stack principle is also going upscale. In south Florida and other areas with a lot of boating activity and shrinking water access, some older dry-stack marinas are being gentrified into commercial yacht clubs that offer far more creature comforts for both the boats and their owners while maintaining the dry-stack concept. One facility yet to be built in Fort Lauderdale has announced: "The marina will offer amenities such as a rooftop pool, spa, locker rooms, and concierge services. Light snacks and beverages will be available by the pool, with dining available in the clubroom. A ship's chandlery will be on-site. Using a barcode system, an automated intelligence system will locate and deliver boats up to 45 feet and 15 tons." Another advantage to dry storage is that, not being in the water all the time, boats don't need bottom paint. They are underway for a huge portion of their time in the water, so all the growth that usually develops on the bottom of boats that are constantly in the water (because they are usually just sitting) never has a chance to get started. This is a huge savings because bottom paint is among the most expensive coatings you can buy, and the cleaning and other preparation that's necessary before applying it also costs plenty.

The system is not perfect. There are three main drawbacks to dry-stack stowage:

- **Size.** While they seem to be building bigger, stronger, and fancier lifting systems and you'll see larger and larger boats being stowed this way, there is still an upper limit. If your boat is larger than this limit, whatever it may be, you'll have to choose a different solution.
- **No electricity.** If you like to have your boat plugged in while it sits—say, to keep the batteries charged or to run the AC on "dehumidify" to prevent moisture damage in the interior—you're out of luck on this score, too. So far, no one has figured out a way to lift boats up onto the stack and also be able to conveniently plug them in while they're up there or unplug them when it's time to launch.
- **Lack of total convenience.** As good as most dry-stack marinas seem to be about accommodating their customers, the system isn't perfect. On a busy weekend you sometimes have to wait for your boat even if you call well in advance of your intended launch time; the lifts can only move so fast and still be safe. And many spur of the moment outings will be out, period, if you get the desire to go boating after the marina has closed.

Dockominiums

In recent years, many apartment buildings that were formerly rentals have been converted to condominiums. Similarly, many marina owners have concluded that selling slips (either wet or dry) could be more lucrative than renting them and so have converted their property to dockominiums and/or rackominiums. This practice is becoming more and more widespread, particularly in California and Florida, though it is catching on elsewhere, too.

The apparently steady decrease in ease of water access we're facing can be a huge impetus toward buying your slip if you have the opportunity. Add to this the thought that as the demand for dockage grows and the supply doesn't keep pace, the slip you buy today should be worth far more tomorrow, which is another incentive to buy. I'm not suggesting that you shouldn't. But I do recommend that you take a very careful look before you leap into a dockominium; they are not without their problems.

Can You Really Own It?

In many cases, you can't own the land beneath the slip; underwater land remains the property of some government entity (most often the state) and at best can only be leased, not purchased. And more often than not, the lease cannot be issued "in perpetuity" but must have a set ending date, which means that at some point in the future the lease will expire. When that happens, what you "own" with your dockominium deed will be worthless. And if this weren't bad enough, in some places the whole concept is illegal. In Wisconsin, for example, the state supreme court ruled the sale of boat slips by a marina there was invalid. The court held that the sales violated state law, which provides that lakes and rivers belong to all Wisconsin citizens. The problem was that the marina in question didn't even have a lease on the land under the slips they were

attempting to sell but had only riparian rights, which usually cannot be sold or transferred separately from the adjoining land. While riparian rights apply to underwater property, they actually attach to the adjoining dry land and give the dry land owner some specific rights to the *use* of the adjacent underwater land, but usually not the right to sell it.

There are exceptions. Half Moon Bay Marina in Croton-on-Hudson, New York, has been selling dockominiums, or permanent rights to plots of land about 8 feet below the surface of the Hudson River, and it's all perfectly legal. Steel Style Development Corporation, the developer of Half Moon Bay Marina, owned the property for sale despite its being underwater. Before it could start selling dockominiums, the company had to get approval from the village of Croton-on-Hudson to subdivide the underwater property—just as it would have been required to do with any other parcel of land. In this case, the village planning board approved the plan; dockominium owners receive a deed and title. The purchase provides the buyer with a permanent home for a boat as well as some potential tax advantages and, quite probably, capital gains.

The right to sell transfers to each individual slip owner just as it does with condos ashore, so slips can still be available for purchase long after the developer has sold out (though prices will undoubtedly rise!).

But in other places, the picture isn't always so rosy. In January 2007, a South Carolina newspaper reported that the South Carolina Ocean and Resource Management office was in the process of determining whether dockominiums "need some form of regulation." And the opposition of local residents in Murrells Inlet, South Carolina, resulted in one large dockominium development deal falling through before it could get started. And that's not the only project to face rough going.

Dockominiums are probably here to stay and most likely will grow in number. But if you opt for buying one (or are, perhaps, forced into buying your slip in order to keep it), be sure to have the paperwork reviewed carefully by a competent real estate attorney before you sign anything. While the dockominium concept is sound in theory, as Yogi Berra said, "In theory there is no difference between theory and practice. In practice there is."

Incidentally, don't think that the increase in owned dock space necessarily means a loss of rentals. Just as some people buy condominium apartments as investments and then rent them to others, many dockominium slips are being purchased by individuals who realize the value of water access, though they often don't even own a boat. These people then place those slips on the rental market, often through a "shared revenue" plan with the marina management. Some slips have been developed where they may not have otherwise been feasible because the dockominium structure was used to finance the project. So I'd say that the dockominium concept is not necessarily bad, but rather one that needs to be viewed with both interest and caution.

Behind Your House

Talk about convenience! Just walk out your back door and there you are. This idea is appealing to those who own waterfront homes and decide to buy a boat. But often it is practical only if the pier is already there. Depending on tidal range, bottom contour, the extent of navigable waters, and other variables, building a suitable pier can be an iffy proposition—problematic and costly at best and perhaps impossible at worst. You usually can't own the land behind your house any farther than the mean high water mark. Your deed may include riparian rights, but outright ownership of underwater land is usually impossible. You may well have the right to build a pier out to navigable depths, but you will still have to get permission to do it. And, given the many different government agencies and environmental (as well as navigational) restrictions that may be involved, this usually means getting many permits, all of which can be far more complex than the simple building permit you need for a structure ashore—though you'll need one of these, also. All this permitting can be expensive.

The Realities of Waterfront Construction

An attorney I had aboard a charter pointed to a modest wooden pier behind a private home and said, "Captain Bob, you see that dock over there? Well, it cost the owner $150,000 in my fees and permits alone before he could even drive a single piling. That's $150,000 *before* any construction could begin, and I have no idea what that may have cost. What's so bad is that without my work there would have been no permits, and without the permits, there could be no dock. So he had to spend the money. Ridiculous, isn't it?"

I can't say what it might cost to get the permits and construct a pier where you live, but it probably wouldn't be much different. I should also warn you that the permitting process can take time. When Hurricane Andrew left its mark on south Florida in 1992, I had recently moved off a boat and was living in a waterfront apartment on an island in Biscayne Bay. One feature I enjoyed was a boardwalk that ran around the corner of the three-building complex and overhung the bay. Andrew wrecked it, tore it to smithereens. Since I had chosen that complex partly so I could enjoy the boardwalk, I was a bit concerned when it still hadn't been rebuilt after nearly a year. So I asked management if they were awaiting an insurance settlement. "No," they answered, "we got that almost immediately. We're still waiting for our permits!" And that was for a structure that was "grandfathered," one that had been there before. So again I must suggest that keeping your boat behind your house is a great idea if you already have the pier. If not, you can look into building one, but don't be too surprised if the pier turns out to cost nearly as much as your boat. Maybe even more!

Behind Someone Else's House

Many people who desire to live beside the water have no desire whatsoever to go on it. So they buy a beautiful waterfront home with a pier behind it and never even think of also buying a boat to keep there. The pier sits empty.

I've talked with waterfront property owners and discovered that some piers sit empty because the folks who own them don't want anything, not even a beautiful boat, blocking their view of the water. Not all property owners feel this way. So, in communities that allow it (in many coastal communities, zoning ordinances prohibit rental of private piers), waterfront homeowners will rent their docks to boatowners who don't enjoy the good fortune of having piers of their own. I can't say whether this is possible

Figure 6-3. Behind your house doesn't necessarily mean in the water; you can also keep your boat high and dry on a lift. Because of the lift distance, this option is less practical in areas of extreme tidal range than it is in south Florida, where our range is about 2½ to 3 feet.

where you live, but it could certainly be worth looking into.

Mitigation Slips

Many of the waterfront developments that displace major marine complexes are now being required to include some dockage as a part of their project—mitigation for having reduced water access in general. While the total number of resulting slips is often less than what was there previously and the development's condo owners may get first dibs, there can still be a few slips available to the general public. It doesn't hurt to ask. When you're looking for a place to keep your boat, you should leave none of the proverbial stones unturned.

In Your Driveway

Keeping your boat on a trailer in your driveway can possibly be such a viable option that it deserves a whole chapter's worth of attention. So I won't add another thought here other than to say please see the next chapter.

Quick Tips

Always make sure it's legal and proper to do so before you rent a private pier. Even if you and the homeowner strike an amicable deal, you could both be losers if the rental violates local codes. In most cases, being moored illegally will void your insurance (and, usually, the homeowner's insurance as well!), which means that in the event of a loss, you'll both be on your own. Further, since your contract with your lender may require that you maintain a certain level of insurance for the duration of the loan, voiding that insurance by being illegally moored could put you technically in default, which would only compound your problems. Always check with your city officials before you rent a private pier.

It's a Wrap — WRAP

✔ Water access is a growing problem that needs our attention before it disappears completely.

✔ In some areas, separate winter storage is necessary also.

✔ Wet-slip marinas are convenient, but slips can be scarce.

✔ Dry-stack marinas are less convenient, but not by that much.

✔ Dockominiums are a viable option in many areas, but they definitely call out "Buyer beware!"

✔ Other possibilities exist, including private piers behind private homes.

✔ Keeping your boat on a trailer is another viable option.

CHAPTER 7

THE JOYS OF TRAILERING

Do I Need to Read This Chapter?

You should read this chapter if you want to discover

- ✔ What constitutes a trailerable boat.
- ✔ The advantages of keeping your boat on a trailer.
- ✔ The disadvantages of trailer boating.
- ✔ A magazine devoted exclusively to this aspect of boating.
- ✔ Some legal and practical technicalities involved in taking your boat on the road.

WHY A TRAILER?

Perhaps the greatest advantage to keeping a trailerable boat on a trailer is that you can use your boat anywhere. All you need is a waterway you can get to by highway that has a launch ramp or two to permit water access. You can go boating on salt water, fresh water, lakes, rivers, bays, or ocean; on places close to home and also on those that are so far away that reaching them via water alone would be unrealistic, if not impossible, for the boat you have. There are other advantages to having your boat on a trailer, and I'll cover them all before the chapter ends, but the key to it all is having a trailerable boat.

WHAT, EXACTLY, IS A TRAILERABLE BOAT?
The Legal View

In simple terms, a trailerable boat is one you can tow anywhere at any time without having

to get a permit and without facing any limits or restrictions (other than, perhaps, the gross weight restrictions placed on certain roads and bridges). The boat's beam is a prime consideration. Since this is another of those matters the federal government has left to state law, we could be facing fifty or more different answers to the question "What is trailerable?" Fortunately, there are only two. Most states set the unrestricted width limit at 8 feet 6 inches, though at present Kentucky and North Carolina decree it's only 8 feet 0 inch—so close and yet so different.

In many states you can tow up to a 10-foot-wide trailer without the need for a follow car or a special permit as long as it is clearly labeled with an "Oversized Load" sign and you do your towing only during the daylight hours of weekdays. But this isn't universal. So let's say trailerable means an 8-foot, 6-inch beam *with two exceptions.*

Of course, there are also length, height, and weight restrictions, but the nature of boats is such that it's unlikely that any vessel with an 8-foot, 6-inch beam would ever be too long or too heavy for any existing state laws.

The Practical View

Other aspects beyond legal restrictions affect trailerability, one of which is the boat's ease of launch and retrieval. Merely fitting on a trailer and being within the legal size limits aren't always quite enough.

The Wrong Boat for Trailering

Years ago, I had a neighbor who had wanted a boat for years, and when he was able to afford one, he got it—a 26-foot inboard cabin cruiser with a flying bridge. It was a nice boat. But not for him. He wanted to use his boat not only on the ocean at our hometown's doorstep but also on some nearby lakes. But given the nearly 11-foot tidal range in our native state of Maine, he could not launch or haul an inboard boat of this size at his convenience. To use the ramp on the estuary from which we gained access to the ocean, he had to wait for the right stage of tide—half flood or higher. So often the boat was stuck on land when he wanted it in the ocean, or in the estuary when he wanted to take it to a lake. His inboard cruiser could sit on a trailer, and he could tow it without a permit, but practically speaking it was not trailerable. No wonder he traded it the following year for a 19-foot outboard runabout that was trailerable and suited his needs perfectly.

The Limits Don't Really Limit

The limits on size and type of boat that you have to accept if "on a trailer" is the most practical answer to the question of where to keep your boat do not in any way have to limit your boating activity. I have a friend who lives in the San Francisco Bay area. He has had the same trailerable boat for years—a 24-foot sterndrive cabin cruiser built in 1972. And over those years he has taken his boat, in his words, "from San Francisco to Glacier Bay, Alaska, down to almost Rio Ochas, Guatemala, and all points in between," which really wouldn't have been practical if the boat was not trailerable.

Other Advantages

Cost

While there will be some added expenses when you buy the boat and trailer, when it comes to eliminating ongoing payments you can't beat keeping your boat in your own driveway. It's basically free! Every other

Quick Tips

When you load gear into your boat for highway travel, the weight should be concentrated over the axle(s). After you get the boat into the water, you'll probably have to rearrange things to allow the vessel to sit *on its lines*, which means exactly level—not down by bow or stern and not listing to either side. The slight effort required to rearrange things is usually easier than all the lugging you'd have to do in going from house to car and from car to boat. Depending on the marina and the proximity of parking lot to slip, trailering is often much easier in the gear-handling department.

stowage option has at least some continuing expense.

And, as noted in the last chapter, boats in dry storage don't need bottom paint or any of the expense it involves. Because boats on trailers are definitely in dry storage, this saving applies to them also.

Convenience

No matter what size your boat may be, every time you take it out there will be things you have to bring from home. Food, drink, and other consumables top the list, but there are more. If your boat sits in a marina, you have to lug the stuff from house to car and then from car to boat. If your boat is sitting outside your house on a trailer, the lugging is directly from house to boat, which is much simpler.

Ease of Maintenance

If you opt for do-it-yourself maintenance, even if for just a portion of it (see Chapter 12), keeping your boat at home beats having it anywhere else. You can do things whenever you have a spare moment because your boat is so handy. In many cases, you can accomplish something positive and actually finish a job in less time than it would take you just to drive to your boat if you kept it in a marina. Considering the amount of maintenance even a small boat can require, this can be a huge plus.

Security

This can be a bit touchy because there is no such a thing as 100% security. But in most cases, your boat will be safer in the driveway of a quiet residential neighborhood

Figure 7-1. Trailerable boats offer many practical advantages, not the least of which are that you can keep your boat at home and have an almost unlimited choice of boating areas.

Don't Forget

Before you get too excited about the idea of keeping your boat at home, consider two realities:

First, if your boat is going to sit in your driveway, it has to fit in your driveway. Make sure you have room for your rig with enough to spare that it won't be a burden. Nothing can kill the joy of boat ownership any quicker than cursing your boat every time it interferes with the enjoyment of other household activities by being in the way.

Second, your community must allow it. Some have zoning ordinances that prohibit storage of any vehicles other than passenger cars in residential neighborhoods. Anything else, even a beautiful boat on a trailer, may be considered visual blight and thus be outlawed. Be sure to check your local zoning regulations before committing yourself to a boat and trailer you can't legally keep at home.

than just about anywhere else. Between the comings and goings of family members, the watchful eye of nosy neighbors (which is a good thing, in this case), and the reality that you have but one boat (thieves often pick from where they have a greater selection), "at home" is often the safest place for your boat and its gear. Just never become so complacent that you don't take proper security measures, such as using trailer locks and

prop locks and keeping easily removed gear in the house. Even in very secure neighborhoods, theft happens.

THE REALITIES OF TRAILERING

While this book is about buying a boat, if you decide to keep yours on a trailer, there will be related aspects that often involve some other large purchases as well. Trailer boating is about more than boats. The world of trailer boating is broad enough that there is a magazine devoted to it exclusively. It's *Trailer Boats*, from Elhert Publishing. Founded in 1971, *Trailer Boats* is a national magazine dedicated to the hard-core boating enthusiast, with articles on trailerable boats and everything related to trailer boating—they even test tow vehicles. If you get into trailer boating, this magazine can be very helpful.

The Trailer

This is obviously the first extra you'll need. As I stated back in Chapter 4, the trailer historically was one of the first elements to be packaged along with the boat and motor. Aside from the economic advantages, trailers became a part of the first packages to help diminish buyer confusion. A reality of trailer boating is that boat and trailer must fit like hand and glove. Foot and shoe might be a better analogy, since shoes come in a far greater variety of styles and sizes and also provide some critical support. The trailer must fit the boat perfectly in several ways—and also provide critical support. As a result, the marketplace offers many types, styles, and sizes of trailers. When faced with these added aspects to consider after having already gone through quite a few in deciding on the boat itself, many potential buyers simply gave up and didn't buy at all. Smart dealers soon realized that if they included a perfectly matched trailer in the deal, the chances of actually making the sale increased exponentially. This is another advantage to buying a used boat; if it is trailerable, the trailer is generally sold with the boat because the sellers will most probably need a different trailer for the new boat they are buying as soon as they sell the old one. Just make sure it really is the proper trailer for the boat.

In case you aren't looking at a package (and even if you are, this information will help you to evaluate the suitability of the whole deal), here are some factors you'll need to consider in selecting a trailer:

- **Type of support.** Some trailers use rollers while others use bunks (also called bunkers), lengths of wood bolted to the frame and covered with outdoor carpeting (or other soft plastic) to protect the hull from actually touching wood, which could scratch. In my opinion, the best trailers are hybrids that use both: rollers in the center under the keel (or the bottom of the V), with bunks on the outsides to offer better longitudinal support for the boat as a whole. If the trailer for your boat has bunks, make sure they extend all the way to, and slightly past, the transom. The hull of a trailerable boat can carry a lot of weight at the stern and needs support all the way back to prevent the development of a downturn, or "hook," that can adversely affect your boat's performance (see Chapter 9).

- **Type of frame.** If you plan to do all your boating in fresh water, painted steel is fine. It can rust, but normal maintenance is usually sufficient to keep ahead of it. If you plan to enter salt or brackish water, even if just occasionally, your trailer should be made of aluminum or galvanized steel. Either will stand up to salt much better than painted steel.

- **Suspension system.** Fixed axles with leaf springs are most common. They cushion the ride somewhat but do nothing to damp the motion; the boat will bounce, which is why tying it down properly must be a part of your prehighway preparations. The independent suspension of torsion axles offers a much better ride for your boat, but not only do these axles cost more to begin with but water can intrude and do internal harm that remains totally invisible until the damage has been done, which means torsion axles can be more expensive to maintain. But there is another benefit to having them: often, the trailer and boat can sit lower, which is better both on the highway (a lower center of gravity means less sway) and when launching and retrieving.

- **Number of axles.** Two-wheel trailers are common, but as the load increases, so must the supporting cast. Four wheels or even six become necessary to spread that load when you tow a larger boat. This is another area in which a good

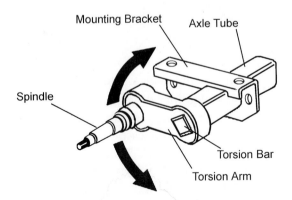

Figure 7-2. Torsion axles provide your boat with a smoother ride than the more common leaf-spring suspension, but they cost more. *(Dexter Axle)*

package helps, in that smart dealers will always match the trailer to the load as perfectly as possible; they don't want you disappointed for any reason.

- **Load capacity.** This is largely a matter of frame strength and the number of axles, though it also considers the weight ratings for the axle(s) and suspension. By law, trailers are classified by the maximum amount they may weigh when fully loaded, and they will have a capacity plate that states the trailer's gross vehicle weight rating and gross axle weight rating, plus the minimum tire rating needed to allow the weight ratings, along with the manufacturer's name and the trailer's serial number.

  Remember, gross vehicle weight includes the trailer itself *plus* the boat, motor(s), fuel, and all other gear you carry aboard. Make sure the trailer you buy is fully adequate. And remember, too, when deciding on adequacy (and also when actually using your trailer), knowledgeable people suggest that you never exceed 85% of a trailer's total rated capacity.

- **Tires.** Always use tires made specifically for trailers. They have tougher sidewalls (which will be marked ST—meaning Special Trailer service—along with the tire size) and are made of a rubber compound formulated to better withstand the wear and tear of towing. This rubber also holds up better to the ravages of UV radiation, which is good because trailer tires are usually more openly exposed to sunlight. Always use the size and type specified on the trailer's capacity plate—a trailer's capacity rating is based on using specifically rated tires.

- **Brakes.** Most common are the so-called surge brakes, which are hydraulic and

activated by a mechanism in the trailer's coupling that senses the pressure of the trailer continuing to move forward (surge) when the towing vehicle's brakes are applied. As with towing vehicles these days, trailer brakes are more and more often the disc type, though drum brakes still abound. Surge brakes are used because they are automatic and also because the mechanism is better suited to being submerged than most of the other options, such as the electrically operated trailer brakes you can control from the tow vehicle and the automatic operation that occurs when the tow vehicle's brake lights are energized. While the ability to brake the trailer alone is nice (it can help reduce sway), it's generally better not to depend on electrical devices for parts that will be submerged, and this includes wheels! Remember, too, that with multiple-axle trailers *all wheels must have brakes*. Failure to install brakes all around will result in poor braking performance, overheating of brakes and wheel hubs, and significantly reduced brake pad life.

- **Bearings.** These are critical—and a potential problem. The problem is twofold. It starts with trailer wheels normally being smaller than the tow vehicle wheels, which means they must make more revolutions to cover the same distance. This makes the bearings run hot. Then, when you launch your boat you dunk them into the water, where they cool immediately, creating an internal vacuum that draws in some of that water. This can cause internal rust and corrosion that leads to bearing failure. The answer is to keep the bearings continually immersed in either marine grease or oil to keep the water out. The most common

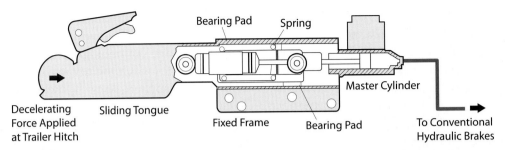

Figure 7-3. This drawing of a boat trailer coupler shows the inner workings of a surge brake actuator. When the towing vehicle slows or stops, momentum carries the trailer forward and the resulting deceleration force pushes the sliding tongue back into a fixed frame attached to the main tongue, causing the master cylinder to send brake fluid to the wheel cylinders, which activate the brakes. *(Atwood Mobile Products/Joseph Comeau)*

solution is spring-loaded bearing protectors, which are seals that use spring pressure to counter the water pressure and thus help prevent the water from entering. You just have to periodically inspect the bearings and repack them with fresh grease at regular intervals. You can also install oil-bath hub kits, which have see-through caps so you can know there's proper oil inside. Either way, your trailer hub bearings are never a "buy 'em and forget 'em" situation; they need constant care and attention.

The Tow Vehicle

Long gone are the days in which you could simply throw a bumper hitch on the family car and haul your boat. Chances are that if you don't already have one, you're going to also buy an SUV or a truck to do the towing. You'll want a vehicle that is also rated for towing the load class at which your trailer is rated (GVWR). *Trailer Boats* has a searchable database of tow vehicle ratings at www.trailerboats.com.

Four-wheel drive is almost mandatory (to better handle steep and slippery launch ramps), and if your towing will cover any distance at all (and it probably will once you get the trailer boating bug), you'll also want

the vehicle to have all the towing options offered by the automaker, which means heavy-duty brakes, beefed-up suspension, oil and transmission coolers, and probably an oversize radiator. Towing puts a lot of strain on the towing vehicle's engine, and the cooler you can keep it, the happier it (and you) will be. A transmission temperature gauge is also a good addition, just so you'll really know what's going on. Towing with a vehicle that isn't up to the job will be a disappointment at best and a disaster at worst. You'll be wise to invest in the truck or SUV you really need.

Once you've invested in a proper tow vehicle, be sure to maintain it well. Your owner's manual will normally show separate maintenance schedules for normal operation and for heavy-duty use. I probably don't have to tell you that towing is heavy duty! If you follow the stricter maintenance schedule, your vehicle will serve you better for longer—and you'll also be better protecting that investment you made.

The Hitch

Hitches, which are essential for connecting the trailer to the tow vehicle, are also classed similarly to the trailers themselves: by the trailer's GVWR.

Class I This class is for towing loads of up to 2,000 pounds with a 200-pound maximum tongue weight. There are three basic types: the bumper mount, the bumper/frame mount, and those that are part of a step bumper.

Bumper hitches are not really meant for serious towing; today's impact-absorbing bumpers, by design, lack the heft that's needed to do the job. They have way too much give to withstand the bouncing a trailer tongue will impose. Unfortunately, this is generally true of even those rugged-looking step bumpers you see on some pickup trucks. For Class I loads, the best bet is a bumper/frame hitch.

Class II Meant for towing loads of up to 3,500 pounds (350-pound tongue weight), all of these are frame mounted, which would seem a good idea except that many vehicles that are otherwise capable of handling this sort of load don't have frames—most of today's automobiles and smaller SUVs employ frameless unibody construction. This means that the hitch must be bolted to mere sheet metal, which will need the extra bracing of a reinforcing piece of thicker metal, often called a backing plate, to be strong enough to bear the load over time. Vehicles that are factory rigged for towing will usually have this needed reinforcement, though aftermarket installations may not. This backing plate, and the strength it offers, is crucial enough to make it a definite checkpoint if you are having the hitch installed locally.

Class II hitches come in two varieties: those with a permanently attached ball and ones with a square opening (called a receiver) into which you insert the drawbar on which the ball is mounted. With the latter option, you don't have to have anything sticking out behind your vehicle if you are not towing; you can remove the drawbar when you don't need it.

Class III These hitches can handle tow loads of up to 5,000 pounds and tongue weights of up to 500 pounds. They are all frame mounted and employ a receiver and drawbar rather than having a permanently attached ball.

Class IV Now we're up with the big boys. These hitches are rated for towing loads up to 10,000 pounds with allowable tongue weights of 1,000 pounds. Once you start towing loads of this category, several other factors come into play because such loads affect handling all around. A full discussion is beyond the scope here, but be aware that both tow vehicle and trailer must be set up for optimum performance and balance, with the objective of having all of the tow vehicle's wheels bear their proper share of the load.

Class V These are not yet that common, but a number of manufacturers do offer them. They can handle tow loads of up to 12,000 pounds and tongue weights of up to 1,200 pounds.

Having a Ball

Hitch balls come in four sizes: 1⅞ inches, which can handle up to a 2,000-pound tow rating (and sometimes more); 2 inches, which handles up to 6,000 pounds; 2⁵/₁₆ inches, which can handle up to 10,000 pounds (or more); and the new 2½-inch ball, which is required by the new Class V hitches. While a full discussion of all the details is beyond the scope of this book, you should at the very least be aware of the importance of matching the hitch ball size to both the load

Quick Tips

You may have noticed a thread running through all the classes: maximum tongue weight is 10% of the trailer's allowable total weight. The boat and its load must always be balanced on the trailer so that the actual tongue weight never exceeds this limit.

Quick Tips

A weight-distributing (aka load equalizing) hitch helps spread tongue weight more evenly between the tow vehicle's front and rear axles and the trailer's axles, which helps improve on-road handling characteristics. The system consists of a frame-mounted receiver hitch and spring bars that attach to both the drawbar assembly and the trailer frame. While these systems can improve handling on the highway, the spring bars, which are available in different tension ratings, must match the load and also be set parallel to the surge coupler, or the system will cause problems by reducing the tow vehicle's rear wheel traction or interfering with the proper operation of the surge brakes. As with many things in life, a weight-distributing system will be a help only if it is perfectly set up and precisely matched to the job at hand. If you will be towing a heavy load, it's worth looking into.

involved and the size of the trailer's coupler. If the coupler is too large for the ball, it can bounce off, which is obviously not a good thing even if you have all of the other safety measures installed.

Other Safety Gear
Some states require some or all of the following items, while others do not. But they are all a good idea regardless. You should have them if you plan to trailer your boat.

- **Safety chains.** These go between the trailer frame and the hitch and should cross beneath the tongue to form a cradle that will catch the tongue if the coupler detaches itself from the hitch ball.
- **Closed-loop fasteners.** Safety chains end in hooks that are put up through holes or pad eyes in the drawbar or hitch. If you face the hook back toward the trailer as you insert it, you lessen the chances of it bouncing out. But if the hooks have retainers that spring shut to form a closed loop after they are inserted

in the pad eyes, the chance of their coming free is near zero.
- **Breakaway connector.** This is a length of wire rope that connects the surge brakes to the hitch. If the trailer disconnects from the tow vehicle, it applies the trailer brakes immediately.

- **Coupler lock.** This can be as simple as a cotter pin, a push-to-release pin, or even a padlock for greater security. In whatever form, it prevents the coupler release from opening unless you want it to, which can also prevent the accidental detachment of trailer from tow vehicle.

Some of these items, and perhaps even all of them, may be required by law in your state. Check with your local authorities. But since they are all such good ideas, why not just install them anyway? Eventually, you'll be glad you did.

YOU'LL NEED SOME EDUCATION, TOO

If you opt for trailer boating, you'll have to learn some different driving techniques. You'll be operating an assemblage of vehicles that's much greater in total length and also probably heavier than anything you've driven before. What's more, it bends in the middle! And if you think this will present problems when you are going forward (you'll have to make wider turns than you're probably used to, and stopping distances will increase), just wait until the first time you try to back it up to go down a ramp. And yet, all it will take is practice—perhaps in a large empty parking lot where you have plenty of room to make the mistakes you'll learn from without doing any harm—and you'll be handling your trailer like a pro.

After you've contemplated all of the above, you may conclude that trailer boating is too challenging to bother with. It isn't. There are just a few more details to consider. But once you have a proper rig assembled and have learned how to handle it, keeping your boat on a trailer can be the easiest, simplest, and most convenient way to go boating. It certainly is popular and probably has more dedicated adherents than any other form of boating, so it is well worth considering, especially if other "where to keep it" options present a problem where you live.

There's one other detail I'd better mention before we move on: a trailer is a vehicle that must also be registered in the state in which you reside. You can apply at the same place where you register the tow vehicle; their reregistration cycles will normally coincide.

It's a Wrap

WRAP

✔ Trailer boating offers the broadest selection of boating areas—they'll be nearly unlimited.

✔ Keeping your boat on a trailer can be the least expensive way to store it.

✔ The trailer must fit the boat perfectly.

✔ Your tow vehicle must also match the load.

✔ Trailers, hitches, and tow vehicles themselves are all classified by the GVWR of the trailer, which is the trailer's total weight, including the trailer itself, plus the boat, motor(s), fuel, and all gear aboard.

✔ Trailering demands that you learn some new driving techniques, but they are not really difficult and require only practice.

CHAPTER 8

CHOOSING THE RIGHT DEALER

Do I Need to Read This Chapter?

You should read this chapter if you want to discover

- ✔ Why buying from the right dealer is as important as buying the right boat.
- ✔ What to look for in a dealership.
- ✔ Why price isn't the only thing to consider in buying a new boat.
- ✔ How to judge a dealer's service department.

WHAT MAKES A DEALER "RIGHT"?

This could be the most important chapter in the book. Yes, buying the wrong boat for your needs can take much of the fun out of the sport. But so can buying the right boat from the wrong source. *Where* you buy can be critical, especially when you're buying a brand-new boat. Boats are a perfect example of the reality that nothing made by human hands can be perfect. You will have problems with your boat no matter how conscientious you are about maintenance—though proper maintenance will almost always reduce those problems in both number and severity, so you should never neglect it. And this is as true of brand-new boats as it is of used. Powerboats are most often a floating bundle of problems waiting to be solved. That stated, let me quickly add that the vast majority of the problems will be minor and no challenge to a good service department;

they will be quickly resolved. And with a new boat, nearly all of them should be covered by warranty (see Chapter 13). On the whole, the pleasures to be derived from powerboating far outweigh the minor aggravation these problems can cause. This will be especially true if you've bought your boat from the right dealer, whose service department will have you up and running again quickly.

Look for Certification

The Marine Industry Dealership Certification Program is designed to ensure consumers that buying and maintaining a boat are pleasant experiences. Certified dealers support the Marine Industry Consumer Bill of Rights, which is reproduced in the accompanying sidebar. Not all good dealers will bother to get with the program. But you can bet a bundle that the dealers that

Marine Industry Consumer Bill of Rights

Preamble

Our dealership subscribes to the Marine Industry Dealer Certification standards established to insure that your boating experience is as enjoyable as possible. This includes adhering to a Consumer Bill of Rights. Should we fail to live up to any of these commitments, please let us know so that we can address the matter immediately. Our goal is to enhance your boating experience by providing trained, friendly employees, quality products, and reliable services.

You have the right to:

Sales

- The assistance of a capable and knowledgeable sales consultant.
- Advertising and representations that are truthful and factual.
- A written disclosure of all details associated with a purchase.
- An explanation of the proper usage and operation of products.
- Products properly prepared, inspected, and tested before delivery.
- The delivery of new products as scheduled.
- An explanation of all maintenance requirements and schedules established for your product.
- An explanation and written copies of warranties on all products and major components.

Service

- The explanation of maintenance/repair plans including estimated repair time and cost.
- An itemized list of all charges (both warranty and retail) with thorough explanation.
- Prior approval of changes in repair costs or additional charges should they occur.
- Maintenance/repair work done right the first time by knowledgeable trained technicians.
- Maintenance/repair work completed when promised.
- Timely notice of changes in service delivery time if delays are experienced in repair completion.
- Inspect any replaced/damaged components upon presentation of the invoice/work order.

Operations

- Fair, open, and honest treatment without discrimination.
- Respectful, professional, and accurate responses to all your product questions and requests.
- Privacy and confidentiality of customer records.
- Voice any concerns, directly with our management team, if we fail to fulfill our commitments or meet your expectations.

(Courtesy NMMA)

do opt to go this route will be among the better ones. You can find a list of certified dealers at www.discoverboating.com/buying/certified/dealers.aspx.

Check Their CSI

The best dealerships will be quite proud of their high CSI (Customer Satisfaction Index) ratings, which reflect a high degree of satisfaction among their customers. Chances are that if a dealer you approach has a high CSI, you'll soon know it. More important, you should discover from the way you are treated from the moment you enter the store exactly why that dealership rates so highly. Although it is perhaps overdue, the industry as a whole is beginning to realize what the best dealerships have always known: it isn't just the one sale that matters; success comes from building lasting customer relationships that can span many years. A good dealer doesn't want to just sell you a boat; s/he wants you to be so sufficiently satisfied that you'll keep coming back to ultimately buy many.

A Good Service Department = A Good Dealer

While you would hope to not need it often, a quality service department is one hallmark of a good dealership. And since you *will* need service on occasion regardless of the quality of the boat, it's best to buy your boat from a dealer who will really serve you well.

Signs of a Quality Service Department
You can never be 100% sure of a service department until it does some work for you, but there are some plainly visible signs that can reveal a lot in advance:

- **It will be busy.** While this could be considered somewhat of a negative (with a

Quick Tips

In 2001, a study by J.D. Power and Associates showed that while many boat dealerships recognized the importance of good service, many others did not and thus their customers were less than satisfied with the service they received after the sale, even when they were essentially happy with the boat itself. This study served as a wake-up call to the industry, and since then many more dealerships have joined the program and upgraded their service departments. But there are still dealerships that consider each individual boat sale to be the only objective—service and potential future sales be damned. So it pays to be aware. Always look for a good service department when you're shopping for a boat.

busy service department, it's hard to get work done as soon as you want it), it usually means that enough people are satisfied with the work to keep coming back, which is really a good sign.

- **It will be neat and orderly.** Neatness is both a sign of and an allowing factor for efficiency. Efficient workers not only tend to keep an orderly workplace, it is nearly impossible to be efficient in the midst of chaos. A neat workplace is usually a sign of careful workers and a good indicator of quality workmanship.

- **It will have certified mechanics and technicians.** While the boating industry doesn't as yet have an equivalent of the auto industry's ASE (Automotive Service Excellence) certification program, it is working on it. The ABYC, which sets voluntary standards for boats and yachts, has undertaken a training/certification program that is steadily expanding in scope. Engine makers usually have training/certification programs for mechanics, as do most electronics manufacturers for retail-level technicians. A good service department will have certificates on display.
- **The service manager will be a good people person.** As suggested in the Consumer Bill of Rights, you should expect to receive a thorough and detailed explanation (in understandable layperson terms) of just what needs to be done and why. The service manager should also be able to estimate how long the repair should take, barring the unexpected. You won't be able to judge this totally until you bring a boat in for work, but you can spend a few moments observing the way the manager and staff seem to treat others. Customers that leave the facility looking relieved are usually a good sign. You should also take a moment to get acquainted with the service manager; you'll be working with him quite often if you buy a boat there (at least through the warranty period, if not longer), and you should feel comfortable with his approach and demeanor.

Other Signs of Quality

A quality service department is just one of many factors that suggest you've found a good dealer. Among others:

- **Salespeople who listen as much as they talk.** It's natural for them to tout the brand(s) they sell, but before a good dealership's associates suggest a model to look at, they will ask a lot of questions and listen carefully to your answers. They've been trained to think "not one boat but many," and the last thing a good salesperson wants to do is put you in the wrong vessel—s/he knows that if you aren't basically happy with that first one, you'll probably never buy another.
- **You won't feel pressured.** Sure, they want to sell boats; it's their business. But good dealerships recognize that one big cause of buyer's remorse is the feeling that you've been pushed into making a purchase you really didn't want. Good dealerships also recognize that, regardless of the size of the boat and its price tag, a boat is a major purchase that no one wants to make hurriedly. So they don't push; they don't present offers "good today only."
- **You'll have all your questions answered.** Even if the initial response is "Golly, I've never had anyone ask that before and I really don't know," at a good dealership this will be followed immediately with "but let me go see if I can find out; there has to be somebody here who has the answer, or at least knows where we can get it. Excuse me, I'll be right back."
- **They'll have a limited number of "sales."** Yes, *all* dealers have special promotions from time to time. In today's marketplace, no business can afford to just sit and wait for customers to come in. Sometimes a special occasion is necessary to increase consumer interest. But good dealerships don't constantly

present one promotion after another, week after week after week. This isn't to say that you won't be able to bargain and maybe get a price below the initial

Price isn't everything. While you never want to pay more than you have to for anything, especially when it's a big-ticket item like a boat, remember that the facilities and services that result in a good dealership have their costs, too. Consequently, a good dealer will usually have higher overhead and thus will probably be unable to match the prices offered by those who are interested only in selling that one boat. So shop around, compare prices, and even bargain for the best price you can get. But always be prepared to pay a little more for the long-term advantage of buying from a dealership that will continue to treat you right long after the sale.

offer; it always pays to try. Just know that good dealerships don't need the carnival atmosphere that usually accompanies a steady string of hyped-up promotions. Don't be turned off by End of Season, End of Model Year, or even Anniversary sales—events like these are not out of line. But beware of dealers that seem to need an excuse for advertising cut-rate prices every single week.

WRAP

✔ Dealer certification is a good sign of quality.
✔ A good service department is an even better sign.
✔ Good dealerships treat their customers right even when they're just looking—you should never feel pressured.

BE YOUR OWN SURVEYOR

Do I Need to Read This Chapter?

You should read this chapter if you want to discover

✔ Questions you should ask at the outset.
✔ How to recognize a basically good boat.
✔ How to recognize boats that aren't so good.
✔ Specific problem areas to examine closely.
✔ Strong points to consider as pluses.
✔ Warning signs that should send you running away (or at least walking very rapidly).

Do I Need to Read This Chapter?

NARROWING YOUR CHOICES

You should have a professional marine surveyor examine any boat you are seriously planning to buy, even if it is brand-new. But long before you get to the stage where you'll want to bring in a professional, you can help refine your decision by conducting some careful inspection on your own. This is important for any boat and critical when it has acquired some age. This in no way means you won't also need a professional survey. But few of us can afford to hire a survey of every single boat we might consider; the cost would be prohibitive. So, by tossing out the definitely undesirable (and even the marginally acceptable), you can narrow your choices to the one boat you really want.

READING THE TELLTALE SIGNS

Since used boats usually display more problems because the passage of time allows troubles to multiply and intensify, we'll discuss them first. Then we'll move on to tips for evaluating new boats and wrap up with suggestions for conducting a thorough sea trial of any boat. Don't read this as a condemnation of used boats; they often are extremely good buys. But since proper maintenance is so important to a boat's condition and because a lack of it so often manifests itself in bad conditions getting worse, the longer a boat has been around the greater the odds of finding things wrong with it. And yet, a used boat can be an even better buy than a new one if the owner has maintained it well, especially if s/he has made improvements.

Quick Tips

Carry a notebook. You'll want to note the things you like and dislike about each boat you examine. Keeping these notes strictly by memory could soon have you more confused than you were before you started. A microcassette recorder can be better than a notebook, and a compact camcorder could be even better. Dictate comments as you go through a boat, and then play the tape back to review them. Another huge advantage to recording rather than writing is the amount of detail you can include, and it eliminates the need for using potentially indecipherable shorthand or cryptic symbols to fit everything into a notebook. You have the option of later transcribing your recorded notes to paper, but I've found this to be generally unnecessary. Recording the answers to any questions you ask is also much more accurate than either trying to remember them or writing them down.

Even a used boat in less-than-average condition can be a good buy if the price is right.

Start by Assessing the Seller

Before you examine the boat itself, try to get to know the seller. You can learn a lot about a boat you may have yet to even see by appraising its present owner:

- **Does s/he seem to be organized?** If so, it's a good sign; organized people usually see that maintenance is done properly no matter how busy they are. Disorganized folks just never have the time. This doesn't mean you shouldn't deal with a disorganized seller but, rather, that doing so should trigger a bit more caution.

- **Does the seller really know the boat?** When you ask basic questions—What's the normal cruise speed and what throttle setting (in rpm) produces it? What's the fuel consumption and range at this speed? What's your oil-change interval?—the seller should be able to respond quickly and with assurance. If s/he can't answer basic questions easily, it is sign that perhaps you shouldn't believe much of anything s/he says about the boat. But there are other questions you should also ask: Who did you buy the boat from and when? Why are you selling it? Who has been your mechanic and how do I contact him? Have you ever had an insurance claim? If so, what did it entail? And last, but far from least, How long has the boat been for sale? The answer is important because boat sellers, whether they are individual owners or dealers with a large inventory, are much more likely to bend further during negotiations if the boat you are considering has been on the market for a long time.

- **Does s/he seem honest?** Consider the answers to your questions and the seller's sales pitch in general, and ask yourself if they seem reasonable. Most boatowners will tend to exaggerate; almost every boat you look at will be "the greatest ever." But the more realistic and candid the seller's statements, the better the odds you can believe them. If you find yourself doubting too much of what the seller says, you'd better walk away.

- **Can s/he produce the boat's paperwork (its certificate of number or federal document)?** The answer had better be yes, and the paperwork should show that the seller owns the boat and has the right to sell it, or you need to exit quickly. The lower the asking price, relative to current market value, the more cautious you should be. There can be many reasons for a bargain, but a common base for an asking price that's unrealistically low is that the boat was stolen and thus any money the seller receives will be 100% profit. Getting rid of the boat quickly is the seller's goal, so s/he sets a price low enough to help accomplish this.
- **Does s/he show some reluctance to sell?** Even sellers who are eager to sell a boat because they have their heart set on another one will usually harbor enough lingering feelings for their "baby" that there will be at least a degree of attachment they can't hide. If you can't sense this, it could be a sign that things are not exactly as the seller claims them to be. This doesn't mean you should walk away, but it should suggest caution.

Once you believe you're dealing with someone who is honest and will treat you fairly, you can proceed. But if you have even the slightest feeling there is something wrong, listen to your gut and walk away.

Most of these cautions apply if you are dealing with an owner directly. When you work with a dealer or broker, it's different. First, understand that selling is their profession, and while I don't intend to demean them personally or professionally, I would be remiss if I didn't remind you that professional salespeople are smoother than the

Quick Tips

Compare the numbers! A boat registered with a state will normally have its registration numbers on the bow. If it is federally documented, there will be an official number displayed clearly somewhere inside, quite often in the engine compartment. Every boat will have an HIN on its transom. Make sure the boat's numbers match the paperwork and that your purchase agreement—whenever you find a boat worthy enough to warrant one—contains the exact numbers (particularly the HIN—it is a boat's most significant identifier).

average individual and that persuasive banter is a part of their game. Plus, they will know the boat only to the extent they've been able to learn things from the owner, so almost everything they tell you will not be personal knowledge. But a good broker or salesperson will guide you to only those boats that appear to best suit your needs and desires, so you should never consider their suggestions to be irrelevant. Even when working with a reliable broker, it can be worthwhile to try to meet the boat's owner, if only for a short get-acquainted conversation. This will allow you to learn things you'll never discover any other way.

Then Assess the Boat

Although you'll ultimately want a sea trial of any boat you are seriously considering, your best initial view will be when it's firmly on land. Neither you nor the boat's owner will likely want to pay for hauling a boat you are just somewhat interested in, so this may not always be possible. But considering that most boats spend at least some time on the hard, you shouldn't regard it as totally impossible, either. And, for many reasons, on-land examination is usually easier with the boats for which it counts the most at this stage, so it often works out nicely.

Carry a camera, too. It doesn't matter whether it's an inexpensive single-use type from your neighborhood drugstore, a fancy digital SLR, or something in between. Use whichever is most comfortable for you—you don't want fumbling with a camera to get in the way of your examination. Take a picture of every major item you make a note about, and keep track of which photo goes with which note. Looking at the pictures when reviewing your notes will make it much easier to narrow your choices. By the way, a tape recorder can help here, too. As you take pictures, state which exposure number goes with each comment. This can be faster and more accurate than written captions. And if you use a camcorder, you'll have your comments and moving pictures all in one.

Is the Bottom Straight and True?

One of your first considerations should be the hull's lines. Regardless of the boat's *deadrise* [the angle of the V, measured from the horizontal], unless the hull design includes a *step* or two [steps are horizontal variations that blatantly reveal the appropriateness of the term], the bottom of the V should follow a straight line from the forefoot back. If it droops or sags in the middle (known as hogging), the boat won't plane well. If it droops at the transom (called a hook), the boat may perform as if it had trim tabs always set slightly down. A little hook isn't necessarily bad, particularly if the boat isn't equipped with tabs; hook

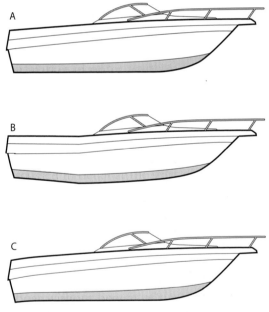

Figure 9-1. The bottom of most powerboat hulls will be straight and true (A). If the boat has been supported improperly while on land, it can develop a sag in the center, a distortion known as hogging (B). Improper support can also cause the transom to droop (C), which is called a hook. Note that in real life, the deformation will rarely be as obvious as in these drawings, which have been exaggerated for emphasis. But if there is any distortion at all, you will be able to see it if you look closely. *(Joseph Comeau)*

can sometimes help a boat to get on plane a bit quicker. But since boats tend to perform better if they still have their designed hull form, you should be wary of any distortion, no matter how slight.

Quick Tips

Boats in the water are supported evenly over their entire bottom. Boats on land should receive similar support, but obviously it can never be exactly the same. Unless the resulting spot support comes close to being distributed evenly overall, hull distortion is inevitable. This can be more of a problem with small boats because the larger ones usually spend more time in the water. Most commercial support systems, such as dry-storage racks and lifts (see Chapter 6) or trailers (see Chapter 7) have been designed to provide adequate and even support—as long as they are sized correctly. The problems arise when owners devise their own support systems. Full-length longitudinal supports that extend all the way to slightly past the transom will always do the job. A few blocks or posts here and there usually will not. Larger boats are often shipped on cradles that should be kept for future on-land storage because they fit the hull and offer perfect support.

Other Exterior Signs

Props Look closely at the drive system. The prop(s) shouldn't have any but the very slightest of dings or nicks—preferably none. Look also for pitting on the surfaces of the blades. This is usually from cavitation, the term for air bubbles exploding against the prop, a result of its failure to bite the water properly. Cavitation is a sign of poor performance, and the pits it leaves behind are another red flag with meaning that goes beyond the prop damage itself.

Zincs Sacrificial anodes, popularly called zincs, that are attached to various pieces of underwater metal (and sometimes the hull itself) should be in good shape: no longer shiny but nearly whole and relatively clean. Zincs are used because their alloy is higher on the galvanic scale (less noble) than the metals to which they are attached and thus will protect these underwater components by reacting and dissolving more quickly when stray electrical current is present, which is why they're called sacrificial. Badly eaten or missing zincs are a sign of poor maintenance at best (they do have to be replaced periodically, even under normal circumstances) and of serious electrolysis at worst—if they deteriorate too rapidly for routine maintenance to keep up, it is most often a result of excessive stray current, a sign of internal electrical problems. For either reason, missing or badly deteriorated zincs are a red flag that should raise some serious questions. If you are wondering how you can possibly see zincs that are no longer there, take heart. Where they *were* is usually so obvious that missing zincs are among the easiest defects to spot. You should also be cautious of zincs that look too new. Unless the bottom has been recently painted, in which case you can assume a thorough bottom job has been done (which usually includes installing new zincs), you have a right to question why the zincs have just been renewed. Ask! While new zincs can be merely a sign of good maintenance, the need for frequent replacement can also be a sign of trouble—under normal conditions, they'll last as long as the bottom paint.

Drives An outdrive or outboard lower unit should be relatively clean, though some marine growth on the *skeg* [the thin blade that extends below the prop] is inevitable and shouldn't bother you at this point. Observe the efficacy of the drive's trim/tilt system by having the seller activate it while you watch from astern.

Conventional shaft-and-strut running gear isn't that easy for an amateur to evaluate, but you can see if the prop is clean and free of dings, check the shaft zinc and others for abnormal deterioration, and see if the shaft is straight. You do this by having someone rotate the prop while you observe the shaft from the side. If it isn't straight and true, you'll be able to see the wobble. If it's okay, you'll have a hard time detecting any rotation at all because the shaft will not seem to move. Also check to see if you can deflect the shaft within the cutless bearing in the strut. Look at the ends of the bearing, which, if okay, will have the bearing surfaces touching the shaft evenly all around. Slight bearing wear is inevitable but nearly impossible to detect visually. On the other hand, obvious wear is a very bad sign and a good reason to question other aspects of the boat as well.

Hull Condition Take a close look at the hull overall with an eye toward spotting any

uneven surfaces or signs of patching, which can mean the boat may have been in an accident. If you can't examine the boat on land, improve your exterior view by having it docked at a floating pier so you can at least get a good look at everything from the waterline up. Be sure to have the boat turned around so you can examine both sides.

Trouble Spots

In every boat, there are a number of areas that can be particularly prone to defects. By checking them first, you can save yourself considerable time and effort. If you find problems early on, unless they are very minor, you can scratch that boat off your list and move on to the next one. Conversely, if you start where troubles are more likely and don't find any, the chances are good that other aspects will pass muster also.

Transom This can be a huge weakness in fiberglass boats with transom-mounted power plants or drive systems that must penetrate the transom. These craft usually have encapsulated plywood cores to make the transom stiffer and better able to handle the forces induced by the drive system. This is a common practice. But wherever the transom is cut or drilled, as it must be to bolt on outboards or allow an external drive to connect to its inboard power source, there's the potential for water to get in. When that happens, the plywood starts to deteriorate because even marine plywood isn't meant to have water in its inner plies constantly. But it can get there through the slightest opening that isn't thoroughly sealed.

Try to flex the transom by grabbing the extreme lower end of a drive to see if you can get it to move. If the transom is sound, you won't be able to budge it—the forces it must handle underway are much greater than any human can apply, even using the drive for leverage. Note that if the drive's tilt mechanism is worn, you may be able to move the drive a bit, but look closely at the transom itself, especially where the engine or drive is attached. If the transom is sound, it shouldn't budge. Even the slightest movement is a sign of trouble that will only get worse with time. Though minor deterioration can be repaired and future damage halted if the problem is caught early enough, I would only consider buying a boat with transom problems if they are slight and everything else about the boat is perfect.

Foredeck This area is often cored also, though rarely with plywood. It can be end-grain balsa, one of several closed-cell plastic foams, or (more rarely) a honeycomb material. What it is doesn't matter. If there's a good core-to-skin bond, the coring will help the deck to be stiff enough that you can walk on it with little flexing underfoot. But if this bond has become unstuck, you'll be able to cause considerable flexing by standing anywhere and bouncing up and down. Test in several places and note if there's any difference. There shouldn't be. Don't be alarmed if a forward cabin top flexes slightly; these are often less stiff than deck areas, and a bit of movement can be normal. But be concerned if any nonskid-covered surfaces are even slightly less than totally resistant to movement. They are meant to be walked on and should be up to withstanding body weight without flexing.

Toe Rails These aren't trouble spots unless the boat doesn't have them. And even then, it's not a major problem. But finding them is a major plus. Toe rails around

Quick Tips

Check the nonskid itself. Walkways need it to provide better footing when wet. But some of the least slippery surface finishes are often also the toughest to keep clean. I really like the tiny pyramids molded into the walkways of many production boats. The raised points provide resistance to slipping while the openness and symmetry allow for easy cleaning. A molded-in or painted-on sand-type surface is more common, and though it works well in the nonslip department, at least when new, its randomness makes it less easy to clean. This type also tends to wear down more quickly and needs to be renewed more often.

the foredeck (and usually the side decks) let your feet know that they're about to run out of decking—that stepping any farther *outboard* [away from the center] will leave you with nothing to stand on. These rails can be, as they were in the days of wooden boats, a low-rising attachment of wood, plastic, or metal (usually aluminum) that can actually serve as a stopper if your foot slides toward the edge. Or they can be, as is more often the case today, a part of the molded deck structure and can range from a mini bulwark that extends several inches above the deck and is a genuine foot-slide stopper to merely an aggressive upturn of the deck just before it becomes the gunwale. While this rail may not be sufficient to actually stop your foot from sliding overboard, it can still be enough to let you know you're approaching the edge. Either way, toe rails are a definite plus. Whether a boat has them will depend largely on its age. They mostly disappeared in the early days of fiberglass as a result of the changes in design needed to accommodate ease of molding. In the past dozen years or so, molding techniques have advanced and the rails have again become common, though they aren't universal. Most European regulations require them, and U.S. builders that also sell overseas now include them in their current designs.

Deck Hardware   Look closely for telltale stress cracks around the bases of handrail

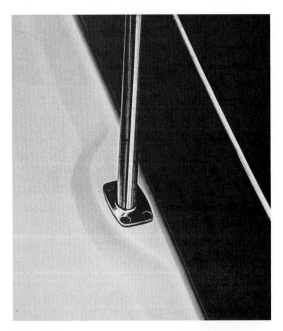

Figure 9-2. This toe rail is a slightly raised gunwale. It serves its purpose of helping keep your feet on deck where they belong by letting you know when you've reached the edge.

stanchions and other deck hardware. The stanchions should be solidly mounted and essentially rigid. If you can move any of them, look closely to see whether this is from loose mounting bolts or a spongy deck structure, which—like the previously mentioned transom damage—is a result of unwanted water intrusion, most probably from improperly bedded mounting bolts. The former is probably easy to fix. The latter is possibly fixable as well, but probably at a much greater cost. I would walk away from any boat with a spongy deck structure.

Look for ample cleats, chocks, and *fairleads* [metal-lined openings that allow a line to pass through a bulkhead or deck], and make sure that there are no sharp or rough edges that can damage your lines. The unseen inner edges of fairleads can be particularly troublesome, so stick a finger in and feel; just be careful not to cut yourself if there is a sharp edge.

Wiring   Look under and behind the console if you can—there's often a hinged access panel beneath the console but not always. You can also ask to see what's on the other side of the electrical panels, which may require removing a few screws, so you need the owner's permission. What you are looking for is neatly bundled, well-supported, color-coded, properly labeled wires with clean ring-type insulated crimp-on terminals. What you may actually see are signs of potential trouble: terminals or contacts that appear burned; wires spliced together with the connections covered by layers of electrical tape; jumbled, tangled wires that are totally unidentifiable. Try to examine both the low-voltage DC system and also the house power 120- or 240-volt AC circuits. While used boat electrical systems can often be in less than perfect shape, they don't have to be. A well-maintained boat of any age will still have neat wiring. And splices, if any have been made, will have crimp-on connectors, preferably covered with heat-shrink tubing that helps keep moisture out. While electrical tape can serve the same purpose, it also conceals the kind and quality of the joint it covers, so taped connections must fall squarely in the questionable column. Wire nuts, the twist-on connectors so common in household wiring, are a definite no-no for boats; they just don't stay put when subjected to vibration. You shouldn't find any wire nuts in boat wiring, but if you do, plan on replacing them immediately if the boat turns out to be otherwise fine and you buy it.

Ground fault circuit interrupters (GFCIs) on the 110-volt house-current outlets in the galley, heads, machinery spaces, and weather-exposed locations such as the cockpit are another huge plus. GFCIs sense any current leakage or a faulty ground circuit and will trip the breaker to prevent your getting shocked if you happen to provide an unintentional but convenient path to ground. ABYC standards require them now, so new boats often will have them while older boats generally do not. GFCI-protected outlets are another of those items that are a major find in an older boat but only a minor issue when absent—they can usually be added with little difficulty or expense. Knowing you'll want to do this is another item to note carefully and add to your to-do list if the boat turns out to be the one you want.

Among the important places to inspect is wherever wiring penetrates a bulkhead or deck. The opening should surround the wires with a round-edged soft plastic or rubber grommet (or at least a soft protective bushing) to prevent them from rubbing against the structure—the edges of the hole itself are usually hard and often sharp. If the opening lacks this protection, insulation will eventually wear through, which can produce a short circuit that will be trouble at the very least and a possible fire starter at the worst.

Hatches, Doors, and Ports These are all necessary. But every single one of them should open easily, close tightly with equal ease, and do its job of keeping water and weather out when closed. Unless your examination reveals that the answer here is "all of the above" for each and every one, you'd better walk away. Pay particular attention to surfaces around, and especially under, these openings. Any sign of water intrusion is a red flag, even if there's no obvious damage as yet. Equally bad are hatches or doors that don't quite fit their openings and thus either leave gaps when closed or don't quite close at all. Either is less than satisfactory and a very good reason to look for a different boat. Give the boat points for some sort of flexible seal that compresses when the hatch, door, or port is closed; these seals are the best way to keep weather on the outside where it belongs.

Cabin Ventilation Use your nose. When you first enter the cabin, you shouldn't detect any "off" odor or mustiness. Even if the boat has been closed and unused for a while, there should be sufficient ventilation to keep the air fresh. You can make an exception if the cabin is air conditioned and the AC hasn't been on; air-conditioned cabins need to be tight for better cooling efficiency. But all other enclosures should have a sufficient circulation of fresh air without opening a hatch or port. If this boat doesn't, it means you'll have to open one or more of those hatches and ports to gain ventilation; when the weather is inclement, this can also let in rain or spray. Keep looking.

Similarly, you shouldn't smell fuel or anything else associated with the engine compartment. The bulkheads should keep the different compartments effectively isolated from each other. If you smell anything inside the cabin that's different from what you smelled outside, be suspicious. Even the pleasant odor of a room deodorant can suggest the seller is trying to hide something.

Also note the general condition of the interior. Obviously, the older the boat, the more wear you'll probably observe. But all of it should match. Be suspicious of any area

that looks much better or worse than its surroundings because either can be a sign of something more serious. Worse-looking places may have suffered some particularly disturbing damage, and anything too new in the midst of older-looking materials suggests a recent replacement. In either case, you should always ask why and then weigh the answer carefully.

Engine Compartment

Look for signs of maintenance and care: clean, reasonably dry bilges; engines with clean, oil-free exteriors (perhaps with oil-absorbing pads beneath them, which should also be reasonably clean); and no clutter or

Quick Tips

Give points for a boat that has fiddles, which are to countertops, tables, and shelves as toe rails are to decks: raised edges that keep things from sliding off in a seaway. Fiddles were actual mini rails in the days of wooden boats, and they also largely disappeared in the early days of fiberglass, even when the interior cabinetry was mostly wood. Fiddles are becoming more prevalent in newer designs, at least in the slightly raised edge variety, though they are still far from universal. But fiddles are such a big help in keeping things in place that, in my opinion, they add value to a boat.

Figure 9-3. A fiddle can be an added piece of wood trim, as shown on this table, or merely a molded-in raised edge similar to that in the toe rail photo on page 118.

The area beneath an engine should be designed for containment whether it is an inset pan or merely an enclosed area with no holes or drains to the rest of the bilge. The purpose is to keep any leaking oil from mixing with normal bilge water and thus becoming capable of being pumped overboard. This is a federal offense that can result in fines up to $5,000 and possible imprisonment. Placing oil-absorbent mats beneath an engine is beneficial, but not all owners or captains bother to do this. New boats and fairly new used boats will normally have built-in containment—it's been the law for a number of years now—but older used boats may not. Always check to be sure it's there.

trash. A less-than-ideal bilge isn't necessarily a sign to walk away, but it should provoke a higher degree of caution; look at everything else a little more closely.

Check hoses for cracks and other signs of deterioration; you shouldn't see any. All hoses attached to through-hull fittings below the waterline should be double clamped (not only at the through-hull but at every other connection as well), and all clamps should be tight and rust-free. Always check the tightening screw; on cheaper clamps it usually isn't stainless, and all too soon it can rust away and fail to hold the clamp tight, which then allows the assembly to leak. The seacocks or valves on intakes should be easy to open and close. Suction hoses should be reinforced to prevent collapse, and any strainers should be clean and clear.

Bilge Pumps Every boat should have at least one automatic electric bilge pump—and the more the merrier. A boat cannot have too many bilge pumps. Most of them are automatic by virtue of an external float switch that closes the circuit to operate the

pump when rising water lifts it. You can check their operation by lifting a float manually. If this doesn't start the pump, you know rising water won't turn it on either. Fortunately, bad bilge pump switches are usually a minor problem that can be fixed quite easily. But knowing that this needs to be done is worth the time it takes to find out.

A manual bilge pump for use in case of electric pump failure or to increase pumping capability in an emergency is a welcome find. But built-in manual bilge pumps are rare on American powerboats. If you find one, consider it a definite plus. If it also has

Figure 9-4. You should find a strainer with a removable basket (for cleaning purposes) on every raw-water intake to prevent grass, weed, silt, or other junk from passing through to clog the finer passages down the line. *(Perko, Inc.)*

Quick ⟨💡⟩ Tips

Because engines pump a lot of raw water, they are much more efficient than the electric pumps normally installed in production boats when it comes to removing excess bilge water. They make excellent backups, easily handling volumes that would overwhelm the basic pumps—or even a manual backup. Being able to use the engines' pumps in an emergency can be a life-saver. Note the secondary valve and alternate pickup on the installation in the illustration. In the event of serious hull damage, each main engine's raw-water intake can be from the bilge instead of from the water beneath the bottom. Arrangements of this sort are not that common in pleasure craft, though many commercial vessels have them. If you find one on a boat you're looking at, consider it a major plus.

a manifold and hoses to pump other compartments, that's even better. Just don't be disappointed when you don't find them; American builders tend to install manual bilge pumps only on boats intended for the European market, where just about every country demands them. As I sadly have to state so often, our U.S. Coast Guard standards for pleasure boats are pitifully lax.

The Engine(s)   Check the lube oil. The level should be at or near the Full mark on the dipstick—certainly above Add. Too much oil can be as bad as too little, however, and possibly a sign of other problems. Dark oil is normal, though it shouldn't feel gritty. A milky appearance usually means there's

water or coolant in the oil, an indication of internal leakage that should be a red flag. This is a good time to ask about oil change intervals. Every 100 hours or so is normal, which can be just once a year for many seasonal boaters. Also ask if the owner has used an oil analysis program; if the answer is yes, ask to review the reports.

Look at the belts. They should be flexible and clean with no cracks and no sign of wear, such as worn or frayed edges. A

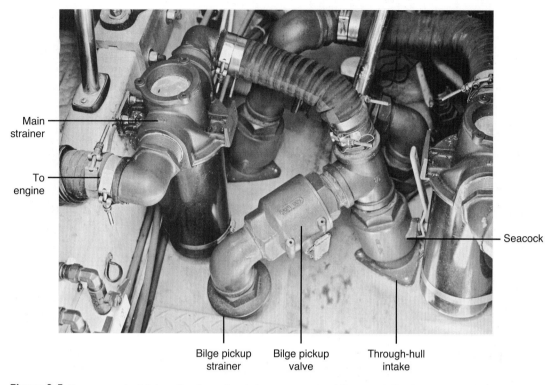

Main strainer

To engine

Seacock

Bilge pickup strainer

Bilge pickup valve

Through-hull intake

Figure 9-5. These raw-water intakes allow the engines to become emergency bilge pumps. Simply open the bilge pickup valve and close the seacock, and the engine pumps its raw water from the bilge. *(yachtaccess.com)*

Quick  Tips

Sending off a sample to be tested at every oil change can be a very good way to learn of impending engine problems before they become serious, and I heartily recommend it (do an Internet search to locate a lab). This is one program that is never too late to start, and you should consider doing it when you buy a boat, even if the previous owner did not. If s/he did, be sure to examine the reports. They can speak volumes about an engine's condition. Internal wear is normal and inevitable, and the oil will contain microscopic particles of the various metals involved. What they are, and how much of each shows up in the oil, can indicate exactly what is wearing and how much. If done regularly, oil analysis can easily detect trends, and anything abnormal (such as a drastic increase in a particular metal, which indicates excessive wear) will shout its presence by the obvious change.

fine dark powder on the belts or pulleys is another visible sign of wear that's easy to spot and possibly indicates a belt that is too tight, which can also cause internal bearing wear you can't see so easily.

Look at the engine compartment and on-engine wiring. It should be neat and well organized with no tangled rat's nests, and the terminals should be free of corrosion. All my previous comments regarding wiring in general apply here, too.

Transmission(s) Pull the transmission dipstick. Whether the gearbox uses transmission fluid or engine oil, it should be clear and new looking. Transmission oil isn't exposed to the combustion by-products that darken engine oil, and any sign of the darker oil you saw in the engine itself usually means a leaking shaft seal, which is repairable but expensive. You don't necessarily have to be alarmed if the transmission fluid level seems low; some gears have to be under power with a resulting increase in fluid pressure before the level can be accurately assessed, and the dipstick marks will reflect this.

Shaft Log Look closely where the shaft penetrates the hull. The stuffing box (also called a shaft log), which keeps water on the outside of the boat, can be a problem. Most older-style stuffing boxes are designed to drip when the shaft is turning so as to lubricate the shaft and prevent wear within the packing gland that keeps most of the water out. This means that a little water in the bilge beneath the shaft log is okay. A lot of water may mean only that the packing gland needs adjustment (it must be tightened occasionally), but it could also mean it needs to be refitted with new packing. Excess water could possibly indicate something worse, but

I wouldn't jump to that conclusion. Note the situation but don't be alarmed. None of the above is cause for rejecting the boat. If there's a major problem in this area, your surveyor will be better able to detect its severity and suggest a correction. If everything looks as it should, you can take this as a plus and move on.

You should definitely give points to a boat with dripless shaft seals, one popular type of which works by using seals more similar to the shaft seals in engines than the old waxed flax packing that used to be so common in stuffing boxes. They also divert some raw cooling water to flow out through the shaft log to help lubricate the seal and also help keep external water out by its pressure. This type of shaft log will be evident by the hose connecting it to the engine. Look closely at the hoses, and be prepared to replace any that appear to be in bad condition if the boat is otherwise fine enough to buy.

Maintenance Log This is a different sort of log. It's a book of records—in this case, records of maintenance and repairs with all the dates, engine hours, and statements of what was done when. Don't be alarmed if the seller hasn't kept a maintenance log; many owners don't. But finding one for any boat you're interested in is a plus, especially if the log shows that maintenance has been performed routinely and in accordance with the engine maker's and builder's recommended schedules.

ASSESSING VALUE

You can get a pretty good idea of a boat's worth by looking it up on www.bucvalue.com. Just remember that the price listed on this site and in the BUC Book will be for an average boat of that make, model, and

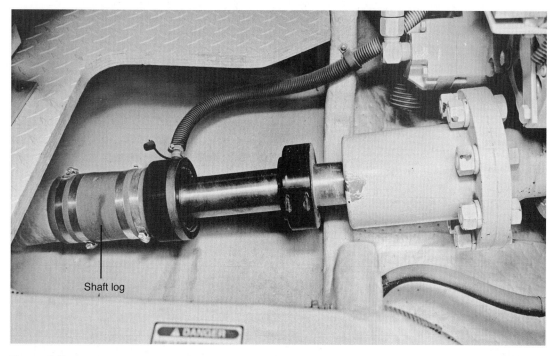

Shaft log

Figure 9-6. The shaft log helps keep water outside the boat where a shaft penetrates the hull, making it a very important element indeed. This is one of the newer dripless types.

age. Before you can establish the worth of any particular boat, you have to determine whether its current condition is above or below average and, if so, by how much. One initial determining factor is the amount of time it has been used.

Engine Hours

I previously noted that the typical pleasure boat owner uses a boat somewhere between 100 and 200 hours per year; since this is a wide range, 150 hours is commonly used as the average. Most boats these days have hour meters—at least for the main engines—which means it is easy to verify the total hours run. You merely divide the hours you see on the meter by the number of years (or seasons) the boat has been in use to see if that use qualifies as normal. Since all things mechanical have a finite life—and thus a

limited number of total working hours—it might seem that the lower the reading on the meters the better; the fewer hours already used, the more there should be remaining. This can be true, but it isn't necessarily so. An engine that hasn't been run much can have significant corrosion damage that quite literally eats into its normal expected life. This means you should be as wary of abnormally low hours as you should of abnormally high ones. Either situation is cause to reduce the boat's actual value.

When assessing significance of the hours run, keep in mind that the typical gasoline marine engine will usually deliver relatively trouble-free service until it reaches 1,000 hours, the point at which many of them develop minor problems. If these problems aren't taken care of while they're still minor, they can turn into major difficulties that may make

Quick Tips

Generally, the best deal is a boat that has been used on the low side of average but at least 100 hours per year. This should be enough for the engines to be in good working order and yet have the maximum number of probable hours remaining. It may help to understand that most inboard gasoline engines in pleasure boats can be run for about 1,500 hours before they need a major overhaul, which means a boat's original engines should be good for 10 years or so. The average marine diesel engine will usually run for more than three times that long and be good for 5,000 hours or more under the same conditions. Just remember that the number of hours that a marine engine runs without trouble is extremely dependent on the quality of maintenance it receives over those years.

the engine's remaining 500 hours of expected life difficult to attain. Interestingly enough, an automobile engine will normally run almost twice as long (3,000 hours on average). Marine engines tend to fail so much sooner because they normally work harder and under worse conditions. As a friend once put it, a boat engine has to work like a vehicle engine that's constantly going uphill.

Still, a well-maintained gasoline engine operated under the best of conditions may well go for *more* than 1,500 hours without major overhaul. But way too many boat engines are not well maintained. And since they must serve under conditions that are considerably less than best—damp salt air, intermittent operation, and basic neglect—they will often quit much sooner. Proper maintenance is so critical to engine longevity that every sign of good maintenance you can detect around the boat as a whole can be taken as a sign of longer expected engine life (considering the hours already run, of course).

Diesel engines are built to higher tolerances than gasoline engines. Even today's lighter, faster-turning models will often deliver 8,000 hours of reliable service before they need a major overhaul (if they have been maintained properly), which is another reason for choosing diesel power if you plan to use a boat a lot. Theoretically, a well-maintained diesel can last the life of a boat. But this is true only if the engines are used—and maintained—on a regular basis. Diesels that just "sit" will tend to give out much sooner, which means too few hours is a bad sign regardless of the type of power.

These numbers are not chiseled in stone, however, and the way an engine has been maintained will usually have a much greater influence on its useful life than how many hours it has run. But generally, a boat with considerably fewer than average hours should be as devalued as a boat with far more.

Overall Condition

Some used boats are absolute gems, while others are disasters that need more work than they're worth. Most fall somewhere in between. And a boat's condition is so important to its value that BUC International recommends adjusting the base, or BUC, value by a percentage based on some arbitrary qualifiers. While a professional surveyor

Quick Tips

One time-sensitive item is an inboard engine's exhaust riser, where raw cooling water meets the exhaust, cools the exhaust manifold, and then exits the boat. Time is especially relevant here if the boat has been operated in salt or brackish water. The riser has two chambers for most of its length, with exhaust in the inner chamber and cooling water in the outer. Just before the exhaust exits the riser, the cooling water is allowed to mix with it so they can leave the riser together. Hot salt water is extremely corrosive. So the more hours on the engine, the greater the chances of corrosion failure of the wall that keeps the exhaust and water separate until the last moment. When this occurs, water can get into the cylinders through the exhaust valves, with disastrous results. Unfortunately, most indicators of potential trouble will be less than obvious to anyone but a professional marine mechanic or surveyor. But it is another reason a greater number of hours than normal should reduce a boat's value. Replacing risers is not a huge job, but it can be time consuming and will inevitably cost a few bucks.

Value Adjustments Based on Condition

OFTEN CALLED	DESCRIPTION	PERCENTAGE TO BE ADDED OR SUBTRACTED
Excellent (Bristol)	Maintained in mint or Bristol fashion—usually better than factory new—and loaded with extras; a rarity	+15 – 20
Above BUC condition	Has had above-average care and is equipped with extra electrical and electronic gear	+10 – 15
BUC condition	Ready for sale requiring no additional work and normally equipped for its size	No adjustment necessary
Fair	Requires usual maintenance to prepare for sale	−10 – 20
Poor	Substantial yard work required and is devoid of extras	−25 – 50
Restorable	Enough of hull and engine exists to restore the boat to usable condition	−50 – 80

Courtesy BUC International

will apply these criteria with a more knowing and critical eye, this will only help when it comes down to the boat you are most seriously considering. In the meantime, you can arrive at a reasonable ballpark estimate of any boat's probable true worth by applying the criteria yourself. A boat in any condition can be a good buy if the price is right.

The vast majority of used boats will be in basic BUC condition, and the value stated in the book (or online) will be appropriate. Most of the other descriptions are self-explanatory, but you might question how a boat can be "better than factory new." Here are some hints:

- **Marine electronics.** This is an area in which equipment seems to make leaps and bounds each year. Even last year's product can often seem outmoded. So a 5-year-old boat with brand-new navigational electronics is much better than it was when new. This is especially true if the owner has added some gear that was not available, even as an option, when the boat was new.

- **Consumer electronics.** Not too many years ago, the standard for video playback was VHS cassettes. Now it's DVDs (and soon it will be Blu-ray). An older boat with DVD players and possibly a plasma monitor and surround sound is better than it was when new, and if it has satellite TV, it can even be *much* better. Satellite or HD radio receivers are a similar upgrade for listening.
- **Mechanical equipment.** Engine accessories can be upgraded also. Many standard-equipment alternators are barely adequate to keep up with the demand placed on batteries by the plethora of electronics we love to have aboard. Larger, higher-output alternators are a prime example of "better than factory new," as are the newer style of AC converters that better regulate battery charging while running on shore power.

Another upgrade would be Airsep air filters on diesel air intakes. These help keep the engine compartment cleaner and reduce wasted lube oil; many builders now install them as standard equipment. Not too many years ago they weren't as common. If an owner has added them to a boat that didn't have them originally, the boat is now better than it was when new.

I think you get the picture. There are many ways that an owner can improve a

Figure 9-7. Now standard equipment on many makes of diesel-powered boats, an Airsep filter on an engine's air intake may be an owner-added upgrade on an older model. Either way, you can take it as a positive sign. *(Walker Engineering)*

Quick Tips

The difference between Bristol value and above BUC value can often be a fine line that may be difficult to discern at first. But after you've examined a few boats that fall short of even basic BUC value, the little things that raise a vessel's worth will be evident. You'll be able to recognize a gem when you see it. If you're in the market for a used boat, look at many before you settle on one. The more boats you examine closely, the more differences you'll be able to see and appreciate.

boat, and if you've done a good job of shopping around, you'll be able to spot them easily. Couple these improvements with a diligent maintenance program, and you will have found a highly desirable used boat, one that's worth much more than its basic BUC Book value. And though no one can guarantee the boat won't develop problems in the future, the chances are it can be less problematic than a new boat. Its break-in hassles, if any, will certainly be ancient history, and a strong record of proper maintenance can go a long way toward minimizing future problems, as well.

CHECKING OUT NEW BOATS

There are ways you can determine a new boat's basic quality, and here again an on-land inspection is the best way to start. Most new boats are displayed this way, either in

Don't Forget

Beware of new-boat shine—it can be blinding. The thrill of discovering all the exciting goodies you'll so often find aboard a brand-new boat can prevent you from seeing the harsh realities that lie beneath. No matter how nice a boat may appear on the surface, don't forget what I suggested back in Chapter 2: a boat's design, construction, accommodations plan, and overall arrangement must be properly suited to your intended primary use of the boat, or you will surely be disappointed. When checking out *any* boat, don't just look around, *examine!*

Measure stowage space, lie down on the berths, check out the cockpit efficiency of a fishing boat, and go through the motions that would be involved in preparing a meal in the galley or taking a shower in the head. Try doing (or at least emulating) all the things you'll eventually be doing aboard if you buy the boat to see if they will be as convenient as you'd like. Less than perfection doesn't necessarily mean you should walk away but does mean that you should make ample notes that you can refer to when comparing several potentially desirable models.

the dealer's showroom or on the lot outside, so examining the entire boat is quite easy. In addition to the basics, such as layout and overall design, there are other important points to consider. My good friend and colleague Charles Nichols once summed them up quite nicely in a Ship's Systems column in *Power & Motoryacht* magazine. With his kind permission, I'll paraphrase and expand on his list in the Ten Clues to Quality below.

Ten Clues to Quality

In each of the following ten points, what you're really looking for is care—in one of several phases of the construction process.

1. **Check the finish first.** While it is true that glitz and glitter aren't essential to a boat's operation, the outward appearance of a brand-new boat can still reveal a surprising amount of information regarding what's hidden beneath the surface. Look for signs of care in the development of the tooling—the plug and mold from which the hull is made—and care in this particular boat's layup. Study the hull surface obliquely, and you can see a lot. Fortunately, shiny surfaces aren't forgiving of imperfections that lie beneath. When you look down along the topsides, you'll see something ranging from absolute perfection—a totally smooth, flawless shine no matter what the angle of view—to disaster, where you can spot every interior bulkhead by its telltale bulge and where flat places are anything but. Most production boats fall somewhere between. Look closely at reflections (overhead lights, especially fluorescent tubes, are a big help, which can make showroom exams ideal). The better the hull, the cleaner, straighter,

Quick Tips

There can be a secondary benefit to sighting along a boat's topsides: if there's a hidden flaw, salespeople will often know about it, and if it appears you are seeing something also, they'll open up and reveal all the details they know about in hopes of preventing you from spotting more. There's no guarantee this will happen, but sometimes the mere appearance of your having above-average sophistication can prompt salespeople to reveal secrets they would otherwise keep to themselves.

and sharper the reflections will be. A little waviness is okay, but walk away from a hull that shows too much.

2. **Look closely at the electrical system.** Much of it is hidden, but what you can see—if you really look—speaks volumes about the system, and the boat, as a whole. Check the distribution panels. Look for an ample number of circuits, including at least a few blank spaces for future expansion. Look for ample metering on the panels. Voltmeters for both AC and DC are the minimum. Ammeters help you avoid overload. If the boat has a generator, a frequency meter is valuable because some equipment is frequency sensitive. With 120-volt AC shore power, a reverse-polarity indicator is also essential. If you can, take a peek behind the panel.

Color-coded wiring and identifying markers on each terminal are good signs. As suggested previously, a brand-new boat should have GFCIs on outlets in the galley, head(s), engine compartment, and any that are outside.

3. **Look closely at the plumbing system.** These systems are also good indicators, though there are fewer places to look. Among the signs of better quality: seacocks or ball valves rather than gate valves on through-hulls, double clamps on critical hose connections (all those below the waterline and anywhere else a broken connection would be more than an inconvenience), and reinforced hose on suction lines.

4. **Look again at the electrical and plumbing systems as a whole.** The neater the workmanship, the better the boat. Look for straight runs with definite turns at each change of direction and solid support along the way. Better wiring will be bundled or run in chases or flexible conduit. Wires that aren't in chases or conduit should have protective grommets (or even watertight glands) wherever they penetrate bulkheads or decks.

   A neat installation also suggests good materials. It's no guarantee, but because the greater cost will be in the labor, a builder will rarely pay someone to do a superior job of installing inferior stuff.

   Look for labels on switches, valves, junction boxes, pipes, and wires. They can tell you more than just what's written on them. Not only will they make it easier to learn your way around your new boat, they also show the builder's care in helping you do so.

5. **See how things fit.** Back when boats were mostly wood inside and out,

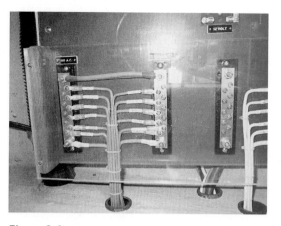

Figure 9-8. Neatness counts! The straight runs, 90-degree bends, ample tie wraps and labels, and the rubber bushings where the wires penetrate the deck all suggest that this wiring is top-notch—a most probable reflection on the overall quality of the boat. *(Nordhavn)*

interior joinery was an indicator of unseen workmanship. It still is, in that good woodwork reflects overall care in construction. Even in a boat that substitutes molded interior components for joinery, you can get a hint of the level of engineering and quality control involved by studying how the modular units fit together. There's still usually some woodwork—galley and stateroom cabinets, drawers, and locker doors, for example. Sloppy fits, if present, will be apparent. Cabinet doors and drawers should either fit snugly with no visible gaps or have gaps of uniform width all around. Anything else equals less-than-careful workmanship. The better things are where you can see, the better the chances of their being fine where you can't. There's no guarantee, but the converse is definitely true. If the builder didn't bother to make sure that work was done carefully where the results are clearly visible, you can be certain the workmanship is even sloppier where it's hidden.

6. **Check for watertight integrity.** In hull lengths up to 25 feet or so, one compartment is okay, but unless you have an open outboard-powered runabout or center console, a bigger boat should have at least two independent, watertight compartments. I'm pleased to report that many builders today are isolating the engine compartment and making all the through-hull penetrations there. This lessens the chances of water intrusion into the cabin area.

There should be at least one bilge pump for each watertight compartment. Ideally, there will be a manual backup for the engine compartment and some means of extending its suction to other areas. The "engine as bilge pump" arrangement shown on page 123 is always a definite plus.

7. **Ask about the hardware.** It all shines when new. But chrome-plated Zamak (a zinc alloy) will not stand up to salt nearly as well as chrome-plated bronze or stainless steel. Many builders are again opting for the lesser shine of Marinium hardware. This aluminum-based alloy isn't quite as tough as stainless, but it is corrosion resistant, has a good strength-to-weight ratio, and seems to stand up very well.

In handrails, welded one-piece units are better than separate sections held together by yet more pieces of connecting hardware. Welded rails are more solid to begin with and will stay that way.

Look for ample cleats, chocks, and fairleads, and make sure that there are no sharp or rough edges that can damage your lines. This is as important with a brand-new boat as it is with a used one. Unfortunately, proper deck hardware is still an area that tends to be slighted in many production boats, though builders are getting much better about this.

8. **Look into the way the hardware is attached.** If the method isn't clearly visible (and it usually won't be), ask. Fiberglass doesn't hold screws well. It's better if hardware is through-bolted using a backing plate of hardwood, stainless steel, or aluminum. Hardwood backing plates are comparatively bulky and require large washers; aluminum plates are good if well constructed; stainless steel is probably the best alternative other than bronze, which is rarely seen anymore. Another good method replaces the core of a deck sandwich locally with aluminum, the hardware being then held by machine screws threaded into the aluminum. Not so good is a hardwood backing plate with wood screws to hold the hardware, though it is slightly better than screws into plain fiberglass.

9. **Look for built-ins.** These include electronics, galley appliances, etc. As I noted in Chapter 4, many boats today are sold as a complete package with nearly all accessories included. For those that aren't, there should still be ample room to add the extras, preferably as built-ins. This means blank spaces on or around the console and easy access to run the wiring they'll need.

10. **Ask to see a hull cutout plug.** Few hull penetrations are molded in; they are cut. This means there is a piece of scrap (or plug) for each hole. Many builders destroy one plug in quality control, but some plugs should still be available, especially when yet more hull

penetrations are made by the dealer. Lack of available plugs for inspection does not mean poor quality, but obviously the more pride the builder and dealer have in the quality of layup, the more likely they are to be eager to show you a piece of cross section.

If you recall the adage about free lunches, you'll realize that each of these quality indicators has its price. The better the boat, the more you'll probably have to pay. But using them can be a big help in understanding why two outwardly similar boats can have such different price tags. Quality costs initially, but it pays in the long run.

THE SEA TRIAL

You shouldn't go this far with every boat you look at. If you decide a boat isn't for you, why waste your time (and the seller's) in a sea trial? But for every boat that makes it to the "could be" stage, a sea trial is a *must*. This is true whether the boat is brand-new or several years old because no matter how appealing a boat may be on land or at dockside, it's only when the vessel is actually underway that you can determine if it's the one for you. And unless you plan to always use the boat all by yourself (a rarity!), be sure to bring some of your probable boating companions with you. While much of your attention should be directed toward the boat itself, always devote at least a bit of your sea trial to observing the reactions (and perhaps recording the comments) of the people you bring with you. If they will ultimately be using the boat also, their input counts.

Start with Cold Engines

With a used boat, you want to begin with cold engines that haven't been started recently, preferably not since at least the day

Don't Forget

A sea trial isn't your average pleasure trip. It can be enjoyable, of course, but you are there for a purpose beyond having fun. You're essentially trying on your prospective purchase much as you would a new suit—to see how well it fits you. Only in this case, you want to see how well it fits from an operational point of view.

before. Problem engines often don't start easily when cold and yet may kick over at the first touch of the switch once they've warmed up. Rough starting doesn't necessarily indicate a serious problem—with a gas engine, it could be as simple as fouled or worn spark plugs, which are easily replaced. But you can leave the cause of rough starting to your engine surveyor if the boat otherwise does well enough to get that far. For the moment, you'll know that the engines don't start easily, which is but one of many details you'll want to note.

Testing as a Passenger

Initially, you'll probably be merely an observer as the seller (or his designated skipper) operates the boat for you. This period shouldn't be entirely passive. As Yogi Berra once said, "You can observe a lot just by watching." See how the boat comes up on plane. Ideally, it will climb out of the hole without excessive bow rise, though many sterndrive boats carry so much of their weight just inside the transom that this is impossible.

Don't be too turned off by a high initial bow rise, but make a mental note to see for yourself how much it interferes with forward visibility until the boat assumes its normal running attitude. Look back to see what sort of a wake it throws at various speeds.

Look for vibrating hardware, such as bow rails, even if you can't feel a thing. It may not mean anything; metal parts often display a sympathetic resonance at certain rpm. But if the vibration continues (or worsens) as speed increases, it is more likely a sign of problems in the underwater running gear.

Look at the Exhaust

Make sure you look back behind the boat from time to time, too, and not just to check the wake. If the engines are in good shape, the exhaust will be white or a very pale gray, meaning it's mostly condensing water vapor. And while a bit of visible exhaust is okay, too much could be a sign of problems. Blue smoke means the engine is burning lube oil and is not at all good—it can indicate worn rings or worse. Dark gray or black smoke indicates incomplete combustion; it's simply unburned carbon. Diesels will often spew clouds of black exhaust when they first accelerate because the fuel-air ratio is off temporarily. This is no cause for alarm because increasing the amount of fuel the injectors spray into the cylinders is the way you increase a diesel's rpm and yet there may not be sufficient air to burn that fuel completely until the engine speed actually increases. This is especially true of turbocharged engines because turbos don't kick in and start pushing more air into the cylinders until a certain engine speed is attained. So don't sweat the black smoke if it shows up only when accelerating a diesel. But *continued* dark smoke from any engine is a sign of maladjustment at best and possibly more serious problems.

Stand Up and Walk Around

Do this at various speeds to judge the comfort level involved. On most boats, standing up and walking around will become more difficult only when speed and sea conditions produce enough bounce to have some negative impact. Generally, the larger and heavier the boat, the less difficulty you'll encounter. Once in a while, however, you'll discover seats that are angled in such a way that rising from them becomes more difficult as the bow lifts to its normal running attitude, despite the ease with which you could stand up when the boat sat at dockside. This isn't necessarily a sign to walk away, but it is something to consider.

See How the Boat Rides at Various Speeds and Angles of Sea

Comfort underway is crucial to your enjoyment of the boat. You should note particularly the boat's behavior in *beam seas* [those that come at the boat 90 degrees from its centerline, hitting it broadside]. All boats tend to roll in a beam sea, but the better ones do so with an easy, comfortable motion that's not hard to take. But some will be unbearable, especially when not moving ahead very fast or at all. If you plan to do any fishing, be sure to see how the boat feels in a beam sea when there's zero headway. You'll be in this situation often when fishing, and you need to know it will be comfortable enough to suit you. *Following seas* [those coming from directly astern, or nearly so] can also be uncomfortable for some hull designs, so note the way they affect your test boat.

When It's Your Turn at the Helm

Though you are about to take a more active participation in your test ride, you should still start by just observing. When you take the helm, make sure you are out of the way of traffic and then bring the throttles to idle, put the clutches in neutral, and stay in one place for a moment. Then look around. Ideally, you should be able to see in all directions whether you're standing or sitting. A lack of perfect visibility from the helm is one price we pay for the increased amenities we have on larger boats. One hundred percent all-around visibility is a given on center consoles and most runabouts. Even on express cruisers and other sport boats, overall visibility is generally good, though there can often be at least one or two blind spots. But once we start adding a cabin or house of any consequence, total all-around visibility can become a challenge. With many cabin boats, the inside helm has limited visibility, especially aft. This is usually countered by considerably improved visibility from a helm on a flying bridge. In all the years I've been working, I've encountered only one boat where visibility from the flying bridge was worse than from below.

Make a note of visibility at rest, and then be sure to check it again—all around—when you get up to cruising speed. It will rarely be exactly the same, but it shouldn't change drastically either. Good all-around visibility is even more important at speed. Note particularly if the bow rail interferes with visibility at certain running angles.

Scrutinize the Console Layout

This is another area in which boats seem to be improving, though even some brand-new models still fall short of ideal. Some designers are more concerned with the overall appearance of the console, its grace and symmetry, than with whether its layout is ergonomic or even marginally functional. But ergonomics matter because the more comfortably efficient the arrangement of gauges,

Quick Tips

There's another thing to check when standing: Does the seat interfere or make standing uncomfortable? Some pilot seats have a flip-up piece that moves out of the way when you stand. Others have a sliding base that lets you push the seat back for more standing room. But some are going to be in the way no matter what you do, though the amount of interference and resulting discomfort can range from very little to total aggravation. Whether this is important to you depends on many things, including the amount of time you spend standing. But you will need to stand sometimes, so be sure to determine how comfortable it's going to be to do so.

switches, and controls, the less tiring it will be to operate the boat for long periods. And if the boat is otherwise a lot of fun, you will be operating it for long periods.

So look around. Can you see and reach everything easily? Is it equally easy sitting or standing? Can you read the compass without strain? Check the electronics. Are screens and controls also within easy reach and line of sight? Don't expect perfection. Cabinet dimensions, such as the depth dictated by the CRT on radars, often take precedence over ease of use or visibility; there's but one place in the console in which it will fit. Just

Get Started

Before you actually do anything, look at the gauges on the console. Are they all working? What do they read? Temperature gauges on freshwater-cooled engines should show between 160° and 200°F, and voltmeters (in 12-volt systems) should show between 12 and 14 volts. Normal oil pressure and gear oil pressure depend on make and model, but on a twin-screw vessel both *port* (left) and starboard gauges should read closely alike (and most gauges have the normal reading about mid-range). Inoperative gauges are not entirely bad in and of themselves, and if the boat passes muster in other ways your mechanical surveyor will report on the matter in depth, so any underlying problems will be revealed. But at this stage you can take inoperative gauges to be yet another sign of poor maintenance and a good reason for further caution.

don't settle for anything less than comfortable. If the boat turns out to be the one you want, you're going to be spending a lot of time here and it shouldn't be a strain.

Grab the Controls

Once you've assessed the console and its surrounds, put the drives in gear ahead and throttle up. Start slowly and get a feel for the way the boat handles. You might even throttle back and put the shifts in neutral to get a feel for the boat's carry forward. Try going astern to see how the boat handles in that direction, again pausing in neutral to note the difference in handling when going astern versus going ahead.

Then, if the area and traffic allow, see what this boat will do. Put the shifts ahead and then gradually push the throttles all the way to wide open. No need to jam them unless you want to test the time to plane because that isn't the kindest way to handle a boat. For one, many engines in this day of electronic control will not throttle up any faster than their built-in computers allow, which is the rate at which they accelerate best. This conserves fuel and allows the engines to operate more efficiently—it's too much fuel too soon that so often produces black exhaust. But even if the engine could rev up instantly (and some gas engines come close), the boat won't actually advance more rapidly until the propellers have achieved their maximum efficiency and are biting "solid" water. And even then, they won't advance to the extent their *pitch* [a theoretical measurement of advance per revolution] would indicate. The difference between theoretical and actual advance is called *slip*, and it is inevitable. But when you spin the props faster than they can bite, slip increases to above normal levels. This not only fails to advance the boat quickly, it can also allow a gas engine to overrev for a moment (diesels can't overrev—they have governors), which isn't really good for them. It also wastes fuel, which isn't good for either the environment or your wallet. Overrevving can also induce cavitation, which isn't good for the props. Advancing the throttles faster than the boat can respond is both wasteful and also potentially harmful.

During acceleration is the time to again assess forward visibility. A perfectly performing boat will show only a slight bow rise, coming up onto plane almost effortlessly in one smooth, steadily rising movement. Many boats will display considerable bow rise and stern squat during which forward visibility is a challenge. Most fall somewhere in between. No behavior is necessarily bad, but if a boat with excessive bow rise doesn't eventually settle down to a running angle similar to the attitude it had at rest (though it's normal for the bow to run a bit higher underway), you should cross it off your list. The lack of visibility is no big deal for a moment or two, but a boat that doesn't level out eventually has more serious problems than you should want to buy into. Failure to achieve a full planing attitude can also be a sign of an underpowered boat, though there can also be other causes.

Once you've attained top speed, throttle back to normal cruise, which should be about 70% to 75% of wide-open throttle (WOT) with gas engines, 85% to 90% for diesels. See how the boat feels at this speed. If the bottom is clean, the running gear is in good shape, and the boat isn't underpowered, it should feel right at this speed. The engines won't be laboring, the ride will be comfortable, and the boat will perform well all around—holding a straight course or turning with equal ease in either direction. If you don't find all of the above, this boat most probably isn't the one.

Look for Some Chop

You need to know how the boat handles when the going gets rough. But Murphy's Law being what it is, you may not be able to find anything but calm water during your sea trial. So do what boat testers do: turn back to ride over your own wake. This is

Quick Tips

Many boats throw less wake at cruise than they do at lower speeds, particularly just before they finally get on plane. If this is the case with the one you're testing, use it to your advantage. Increase the wake by slowing down until you see a good wake behind you. Then speed up, turn back, and cross it. This may still be less than ideal for testing purposes, but it will be better than crossing the shallower wake you throw at cruise.

rarely anywhere near as rough as Ma Nature can dish out when she's in a foul mood, but it will give you some idea of what to expect.

Take It Easy

While a boat's ease of handling at cruise speed is important, you also need to evaluate the boat's handling at the speed you'll use in close-quarters maneuvers such as docking—idle speed. Unless you're a very experienced boat handler, chances are you won't want to actually dock a boat you don't yet own and very well may not buy. But this shouldn't stop you from seeing how the boat handles under such conditions by emulating them out in open water where you can't possibly hurt anything. Try some typical docking maneuvers by making "landings" at an imaginary pier. Your actions may look silly to anyone watching and the seller may question your sanity, but you can learn a lot this way. You know for certain that if the boat doesn't handle well in an imaginary landing, it will be even worse where the hardness of a physical pier and the presence of other boats complicate the procedure by increasing your nervousness.

How Long?

How much time should you spend on a proper sea trial? Stay with it as long as necessary to find out what you need to know. The requisite time is easiest to gauge for boats that are either obvious disappointments or obvious winners. In neither case is it wise to prolong the test. If the boat quickly fails, you should just as quickly say thanks, but no thanks, and move on—no sense wasting any more time on a boat you are not going to buy. And if a sea trial quickly fuels your desire to buy the boat, stop evaluating it and move on to the later stages of the purchasing process: present the seller with a solid offer to buy, and schedule a professional survey.

But when a boat is "Okay, but . . . ," you may have no choice but to examine it further. And if a boat is still in the "maybe" column after a thorough sea trial, just carefully note everything you liked and didn't like and compare the results with any other boats that are also possibilities. Unless you later find a definite "yes!" you can compare these notes to help further narrow your choices.

WRAP

✔ Always try to take stock of the seller before you assess the boat itself.

✔ Try for an on-land exterior exam before you go aboard.

✔ Examine known trouble spots first; this can save you considerable time.

✔ Look for signs of proper maintenance; they are your best clues to quality.

✔ Check the engine hours, and adjust the boat's value downward for more or less than typically normal use.

✔ While used boats are usually more prone to trouble, you should examine new boats carefully, too.

✔ Always have a thorough sea trial to see how well a boat fits your needs.

Don't Forget

Don't forget to check the engine compartment and bilge for signs of oil or other leaks after the sea trial is finished and you're back at the pier. Many times a compartment will look fine when you first inspect it—the seller will have cleaned up any previous spills. But if leaks exist, they will be quite evident if you look again after the boat has been run a while.

CHAPTER 10

BUT YOU'LL NEED A PROFESSIONAL SURVEY, TOO

Do I Need to Read This Chapter?

You should read this chapter if you want to discover

- ✔ Why even a new boat can need a survey.
- ✔ What a marine surveyor actually does.
- ✔ What types of surveys you can have.
- ✔ How to find a surveyor.
- ✔ The two main organizations that establish standards for surveyors.

WHY HAVE A SURVEY?

Because you lack the training and experience of a professional marine surveyor, no matter how closely you look at a boat there will still be much you can overlook. By having the one you finally decide to buy inspected thoroughly by a professional who knows exactly where to look and what to look for, you can save yourself aggravation down the road. This is true for any boat, even a brand-new one, but it is especially important if you are buying a used boat, because the longer a boat has been around the greater the opportunity for things to have gone wrong. Knowing in advance exactly what is wrong is the best way to avoid serious trouble. Unpleasant surprises are never much fun. In an absolute worst-case situation,

what you learn from the survey can keep you from throwing money away on a boat that will present more problems than pleasure. In the more normal course of events, knowing what's wrong with a boat *before* you buy it will allow you to anticipate what you're getting yourself into—that is, what it will take to make things right. Once you are armed with facts from an independent and knowledgeable source, you can negotiate with the seller to either get the defects fixed before you buy or have the probable cost of repairs deducted from the sale price. Either way, you'll be far better off than if you make your purchase in a state of ignorant bliss, which will be the case if you buy a boat without the benefit of a professional survey.

Limitations

As critical as a proper survey may be, and there's probably no aspect of boat buying that's more important, a surveyor will not and cannot see everything. Surveys must be nondestructive; a surveyor is not supposed to take anything apart, which means that any items essentially hidden must remain so. Even the most knowledgeable and conscientious surveyor can't tell you a thing about components s/he couldn't see well enough to examine. So even the most thorough survey may not reveal everything. But after a proper survey, you will know far more about a boat than you did before, and if you've hired the right surveyor(s), you'll know as much as is humanly possible.

TYPES OF SURVEYS
Prepurchase Survey

This is the one we're most interested in. It is also the most comprehensive of all surveys, and having one is strongly recommended for *all* used boat purchases. A proper prepurchase survey will actually involve two surveyors: a general surveyor for the boat itself and a mechanical surveyor for the engines. Sometimes you have to contact the two independently, but often a mechanical surveyor can be hired through the general surveyor. Though the two surveyors will do their work independently, and are normally paid separately, cooperation between them is always necessary and allowing the general surveyor to book the mechanical surveyor usually guarantees this.

Out of the Water

A prepurchase survey will always require a haulout (unless the boat is already on the hard), which you will probably have to arrange and will definitely have to pay for, usually at the time of the haulout or, more likely, before. In most cases, you'll also have to arrange and pay to have the bottom pressure cleaned to remove any accumulated marine growth that might get in the way of a detailed examination. (Your broker will generally arrange the haulout for you, so you don't have to do a thing but pay for it.) Having the boat out of the water allows the surveyor to inspect the underwater running gear (if applicable), which includes the shaft(s), propeller(s), cutless bearing(s), and rudder(s) and their mounting hardware. If the boat has a drive system other than the conventional shaft and strut, this is also when it gets inspected.

Exterior Hull Inspection

The survey begins with a thorough visual examination of the exterior of the hull and bottom, including the propulsion system. As you did in your own inspection, though with a more practiced eye, s/he will look for any signs of collision damage (both above and below the waterline) and its resulting repair. The surveyor will also check the bottom's structural soundness by using sound. S/he will tap the bottom all over using a special rubber or plastic mallet (and, in some places, a ball-peen hammer), discovering problem areas by their distinctly different sound. This is a particularly important procedure since many problems within the laminate and underwater gear often don't show on the surface and thus appear exactly the same as their surroundings; even a skilled surveyor usually can't uncover everything by eye alone. Any suspect areas of the hull, whether from delamination, osmosis, rot, loose fastenings, poor construction, inadequate repairs, or other sources, will be marked for future reference and thoroughly inspected to determine the cause, the extent of the damage, and possible avenues for proper repair, including projected cost.

The surveyor may also test for moisture in the fiberglass using nondestructive equipment (where applicable). This involves more than simply reading a meter. An experienced surveyor will be able to interpret those readings and know whether they are reasonable. All hulls absorb water; it's inevitable. Knowing when to be alarmed requires judgment, experience, and the knowledge of where to draw the line.

A surveyor will also look for blisters, which can happen when water seeping into the laminate by osmosis causes spot delamination of the gelcoat and a chemical reaction that concentrates and increases the volume of water at the spot, which in turn raises the visible blister. Since the underlying cause of blistering was determined in the 1980s, new, less permeable resins and bottom coatings have been employed and blistering is far less prevalent than before.

Deck and Internal Structure

After completing the bottom inspection, the surveyor will climb aboard to inspect all exposed and accessible areas of both the exterior and the interior of the hull and deck, paying particular attention to the details of construction and condition. A surveyor will carefully inspect all structural members for signs of rot, delamination, or separation from the hull and also note the location and condition of all underwater through-hull fittings and seacocks. S/he will go over the entire deck surface with the sounding mallet to help determine its condition and to locate any areas of water intrusion or core damage, and may use an electronic moisture tester as an additional aid in determining the deck's overall condition. The deck inspection will also include close examination of all exposed hardware, such as cleats and chocks, and a thorough check of the stanchions and railings for secure mounting. An experienced surveyor will note the source—and extent—of any problem, including possible repairs and their cost.

Systems Inspections

A surveyor will thoroughly examine the systems on board, including fuel systems, DC and AC electrical systems, LPG (propane) or CNG (compressed natural gas) systems (if applicable), air-conditioning, freshwater and saltwater systems, and sanitation systems. In determining the suitability of the systems installations, the surveyor will use the required standards described in the Code of Federal Regulations (CFR) Title 33 and Title 46, and the voluntary standards and recommended practices developed by the ABYC and the National Fire Protection Association (NFPA). Detailed recommendations will be noted in the reports if any work is needed to bring these systems up to proper standards.

Required Safety Equipment Inspection

The surveyor will consider required safety, firefighting, and distress equipment as well as the navigational equipment, which includes the navigation lights and sound signals. Deficiencies are often found in these areas (and the older the boat, the more of them there will usually be), and the report will include a list of the equipment already on board, its current condition, and any pertinent expiration dates. The report will also include what may be needed to bring the boat up to standards if the surveyor finds anything lacking. This applies particularly to fire extinguishers, which must be inspected annually, and to VDS, many of which have an expiration date (see Chapter 4).

Engine Inspection

This is the province of the mechanical surveyor, who will first examine the engines externally, with an eye toward proper and safe installation (also using the same standards and recommendations) and to note any significant damage or undue wear and tear. S/he will pay particular attention to areas especially susceptible to damage, such as all external belts and hoses, and will also look for signs of corrosion on crucial parts.

In addition to carefully examining the engines themselves (including the generator, if applicable), the mechanical surveyor will also take a close look at the fuel and oil filters, the fuel and oil lines and manifolds, exhaust systems, cooling (both the raw-water and the freshwater components), emergency stop and alarm systems, and the transmissions. Surveyors never start any engine unless the owner—or an owner's representative—is on board, which will be necessary during the sea trial, a process that is required to more fully determine the engines' operating condition.

Sea Trial

The hallmark of a thorough prepurchase survey, a sea trial is generally not required, and thus is rarely included, in all other types of surveys. During the sea trial, surveyors will have neither the time nor the inclination to act as captain. And since you should never take sole responsibility for the operation of a boat until it is actually yours, it is imperative to coordinate the survey with the seller in order to have a competent operator on board, preferably someone who knows the boat.

The mechanical surveyor will visually inspect the engine installations and gather much of the initial survey data while the boat is out of the water and the general surveyor is checking other details. S/he will also most probably draw some oil samples to send off for lab testing.

A thorough engine survey usually includes a compression test, and the figures for each individual cylinder of every engine aboard, including the generator(s), will be incorporated into the report, along with a narrative description of what the figures mean. Underway during the sea trial, the surveyor will have the boat's operator adjust the throttles from idle to wide open, holding for a time at each of certain critical speeds so the surveyor can observe any changes in performance after time. The mechanical surveyor will often use an infrared remote-reading thermometer to scan parts of the engines and their cooling and exhaust systems while underway, looking for hot spots that indicate problems within.

The mechanical surveyor will be particularly concerned with the status of the engines' cooling systems and how well they function after running for a while at normal cruise. S/he will also want to see what happens when the power plants are pushed to wide open, which is usually the point at which poor cooling will quickly become apparent.

Both surveyors will be interested in the boat's response to various controls, including the steering system, and the general surveyor will also observe the operation of most other nonmechanical systems and the boat's general behavior while underway (though the survey report normally won't cover handling or performance characteristics). The mechanical surveyor will concentrate on what's happening in the engine compartment.

The mechanical surveyor may order a crash-stop test, in which the drives are put hard astern as quickly as possible from normal cruise. This is a good test of several factors, including the solidity of the engine mounts. For this reason, most surveyors will not ask for a crash-stop test if the mounts appear at all suspect under visual and tactile examination.

The mechanical surveyor's report will discuss any shortcomings discovered, along with recommendations for any repairs or additions that s/he may feel are needed to improve the situation. A mechanical surveyor will rarely attempt to estimate how many hours of useful life remain in the engines, though s/he may offer a general prognosis.

Appraised Value

The survey report will contain an appraised value, which applies to the vessel *as surveyed*. Upgrades or equipment added after the survey are obviously not covered, and the stated value is applicable for only a short period of time, given the normal fluctuations in the used boat marketplace. The

Though lenders and insurers will also have access to the BUC Book and other price guides, the surveyor's valuation often carries more weight in both camps because s/he has actually seen and examined the boat.

reported value is the *surveyor's opinion* of the market value at the time of the survey, taking into consideration the vessel's structural and cosmetic condition, its equipment level, and other important factors, such as conditions in the local marketplace.

Report Style

The reporting style of most surveyors is straightforward narrative, with detailed descriptions of the conditions they found along with their recommendations for upgrades, repairs, and sometimes even the installation of entire systems that may be required to meet federal codes and/or ABYC or NFPA standards. A good surveyor will also note in the report the specific authorities on which the noted defects and recommended changes are based. A summary of recommendations is commonly provided at the end of the report, which will be broken down into sections to help determine the differences among required actions, recommended upgrades or practices, and suggested actions or changes. The general and mechanical surveyors will each provide a report of their specific observations,

If the engines are not in good shape, you will be told the truth. It isn't very pleasant to learn that the power plants in the boat of your dreams aren't up to snuff. But it's far better to learn this by reading a report before you buy the boat than to find out the hard way after the fact! It's usually less costly, too.

and you may also receive detail and over-all photographs (either on CD-ROM or as prints) along with the written reports, identified for visual cross-reference. For convenience, many surveyors simply print a sheet of images, identified as to what each represents, which they include as the last page of their report.

Terminology

Most surveyors use some common words and phrases when reporting a boat's condition:

- **Appears.** This means that a close inspection of the particular system or component was impossible because of constraints placed on the surveyor by circumstances. These can range from no power being available, to the item being located behind a panel that couldn't be removed without damage, to some other aspect of the surveyor's pledge to conduct "nondestructive" testing. The bottom line: whenever a surveyor uses "appears," it relates to an item s/he's examined only visually.
- **Fit for intended service/fit for intended use.** Either phrase means that, in the surveyor's opinion, the item will do what it was designed and built to do.
- **Serviceable/adequate.** These are surveyors' terms for "okay." I've always preferred "serviceable" for items that aren't too bad, because the connotation is more positive.
- **Powers up.** Generally used with electronics, it means the unit turns on, but nothing more. It says nothing about how well the equipment works.
- **Excellent condition.** This is about as good as it gets; the item in question is new or like new.

- **Good condition.** This means nearly new with only minor cosmetic or structural deficiencies, which will usually be explained in greater detail.
- **Fair condition.** The system, component, or item is functional as is or with minor repairs that will be noted in the report. It can also indicate things that are currently functional but may be questionable as to continued functionality and

A less than satisfactory survey doesn't necessarily mean you have to walk away, though if you made your purchase offer subject to satisfactory survey you certainly may do so if you wish. But if you still find the boat attractive and the survey hasn't uncovered anything that isn't fixable, you can use the report and, especially, the surveyor's estimate of current market value to start negotiations anew. At this point (if the seller is willing—sometimes s/he will then be the one who wants to call it off), you can ask the seller either to correct the deficiencies and you buy the boat at your previously agreed price or to accept the surveyor's estimated value and you buy the boat "as is" at that price and plan to make the necessary repairs yourself. Either approach should be satisfactory.

thus require ongoing close attention. This will normally be further explained with details of the actions required.

- **Poor condition.** The component or system is unusable as is. A good report will contain recommendations for correcting the situation.

Many surveyors will also include the BUC terms of condition (see Chapter 9) and in the Current Value section of the report give an overall evaluation of the boat's current state, from "Bristol" to "Restorable," as a qualifier for its current market value.

Condition and Value Survey

A condition and value survey (CVS) is *almost* as thorough as a prepurchase survey. It will usually be sufficient to satisfy a lender or insurer and is often all you need for a new boat since so many of the problems that may be revealed by a full prepurchase survey only develop over time and thus normally do not exist in a brand-new vessel.

A CVS is generally required by insurance underwriters or financial institutions to help them assess financial risk. An insurance company or lender rarely requires that the vessel be hauled from the water for a thorough bottom inspection or that it be launched if already stored ashore, although a haulout may be required to reinsure an older boat—in which case a comprehensive bottom inspection can be significant. These surveys are also limited to visual inspections. No operational testing or sea trials are performed, unless required by one of the above institutions, which is rare.

Figure 10-1. A CVS usually doesn't require a haulout or even leaving the boat's home slip. But if you're insuring an older boat, especially if the hull is wood, a thorough bottom inspection is a must. *(Frank Rotthaus)*

A CVS is a static inspection that compares the subject vessel to similar vessels of the same age, size, class, and intended service. And while this type of survey isn't as thorough as a prepurchase survey, the same standards apply.

A CVS report format is tailored to the special needs of insurance underwriters and financial institutions and usually omits the descriptive detail that is so valuable to a prospective purchaser. A CVS report should not be used for making a purchase decision on any vessel that isn't brand-new because it simply won't tell you all you need to know. And there won't be a separate engine report in addition to the basic survey report, because there will be no mechanical surveyor involved.

Insurance Survey

This inspection is essentially an abbreviated CVS offered by some surveyors to satisfy the often less demanding requirements of an underwriter when they are insuring a new or nearly new boat. While you, as a prospective buyer, will want to learn as much as possible about the boat you are seriously considering (which means a full prepurchase survey on any boat that isn't nearly straight from the factory), lenders don't need to know quite as much and most insurers will often be satisfied to know even less, especially when the boat is new. They're mainly interested in structural integrity and suitability for its intended use, though most insurance companies require a more detailed survey on older boats. They will also want to know the vessel's fair market value.

An insurance survey is also strictly visual and is usually done while the boat sits in its slip. As with a full CVS, the surveyor doesn't operate equipment or start the engines. The report will be similar to that of a regular CVS, just with less detail and with the emphasis on the boat's *current value*. Though insurers as a whole will usually be satisfied with less information than you or a lender might require, many will still want more than what's contained in the typical insurance survey. Unless the survey has been arranged and paid for by the insurer, always insist on a CVS at the very minimum. And if the boat is not brand-new, only a thorough prepurchase survey will do.

Other Surveys

We'll discuss the other types of surveys more thoroughly in later chapters where they have more relevance, but here is a quick look.

A *damage survey* will often be necessary to help settle an insurance claim; we'll cover this one in Chapter 11.

A *premarket survey* is often ordered by the seller of a vessel before placing it on the market in order to determine a reasonable asking price and discover any unknown defects that a prepurchase surveyor working for a buyer might find. We'll discuss it more thoroughly in Chapter 15.

One big difference between the surveys we discussed in detail at the start of the chapter and the damage survey and premarket survey mentioned here: the first three are usually paid for by the buyer. A possible exception might be the insurance survey, which is often commissioned by an insurance company when a new boatowner has purchased a boat without benefit of survey. Of course, a premarket survey is paid for by the seller, usually well before there is any buyer.

In my opinion, the slight savings you gain by having someone else pay for a survey is not a sufficient reason to buy a boat without also investing in what you can learn from a survey you've purchased. When the insurance company pays for the survey, the report goes to the insurer, not the boatowner. And while items needing immediate attention (if there are any) will be pointed out during the survey (the owner or a representative is normally present), you want to receive, and read carefully, every survey report available. After you've already bought the boat is just a bit late for assessing a survey report!

HOW TO FIND A SURVEYOR
Accrediting/Certifying Organizations
Although marine surveyors don't have to be licensed in the United States, there are two major independent organizations that accredit or certify their members—the National Association of Marine Surveyors (NAMS) and the Society of Accredited Marine Surveyors (SAMS). See the Resources section for contact information.

Get Started

The easiest way is to ask for a referral from your dealer or broker. But always remember that while all good surveyors are truly independent, this doesn't necessarily apply to all surveyors in general; a surveyor recommended by a broker or dealer may conveniently "overlook" minor problems that could hinder a sale. So also ask your insurance agent, your lender, other boaters, and anyone else you can think of who might know whom to suggest.

Quick Tips

Be sure to apply due diligence to make sure you're hiring the right surveyor. There are no restrictions on who may advertise and call himself a marine surveyor, and in the United States marine surveyors are not licensed. When hiring a marine surveyor, request a résumé, along with samples of work (particularly copies of reports on the type of survey you request). You should also ask that s/he provide references from marine lenders, insurance agents, former clients, and other marine industry associates. Then check those references out! Never accept any surveyor at face value.

I believe the most reliable recommendations come from lenders or insurers; it's in their best interest, perhaps to a greater degree than any other concerned party, to have truly fair, equitable, and independent surveys. Thus they tend to suggest surveyors they know will always provide exactly that.

Qualifications
Both organizations have some rigid experience and education requirements that qualify a person for membership. A NAMS Certified Marine Surveyor "must have served as a professional marine surveyor for not less than 5 years, or have served as a professional

marine surveyor for not less than 2 years and have substantial experience in the marine industry that is closely related to the technical requirements of marine surveying." To maintain NAMS-CMS status, members must complete at least 6 hours of continuing education credits each calendar year.

To become a SAMS Accredited Marine Surveyor, a candidate "must be currently practicing marine surveyor with at least 5 years surveying experience, accumulated within the past 10 years, in the field of expertise [in] which accreditation is desired." Accredited marine surveyors are expected to follow a course of continuing education to maintain their accreditation.

Both organizations also have apprenticeship and associate programs under which interested and qualified newbies can learn and gain the experience so necessary to becoming full-fledged professionals.

Integrity

Each organization also has a strict code of ethics that requires its members to accept only assignments that can be completed with professional competence and to decline any assignments in which there could be a conflict of interest. You really shouldn't go wrong in hiring a surveyor who is a member of either group.

SPECIALTY SURVEYS

General surveyors know hull construction, the system requirements outlined by federal codes, and the further recommendations of the ABYC and NFPA. But as we saw earlier in the need for a mechanical surveyor to examine engines, there is also often a need for specialists in other areas, too—for example, electronics. In the course of a routine inspection, a marine surveyor will note

Quick Tips

Marine surveyors most often charge by the foot; the larger your prospective purchase, the more the survey will cost. But when you consider that, generally, the larger the boat the greater its purchase price and also the larger the boat the more time a proper survey will require, this isn't out of line. Think of what buying a bad boat could possibly cost you if you didn't have the survey, and the survey's price will seem insignificant by comparison.

whether gear powers up—that is, comes to life when it is turned on. But s/he won't tell you if the equipment operates according to specs. If you want to learn this, you'll have to hire an electronics technician.

You'll also need a specialist if the boat has a problem with electrolysis, or galvanic corrosion. When this occurs, underwater metal can slowly (or not so slowly!) dissolve almost as if it were made of sugar. Boats usually have sacrificial anodes to prevent this, but a serious corrosion problem will eat them up way too quickly and needs to be corrected ASAP. A general surveyor can detect the problem but will usually defer to a specialist for determining the precise cause and cure.

Firefighting equipment and systems should also be inspected annually and tagged to indicate when the inspection was done and by whom. In the course of a routine vessel inspection, a general surveyor will note only whether the equipment is aboard and in sufficient number. S/he'll also report as to whether the extinguishers are properly tagged and, if so, when another inspection is due—or, perhaps, overdue. But that's all.

If and when the extinguishers need reinspection, you'll have to hire a specialist. The best news here is that the annual inspection of firefighting equipment is one issue aboard that really doesn't require a marine technician; any competent fire equipment service can do the job.

WRAP

✔ You should always have a survey before buying any boat, even a new one.

✔ A prepurchase survey is the most comprehensive and usually also requires the services of a mechanical surveyor to assess the engine installation.

✔ A prepurchase survey should always entail a haulout and a sea trial.

✔ A condition and value survey will generally satisfy the survey requirements of lenders and insurers and may be all you need before purchasing a brand-new boat.

✔ Surveyors need not be licensed, but you'll be better off hiring a member of either NAMS or SAMS, the two major national organizations for professional marine surveyors.

✔ Certain systems can also require close inspection by an experienced specialist in addition to the general survey.

CHAPTER 11

INSURANCE: ANOTHER WAY BOATS ARE DIFFERENT

Do I Need to Read This Chapter?

You should read this chapter if you want to discover

✔ The need for specialized insurance.

✔ Reasons for choosing an experienced marine insurance agent.

✔ The differences between boat insurance and yacht insurance.

✔ Possible policy limits.

✔ How to handle claims.

✔ When you may need a damage survey.

✔ Ways to lower your premiums.

Do I Need to Read This Chapter?

THEY HAVE YOU COVERED

Insurance is an all too necessary evil. A boat can be a huge investment that you need to protect whether it is being used or not (80% of reported sinkings occurred at the vessel's home slip!). You also need protection from having to pay for any damage you and your boat may cause even if it is totally unintentional or not your fault. Boat operators and owners have been sued for tens of thousands of dollars because of damage caused by their wakes. Owners are also legally responsible for the costs of recovering fuel or oil that may be spilled or accidentally released into the environment if their boat is wrecked or sunk. Furthermore,

maritime law gives special protection to anyone who works on a boat, and that includes trade workers performing repair and maintenance.

Of course, if you handle your boat properly, drive defensively, and faithfully obey all the various rules and regulations, you may never have to file a claim. In that case, your premiums can seem to have been a waste of money. But have just one unfortunate incident of any kind, whether your fault or totally unavoidable, and the value of proper coverage becomes crystal clear. The primary trap to avoid is being underinsured, which can happen if you shop strictly by lowest possible premium.

Get Started

Start early: Shop for insurance as you shop for your boat. There are at least three good reasons for not leaving your new boat's insurance coverage to the last minute:

1. To get the best deal, you may have to do some shopping around.
2. Different boats will usually demand different policy details, so there will undoubtedly be different premiums involved as well. When buying a boat, you need to be aware of all of its potential expenses before you commit to purchase, so discovering in advance what a particular boat's insurance premiums will cost you should be part of the process.
3. A boat is usually a major purchase; it could be unwise to leave it uninsured for even a few minutes. If you have a loan using the boat as collateral, lenders will require insurance listing them as a loss payee to protect their interest in your boat, and lenders usually demand that the policy be in place before they'll hand over the money. Also, most marinas will require that you have insurance in order to keep your boat at their facility. So you really can't wait; you need to have the insurance before you can have the boat.

And choose an experienced marine insurance agent. The complicating factor in insuring your boat is that it is rarely as straightforward as insuring your home or car. But neither is it terribly difficult; you just need to find an agent or broker who knows all the ins and outs of marine insurance.

Types of Insurance Agencies

There are two types: *direct* agents, who represent just one company (aka the carrier or underwriter), and *independent* agents, who represent a number of different companies.

A direct agent can be fine if you're buying a small (less than 26 feet) outboard-powered boat. In fact, a boat insurance policy, the type most direct agents are most familiar with, can often be bundled with your homeowner's and automobile policies, for an often considerable savings in total premiums—the insurance company in essence rewards you for being a loyal customer and giving it all of your business, and a direct agent can usually arrange this money-saving package for you very well. For a smaller, less expensive boat, you might also consider the possibility of adding a boat rider to your homeowner's insurance rather than buying an additional policy. This isn't always possible, and even when it is, it's not always the best plan. But you should discuss the pros and cons with your agent before you make a final decision.

There are also several nationally recognized direct agents that have websites for convenient online application (see Resources). What

Figure 11-1. In addition to causing property damage and perhaps some physical injury, boating accidents can have other costs that often run high. But if you have the proper insurance, at least your monetary loss will be covered. *(George Green)*

many of these agents have going for them is that they are boating people also and thus know all aspects of the situation very well. Just remember that a boat policy is generally best only for vessels up to about 26 feet in length. Recognizing that 90% of the boats registered in the United States are under 20 feet in length puts this limitation in perspective; for the majority, a boat policy is fine.

But it's a limitation, nonetheless. And if you buy a larger boat or a small one that's been powered to the max (which is generally considered a greater risk), a boat policy may not be sufficient. In this case you'll want a yacht policy, and most often you'll do better with an independent agent. An independent agent can get you the best policy at the best price because of choice and competition, and a really good independent agent can tailor a policy to suit your specific needs.

This is why you definitely want an agent who is experienced in writing yacht insurance because—unlike boat policies, which can be as simply off the shelf as your typical auto or homeowner's policies—a yacht policy is most often individually crafted, and the more knowledgeable your agent, the better your chances of getting perfect coverage at the best possible price.

THE DEVIL IS IN THE DETAILS
Hull and Machinery

Hull and machinery coverage pays to repair or replace a damaged or lost vessel, engine, trailer, and attached equipment, no matter who or what caused the damage and regardless of why the damage occurred—subject to some limitations, of course. Collision, fire, theft, and accidental sinking are also normally covered. However, losses due to war or seizure by authorities most probably are not.

Normal Wear Is Excluded

Normal wear and tear will not be covered, and damage resulting from negligence or poor maintenance is also not covered because it is your responsibility to properly maintain your vessel and not operate it in a negligent manner.

POLICY LIMITS

Some policies cover only *named hazards*—that is, they pay only if the loss results from one of the types of mishaps specifically named in the policy (fire, theft, sinking, etc.). A named hazards policy is generally less expensive, but it is also less desirable, since it isn't always possible to anticipate every potential cause of damage or loss and if the cause of loss isn't specifically named in the policy, it isn't covered. Note: A named hazards policy may be the only kind available if your boat

Don't Forget

Having an illegal substance aboard can cause your boat to be seized. Say you have a friend who likes to smoke a controlled substance and brings some aboard when invited as a guest. At some point in mid-cruise, you are boarded by the Coast Guard (they do this routinely, so there's no need to panic). In the process of checking the boat for required safety gear, a boarding officer happens to discover the controlled substance. Of course, no one will admit it's theirs. So, under the Coast Guard's zero tolerance policy, in which no amount is considered insignificant no matter how small, the boat can be impounded despite the obvious reality that the boat itself couldn't possibly have had any part in bringing it aboard. You lose the boat! And since most policies won't cover seizure by government agencies, you lose big time. If you have friends who like to smoke "wacky tobaccy," be sure to tell them to leave the stuff at home when they come aboard your boat.

Quick Tips

Negligence is usually defined in two ways. It can be (1) "failure to do what a prudent person would do under the same circumstances," or (2) "behavior that endangers the life, limb, or property of a person." Either way, negligent operation can be a serious problem because not only can it void your insurance but, depending on the nature of the damage it causes, you can face some stiff consequences from the authorities as well—for gross negligence, up to a $5,000 civil penalty and possibly a year in jail!

Quick Tips

Chartering is commercial use. If you plan to recoup some of your boat's operating expense by chartering it to others when you're not using it yourself (see Chapter 1), remember that this will be considered commercial use and thus will void your policy unless you add commercial coverage. Some yacht policies include an option for occasional commercial (charter) use; but if you plan to charter, be sure to get a clear definition of how much activity will be considered "occasional."

is big enough that your cruising plans may include venturing to foreign shores.

All-risk policies are generally broader and cover any kind of loss *except* those specifically excluded. Common exclusions are nuclear war, illegal activities, normal wear and tear, intentional acts, commercial use, and racing.

Other Aspects

Some other normal exclusions may surprise you, such as loss resulting from ice and freezing, loss because of effects of electricity (other than lightning or fire), and loss caused by faulty design or construction of the vessel, often known as latent defects. Latent defects coverage can be included in a yacht policy, but it will usually cost an additional premium.

Repairs, Towing, and Salvage

Hull and machinery coverage pays for repairs up to the policy limit, generally subject to a deductible.

You can also get coverage for towing and/or salvage of your vessel. Some insurance companies offer towing coverage for an additional charge. Of course, with this option you pay to be towed and then get reimbursed later. A better deal would be membership in a national towing service, since they also do the towing.

Engine Coverage

Some yacht policies cover engines for more than just fire and theft and will pay to repair or replace them if they break down. Most often, there will be some restrictions.

What If You Have a Total Loss?

In this case, a yacht policy can pay either actual cash value (ACV), which is usually the BUC Book or depreciated value, or an agreed value, which is set at the time the policy is issued and usually requires a CVS to help determine the vessel's worth. Don't let the need for a survey throw you;

Quick Tips

Latent defects coverage can be complex. These are, by definition, hidden flaws that cannot be detected through routine inspection, which, in the case of boats, would include a proper survey. If you have latent defects coverage, your policy will generally pay for any loss that results from a latent defect but will *not* pay for repairing the defect itself. It is the builder's obligation to deliver a defect-free vessel. Covering repair of the defect itself would be insuring the builder. If you want the repair of the defect paid for by someone other than yourself, you'll have to go after the builder either through a warranty claim (even if it isn't specifically covered by the warranty you got when you bought the boat, there is always an implied warranty that a hull is defect-free) or, if all else fails, through a lawsuit. Consult your attorney as to the best approach.

Figure 11-2. Time was when you could call the Coast Guard for any on-water difficulty. These days they won't respond for anything less than a life-threatening situation. The least expensive towing and assistance comes from membership in a towing service. *(Sea Tow)*

before they will issue any yacht policy (and this is generally true whether the boat is used or new), most insurance underwriters will demand a survey (as will your bank or lender, particularly if you are buying a used boat). Besides, since a CVS is usually less comprehensive than the prepurchase survey you'll probably have done anyway before you buy the boat (see Chapter 10), complying with the underwriter's demand

Quick Tips

Towing and salvage are two different beasts. Whether as a part of your basic insurance or via membership in a towing service, such as Sea Tow or TowBoatU.S., towing coverage applies only when you are out of fuel, the engine breaks down (or simply won't start), you are lightly aground (which is known as a "soft" grounding), or you are in any other simple situation in which you can't get the boat to go under its own power. Rescue from being hard aground or from any stage of sinking is salvage work and is generally *not* covered by towing insurance or basic membership in a towing service. In a salvage situation, you will have to negotiate directly with the salvor that comes to your aid, though some insurance companies will negotiate for you (call their 24-hour hotline) and will pay the resulting fee (to the limits of your policy) if you also have salvage coverage.

for a survey can simply be a matter of providing them with a copy of your prepurchase report. Remember, the underwriters will probably want proof that any deficiencies noted in the report have been corrected. This will usually require copies of repair orders or invoices for the purchase of any requisite equipment that the surveyor found lacking.

All in all, you'll generally come out better with an agreed value policy, although it will probably cost more than one that pays actual cash value. Payout on a total loss is usually minus a deductible of 1% or 2% whether it is ACV or agreed value.

Protection and Indemnity, the Nautical Equivalent of Liability Coverage

Protection and indemnity (P&I) coverage pays for your defense if you are sued for damage or injury allegedly caused by your boat. It also pays the amount awarded the claimant in a successful lawsuit (up to the policy limit) or a negotiated amount if the company can get the other party to agree to an out-of-court settlement.

P&I coverage pays for damage caused by your boat's wake (you are always responsible for your wake and any damage it may cause), by fire spreading from your boat to other boats or facilities, and by ramming, *collision* (hitting a moving object, such as another boat), or *allision* (hitting a fixed object, such as a bridge or pier). It pays medical expenses, if necessary, for guests or other third parties injured aboard and may also pay for guests' personal effects.

A good policy will also provide a separate coverage for your liability under the Federal Longshoremen's and Harbor Workers' Compensation Act. This will cover your statutory liability to temporary shore-based workers, such as mechanics or marina employees, if they become injured aboard your boat. It may further pay "maintenance and cure," room and board and medical treatment, for persons who become sick or injured while working on your boat.

They Must Be On Board

P&I coverage usually extends only to persons who are actually on board the vessel. Off-the-boat activities, such as waterskiing, riding a PWC, or even just swimming or snorkeling, may or may not be covered. It is always possible to include coverage for any or all of these; just expect that you may have to pay more in premiums.

Some policies pay for investigative services used to determine the most probable cause of damage. Some pay for recovery of a wrecked or sunken boat and for cleanup of spilled fuel and oil. But these are rarely automatic—if you want a specific coverage, ask for it. At the very least, be sure to discuss with your agent the cost/benefit ratio of various coverage aspects; only then can you know whether you want them or not. While it is unwise to be underinsured, it is an expensive waste to be overinsured.

Most policies cover damage to you or your boat caused by another boater if s/he is not carrying P&I coverage (uninsured boater coverage). In this case, after paying your claim, your carrier will probably try to recover its loss from the other party, though this infighting will probably be of little concern to you as long as you don't have to pay.

Other Limits

You must provide accurate information about yourself and the boat, including your age, experience, and driving and loss record, as well as vessel type, age, and safety equipment carried (much of which will be confirmed by your condition and valuation

Quick Tips

Set your P&I limit high enough. Maritime law limits a vessel's liability to its own total value. There was a time when this applied to all vessels, but nowadays it applies only to suits that are filed in federal court under admiralty law. In recent years, probably because of the often expensive damage caused by some relatively inexpensive little boats, other courts have decreed that pleasure boat owners are not subject to this limitation and have awarded higher amounts to successful claimants. Smart plaintiffs (or their attorneys) will try to get their cases heard in other courts! Since the purpose of P&I coverage is to protect your personal assets from damage claims, you should select a P&I limit based not on what your boat is worth but, rather, on the value of all the assets that you want to protect, including your home, savings, and any other financial holdings you may have. Your boat P&I policy can also be matched to a personal liability umbrella available through your homeowner's insurance agent to provide excess liability coverage.

survey). By signing the application, you provide a *warranty* (guarantee) that the information is correct and true—and if any of the data you provide should prove to be false, you quite probably will soon find yourself uninsured.

You agree to operate the boat only for lawful purposes and not to engage in commercial activities or racing. Unless you operate strictly within the Sunbelt, you probably will have to agree to an annual layup, a period of time, usually in winter, when the boat is not in use. It is also common to have geographical operating limits within which you promise to stay (and outside which your insurance is void). You must agree to report changes to any of the above, and to pay premiums on time. Incidentally, layup time and operating range are usually negotiable, though increases in time

of use and/or geographical operating limits will often, though not necessarily, increase your premiums. Increasing your geographical range may also require another survey to assess the vessel's (and operator's) suitability for the extended travel.

Failure to comply with any of the above constitutes a breach of warranty, which may invalidate your policy. Your lender may require breach of warranty insurance, which pays the outstanding balance on your loan if you commit a breach of warranty, invalidate the rest of your policy, and suffer a loss. Of course, this will also add to your premium.

It's All Negotiable!
The bottom line is that nearly every aspect of a yacht policy is essentially negotiable: coverage limits (in terms of money, geography, and use), as well as inclusions, exclusions,

endorsements, and, often, even the resulting premium. This why it is so important to choose an experienced marine insurance agent. S/he will have the knowledge and experience to work with you, and the underwriters or carriers, to get you the best possible coverage at the best possible price.

FILING A CLAIM

When you get your insurance policy, be sure you also get a phone number to call in case you have a claim (preferably with 24/7 availability). And be sure to ask whether you call your agent (whom you should call regardless), the underwriter's claims department, or a third-party claims adjuster.

Federal law requires you to file a formal boating accident report with the U.S. Coast Guard or your state marine patrol if you are involved in an incident that results in loss of life, personal injury that requires medical treatment beyond basic first aid, damage exceeding $2,000, or complete loss of the boat. If there is a death, injury, or disappearance of a person, you must file the report within 48 hours. Otherwise, the report is due within 10 days. Your insurance company will probably require a copy of the accident report to process your claim. You can get blank forms from the Coast Guard or state marine patrol, and if officers respond to your accident scene, they will often give the forms to you at the time.

Handling Claims

After an incident, you will probably be upset and feel overwhelmed. Your insurers won't be, however; they deal with claims every day, and the agent or adjuster handling yours will undoubtedly want to see that it is processed as quickly, fairly, and smoothly as possible. Doing so generally means following a routine to make sure they don't

miss anything. So, in addition to a copy of the formal report (if the incident requires one), s/he will most probably ask you for full information about the loss, including location, date, time, and the names of all persons involved and present, the weather, and any other pertinent circumstances. Much of this will be in the formal accident report, if there is one, but chances are the adjuster will want the information in greater detail and usually with your personal narrative. And if the incident didn't require a formal report, the adjuster will still want you to provide all the necessary details. So it's essential that you take good notes. If possible (and this is important, so you should try to make it possible), get the names and phone numbers of witnesses or anyone who participated in any aspect of the rescue or recovery. Buy a notebook or make entries in

Quick Tips

It's your money, so protect it. Be sure to keep receipts for all expenditures, including services, parts, and any other expenses you incur in the course of recovering and repairing the boat. They may not all be reimbursable, but a big stack of receipts will go a long way toward establishing your claim for all the reimbursements to which you are entitled. You may even be paid for your own time if you materially assist in the repair of the vessel.

the vessel's log detailing all the events leading up to, and subsequent to, the loss.

And You'll Need Another Survey!

Before authorizing repairs, the adjuster probably will want to inspect the boat or have a marine surveyor inspect it and file a damage report that will include an estimate of the cost of repair. Be sure to cooperate fully to ensure prompt and full claim payment.

KEEPING PREMIUMS LOW

While the lowest possible premium will usually be far from the best deal, you still don't want to pay any more than necessary. Here are some tips:

- Newer boats (less than 10 years old) are the least expensive to insure. Wooden

Quick Tips

If it's feasible, use the same surveyor who did your prepurchase survey. While the purpose of this survey is to fully assess the extent of the damage and estimate what it should cost for proper repairs, which any competent surveyor can do, the one you used initially will have records, probably some digital photographs, and perhaps even the actual memory of the way things were before the loss and is thus in a better position to estimate the total extent of the damage, which might get you more money.

boats and high-speed boats are more costly.

- Boats with diesel engines generally cost less to insure than those with gas engines, and boats with outboards may also be less expensive to insure than those with gas inboards.
- Your policy requires that your boat carry all legally mandated equipment (see Chapter 4), but you might get a discount for carrying additional safety equipment, such as a VHF radio, GPS, and additional fire extinguishers—especially an automatic fixed system in the engine compartment. An EPIRB (emergency position-indicating radio beacon) and a suitable life raft can also help if your cruising plans will take you far offshore.
- Paying the entire premium at once saves finance charges.
- A higher deductible, a lower P&I limit, and a longer annual layup can each contribute to a less expensive policy. Likewise, named risk and actual cash value policies can cost less, though the savings/benefits ratio will probably suffer as a result.
- Previous boating experience, completion of a boating safety class approved by the National Association of State Boating Law Administrators (NASBLA; see Chapter 14), a clean loss record, and a clean (auto) driving record may get you premium discounts, as will hiring a professional to operate your boat for you. Evidence of a secure place to store the boat may reduce premiums, also.

There Is No Free Lunch!

When you pay less, you most often get less; the lowest-cost policy is rarely the best value. Carefully evaluate all your needs, including what you are protecting, when

Quick Tips

One quirk in the laws on pleasure boating is that the only qualification you need for buying a boat of *any* size or type is that you can afford it. Whether you are able to handle a boat of that size and type is largely overlooked by everyone—except your insurance company. If you've opted for a boat that your underwriters decide is too much of a stretch for your operating experience, your premium will reflect the higher risk. You can usually lower it by hiring a licensed professional captain to run the boat for you. You can also have this captain teach you to operate the boat yourself. And after you've gained enough experience, you should qualify for a lower premium on your own (though it will still most likely be higher than what you have when an experienced pro is running the boat).

Don't Forget

An insurance policy is a contract. Both you and your underwriter are bound by its terms. If you fail to live up to your end of the bargain, you may find yourself uninsured. But also be aware of two other potential problems. First, don't count on oral promises from your agent that are not included in the written policy. No matter what the agent tells you, it is what's in writing that counts—be sure to read and understand your policy.

Second, not all insurers are created equal. Regardless of the coverage your policy calls for, a financially unstable insurer may not pay promptly—or even at all. Best's Ratings, recognized worldwide as the benchmark for assessing insurers' financial strength, are an independent third-party evaluation. Since 1999, A.M. Best has been offering ratings and insurer profiles on its corporate website free of charge (see the Resources section for contact information). Reputable agents normally write policies only with highly rated insurers. But you can conduct your own due diligence by double-checking an insurer's Best Rating for yourself before you accept a policy.

selecting an insurance policy for your new pride and joy.

What About Applying Online?

It's possible. And if you are looking for an off-the-shelf boat policy, it will probably work, especially if you insure your car this way and your underwriter also insures boats. There are also boat insurers that provide online applications. But crafting a suitable yacht policy usually calls for some face time with your agent while s/he questions you to determine your specific needs. Since your reaction to certain questions can be as important as your actual responses, I would say that, for the present at least, you'll be better off to work directly with a human being.

WRAP

✔ Boats require specialized insurance from knowledgeable agents.

✔ Boat policies are generally standardized.

✔ Yacht policies are usually individually crafted.

✔ Hull and machinery coverage protects your property.

✔ Protection and indemnity coverage safeguards your assets.

✔ Filing a claim will most often involve a survey to assess the extent of damage.

✔ There are many ways to lower premiums, but the lowest-cost policy isn't always the best buy.

CHAPTER 12

MAINTENANCE

Do I Need to Read This Chapter?

You should read this chapter if you want to discover

- ✔ The need for care and maintenance of your boat.
- ✔ The options you have for getting the work done.
- ✔ The advantages and disadvantages of each option.

Simply stated, your boat will need care and attention. Truthfully stated, your boat will need *a lot* of care and attention! Your home, automobile, and some of your other possessions require routine maintenance also, but none of them has the potential to sink if things go terribly wrong. And you can usually walk away from problems that develop ashore. The situation is generally less forgiving when problems arise out on the water, so proper maintenance is even more critical for your boat. I'm not trying to scare you or dissuade you from buying a powerboat. But it is my duty to make sure that you are aware of all the aspects inherent in boat ownership and the need for considerable and ongoing maintenance is high on the list.

MAINTENANCE OPTIONS
Your Dealer's Service Department

If you have a brand-new boat that's still under warranty (a topic we'll cover more thoroughly in the next chapter), this really isn't just one option among several—it's your only one. Boatbuilders, engine makers, and the manufacturers of most ancillary equipment are usually quite finicky about who works on things while they are still under warranty. In fact, most of the time, you'll find that you will void your warranty if you allow anyone *but* a factory-certified technician to even so much as take a look.

This is not necessarily bad. In fact, it can be very good. As we saw in Chapter 8, having a reliable service department is one hallmark of a good dealership. Going back to your dealer for service, warranty or otherwise, is often your best move.

Pros and Cons

There are several advantages to having all of your maintenance and repairs done by your dealer's service department:

- **They know your boat and its equipment.** Most dealerships employ only factory-trained (and certified) mechanics and technicians who remain up to date by going back to school on a regular basis.

- **They have the right parts.** Keeping an inventory of factory-approved replacements is generally a manufacturer's requirement of dealerships in order to maintain an authorized sales and service status.
- **They value your business.** Good dealerships will want to keep you as a potential customer for other boats in the future by providing the best service they can on the one you now have. It's a small point, but one that can reign huge when you have a serious problem that needs immediate attention.

Of course, dealer service isn't the only answer and it isn't always your best choice after the warranty period expires. Among the potential drawbacks to having your dealer take care of all of your boat's maintenance are:

- **Inconvenience.** While many dealers now have trucks and roving mechanics that will come to your boat for maintenance and repairs that don't require a haulout, not all of them do as yet. And when they don't, you have to take the boat to the dealer for even routine stuff, which takes some (or maybe a lot) of your precious time.
- **Cost.** Dealer service departments are rarely the least expensive option. The slightly higher labor rates (most often brought about by the requisite factory training of the technicians) and the difference in cost between factory-approved and equivalent parts can add up to a higher bottom line on your service ticket. And if you must take your boat to the dealer, you have to consider that cost, too.

- **Delays.** Good service departments are usually very busy. Even if you're a prime customer and the sales department is grooming you to trade for a larger model, you still have to wait your turn in the service department. This can be frustrating, especially when the service you need won't take that long and you know it. It fact, it can be extremely aggravating when the waiting time significantly exceeds the actual repair time. But it happens.

Dealer service departments can be your best bet long after the warranties have expired because no one knows your boat as a whole any better. Yes, they have drawbacks, but a cost/benefit analysis often weighs heavily in their favor.

Authorized Service Shops

If your boat is outboard powered, you'll probably soon discover that the nearest factory-authorized service facility for your power plants is the dealership itself. This is often also true for gasoline inboards. But if you have a diesel boat, chances are that engine work, warranty and otherwise, will be farmed out to another shop that is either owned or licensed by the engine maker. The company's mechanics will be allowed to work on the dealer's property and will come with the dealer's full blessing, having been called in by the service manager. And if your boat needs other work in addition to the engines, having the mechanics come to the dealer's facility isn't a bad idea; often, the engine repairs can be made at the same time other workers are doing other things. But if you don't need anything but engine service, it's usually easier to have the mechanics come directly to your boat. These authorized shops have a fleet of trucks that roam the shop's allotted territory and carry the mechanics and their tools to wherever they're needed.

Warranty work, even on engines or other equipment that may require the dealer to call in outside techs, should always go through the dealer's service department. This will ensure that all warranty requirements have been met. But once the boat is out of warranty, you can deal with these shops directly. This is true for engines and also for most electronics.

Authorized service shops always employ factory-certified technicians who keep up on all the latest technology by going back to school often enough to maintain their certification. Couple this with total and quick access to authorized parts, and you have a very strong argument for using only authorized shops and their technicians. It is far from a bad idea. But it is not necessarily the best idea. There are drawbacks:

- **Cost of labor.** Maintaining a fleet of trucks, as well as an inventory of most-needed parts, combined with the need for constantly sending techs back to school quickly adds up to a considerable over-head. To cover this cost of doing business and still show a profit, authorized shops have to charge quite dearly for their services. Generally, when you go factory authorized, you pay top dollar.
- **Cost of parts.** Authorized parts usually cost more. Often, they are needed. But many times equivalent parts will work fully as well, and they usually cost less. An authorized facility can lose its certification if it uses anything but authorized replacements, so they won't do it. The result? You pay.
- **Limited scope.** Technicians are authorized to work on equipment manufactured by the company that sanctions them, and

generally they won't work on anything else. If you have mechanics aboard to service your main engines, don't expect them to service your generator also. It will most probably have an engine produced by another manufacturer, and they aren't supposed to touch it.

All things considered, authorized shops can also be a viable option long after the warranty period has expired. They know the equipment far better than anyone else, and often the bottom line on a given repair can be less despite the higher labor and other costs simply because their intimate knowledge of the product allows them to work more efficiently.

Boatyards

In most boating areas, you'll find at least one total-service boatyard (and usually more). These institutions have lifts, railroads, or other devices to get boats in and out of the water easily, large sheds in which to work on them out of the weather, and usually some outdoor work areas as well. In seasonal boating regions, these facilities also generally have sufficient area to store boats ashore during the off-season, and sometimes some of these storage areas are enclosed to provide protection from snow, ice, and the other potentially harmful aspects of northern winters. These yards are great for winter storage because you can usually schedule work to be done during the off-season, which frees up more actual boating time when the weather turns nice.

A boatyard may be associated with a dealership and its service department, but quite a few are totally independent and don't sell new boats, though often they have an allied brokerage service to handle the sale of boats whose owners have decided to call it quits and want to get rid of the headache that used to be their baby while it is in the yard.

The largest yards do everything:

- haulout and launch
- complete repairs of all marine systems
- fiberglass repair
- painting and exterior refinishing
- woodwork and interior repair and renovation
- comprehensive engine service
- other mechanical repairs
- electrical repairs and maintenance
- electronics installation and service
- running gear service (prop and shaft shop)
- machine shop services

In some yards, all of these services are provided by one company, the yard itself. In others, the yard leases shop and office space to subcontractors who have an exclusive on all work they qualify for that is done within the yard as well as the opportunity to bring in jobs of their own. Always in the former, and often in the latter, each visit to the yard requires but a single work order (though it may include many separate projects), and all billing and payment is handled by the yard office, which makes it more convenient for all concerned.

Smaller yards generally don't provide the full scope of services (though they can usually arrange for most of them); they tend to specialize in one or two areas for which some often earn a reputation for being the best. While the large, full-service yards are usually better if you need several things done at once, when you have but one project, say repainting the boat or repowering, you will often do better by seeking the best specialty yard for the job.

Independent Contractors

You'll discover as you get into powerboating that many people work on boats for the same reason others play on them: they *love*

Figure 12-1. Large yards have the equipment to get boats out of the water and move them around with relative ease. Even if you opt to do much of your maintenance and repair work by yourself, you'll still need boatyard services for at least a portion of it. (*Grand Banks Yachts*)

boats! There are mechanics, woodworkers, fiberglass specialists, electronics technicians, and other skilled craftsmen who could easily earn a living ashore but instead choose to be marine technicians because they'd rather work on boats. The strength of this love becomes more evident when you consider that the structure of boats and the location of installed equipment often combine to require boat workers to also have the skills of a contortionist (in addition to their technical knowledge) just to do the simplest of jobs. Working ashore would be so much easier!

The majority of independent contractors are good at what they do. The main drawbacks are that they cannot be currently certified—manufacturers' certification programs normally require that candidates be employed by "authorized" shops—and they also lack the depth of resources usually found in a larger company.

On the plus side, many independent contractors were once certified because they worked for an authorized facility until they decided to go out on their own. And while their technical knowledge may lag behind that of currently certified technicians, it's usually by a narrow margin. Most important: independents are free to use equivalent components whenever the substitutes will work as well, so when you add this lower parts cost to the lower labor fees they normally charge as a result of their lower overhead, you get quality work for less. Independents will also usually work longer and odder hours (often with no overtime charge) than technicians bound by the rules and regulations (and perhaps labor agreements) of a large organization.

Be aware that anyone can call himself or herself a marine mechanic (or any other type of technician) and, lacking the certainty of a universal certification program, you can only guess at any individual's competence—or learn the hard way. Your best bet is to use your ears. Word travels fast on the waterfront, and it's usually easy to get recommendations—or warnings—from fellow boaters. Heed them well, and you usually can't go wrong. You can also use your eyes. If you see someone working on a neighbor's boat, it is probably a good sign—and a better one if they seem to be working on several over a period of time. Try to get acquainted before you need their services. Introduce yourself at the earliest opportunity, and ask for a card or phone number. If you ever have to call, they will perhaps remember you and respond a bit more rapidly than they would for a total stranger. If the tradesman was recommended by a friend, it helps to mention this when you call. Because another drawback to most independent contractors is that, though they may have a helper or two, they essentially work alone. If they are busy on another boat, they can't take care of yours until they're finished with that one, and their rate of response to an unknown caller often depends on the relationship of that new business to current clients.

Once you have employed an independent, s/he will usually respond quickly to a legitimate emergency, often coming to take care of your urgent matter before finishing a current job. This will be especially true if you've paid for past work promptly and have established yourself as a good customer.

Do It Yourself

This has a lot going for it—if you have the time and inclination. Doing your own maintenance offers many advantages:

- **Lowest cost.** Since labor is often the greater part of a service bill, doing all the work yourself can really save some dollars.

- **Greatest convenience.** If you have the time, scheduling the work is entirely dependent on your calendar, not that of anyone else.
- **You really get to know your boat.** If you can take the time to acquire the tools and parts as well as the knowledge of how to use them, you should never feel stumped if a breakdown occurs when you are out on the water underway (and this will happen despite your good maintenance practices—though proper maintenance will tend to reduce such occurrences dramatically).

I found that doing much of my own work allowed me not only to be closer to my boat (to make it more rationally mine), but also to be involved with my boat when I didn't have the time to actually go boating. On those occasions when my schedule prevented

casting off the lines and going somewhere, I still could enjoy my boat by working on it for a half hour or so. While this worked for me because I love picking up tools and using them, it might not work for everyone; don't even think of the DIY approach unless you

Find a mentor. One of the best ways to acquire the requisite knowledge is to watch and learn from a pro. Many independent contractors, and even some technicians working for a large organization, will gladly share their knowledge with anyone who shows a genuine interest in learning. As you learn, they'll gradually wean you from depending on them entirely and will encourage you to take on minor projects on your own. As your knowledge and skill levels increase, they'll take pride in having helped you grow to where you need them less and less. But they will still usually be available for advice (for which you should pay them) and ready to come to the rescue whenever you face a problem that's beyond your abilities. Finding a good mentor isn't always easy, but if your love for boats and your desire to learn are sufficiently genuine, it shouldn't be that difficult, either. A mutual love of boats can be a powerful bond, and a virtual open sesame for knowledge if you allow it.

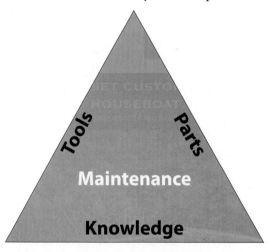

Figure 12-2. Boat maintenance is an equilateral triangle, and if you want to take the DIY route, you'll have to acquire all three sides. Note that both tools and parts rest on a base of knowledge, without which neither will do you much good. Acquiring the tools and parts is easy; all you need is money. Acquiring the requisite knowledge can be more difficult, but once you have it no one can take it away. If this were a TV commercial, tools and parts would have stated costs but knowledge would be "priceless." *(Joseph Comeau)*

like to get your hands dirty. But if you basically enjoy fixing things, maintaining your own boat can be rewarding beyond belief and a huge part of the fun.

One last word on DIY maintenance: you can almost always practice it if you keep your boat in a wet-slip marina. But if the work requires a haulout or other yard services, you may be more limited. Many yards insist that all work done on the premises be conducted by yard employees or authorized subcontractors. *No one else*, including the boat's owner or captain, is allowed to do a thing. Fortunately, there are yards that will allow DIY work and even a few that provide hauling, launching, bottom cleaning, and other services but are otherwise quite dedicated to DIY. If you want to do as much of your own work as possible, make sure you have your haulout at a yard where it is allowed.

Quick Tips

If you opt for DIY maintenance, you'll undoubtedly need additional manuals. Most owner's manuals are geared toward hiring everything done. There are recommendations as to what needs to be done when but usually little info on procedures or specifications. For these you'll need shop manuals, which spell things out in greater detail. Check the Resources section; you'll find sources of tools, parts, and—perhaps more important—valuable technical information and other practical assistance as well.

WRAP

- ✔ Your dealer's service department is your only choice for warranty service and, often, a wise choice for all your service needs.
- ✔ Authorized service shops are a good choice for engine work or electronics.
- ✔ Large boatyards are often your best bet for complicated, multiskill projects or when you need several jobs done simultaneously.

- ✔ Smaller, specialty yards are often ideal on single projects for which they rate as the best.
- ✔ Independent contractors are known for doing good work at lower cost; they are also often quicker to respond.
- ✔ Do-it-yourself maintenance and repair can be enjoyable and rewarding, but it requires an even deeper commitment.

CHAPTER 13

WARRANTIES

Do I Need to Read This Chapter?

You should read this chapter if you want to discover

✔ What boat warranties usually cover.

✔ What they don't cover!

✔ How to maximize warranty service.

✔ The lowdown on extended warranties.

ALL WARRANTIES ARE LIMITED

There is no such thing as an unlimited warranty. And this doesn't apply only to boats. No one could possibly issue a warranty that didn't have at least some limits; to do so would be economic insanity. Even the manufacturer of an absolutely solid product that is unbreakable under normal conditions must, to protect itself from frivolous claims, state in its warranty what normal conditions might be and declare the warranty invalid unless they pertain. Most warranties have several such limitations, and any situation that falls outside the manufacturer-imposed boundaries will not be covered. Nonetheless, buying a new boat usually gives you no-cost repair of most problems that arise during the warranty period.

Automakers Have Spoiled Us

When you buy a new car, nearly every aspect is covered under warranty and you have

Most owners' manuals state the operational, maintenance, and care requirements that are necessary to establish normal use of the product, which is another good reason for reading them thoroughly.

but one place to go for satisfaction: the dealer you bought it from or another dealer that sells the same make. Despite the reality that no carmaker actually builds every component of an automobile, nearly every item involved will ultimately be branded the same—only the tires carry a different name. The carmaker takes full responsibility for the vehicle as a whole, and though different components may be warranted for different lengths of time, as a result of their different inherent lives, there is still just one organization responsible for making things right: the carmaker. And there is a very definite process in the works to handle all the many warranty points that might arise, starting with returning the car to the dealer, who usually says, "We'll take care of it."

Boats Are Different

New boatowners are often surprised to discover that boatbuilders rarely issue a warranty as comprehensive or long-lived as they got with their car. These days, despite Mercury/MerCruiser being a division of Brunswick Corporation, which also has many boat brands, boat engines are rarely branded the same as the boat. In a few cases they are— for example, MasterCraft boats have engines made specifically for them by Indmar, and Yamaha makes engines and boats under the common brand. But most boats possess engines (and other components) that are generally openly acknowledged to have been manufactured by others and merely installed by the builder or, in some cases, the dealer. The bottom line: different organizations are responsible for making it right whenever something goes wrong.

This has produced a fragmented warranty process. Good dealers try to simplify the situation by being the intermediary to the greatest extent possible, but it still often requires several separate warranty claims. The process has also been complicated historically by builders who paid dealers a lower rate for warranty work than they would receive for doing the same repair if it simply came in with a boat not under warranty. This was grossly unfair to the dealers and, fortunately, seems to be changing for the better. Most progressive builders now

Figure 13-1. A MasterCraft LY6 inboard, an uncommon example of a power plant carrying the same brand name as the boat in which it's installed. *(Indmar Marine Engines)*

pay their dealers' standard service rate for all work performed under warranty, and this appears to be a growing trend.

Get It in Writing

All builders now offer a warranty of sorts, but they are not all created equal. The law requires that warranties be available in printed form, to make sure that pertinent details are well established, clearly visible, and accessible to anyone who cares to read them. So be sure you do just that. When you're deciding which of possibly several boats will be the one, the warranty you'll get with each can be a clincher. Given that warranty work ultimately costs the builder, a strong and comprehensive warranty shows you that the builder has faith in its quality control and really doesn't expect to handle many claims; well-built boats usually have fewer problems and thus can carry a stronger warranty.

Not to disparage salespeople, but you absolutely *cannot* rely on any warranty information offered orally. The only warranty that counts is the printed one. Always ask for a copy and read it carefully. Do the same for each boat that interests you.

The warranty that applies in any given situation may be the builder's, the engine maker's, or that of some other component manufacturer, but one major advantage in buying a brand-new boat is that nearly everything aboard will be covered by a warranty. And they will all be valid—as long as their qualifying conditions have all been met. The main problem is that they will rarely have the same expiration date, and keeping track of expirations can be as much of a problem as keeping track of which company is ultimately responsible. This is another area in which having a good dealer can make all the difference. It's a part of that "best dealer" desire to build long-standing customer relationships in order to sell a number of boats over the years rather than just this one. So the bottom line is essentially the same for boats as it is with cars: take the thing back to where you bought it! A good dealer will help with warranty claims to the extent that the best of them will say, "We'll take care of it."

Don't Forget

Boats are not yet as reliable as either cars or the consumer electronics we love so much. As one writer commented in a blog on marine warranties: "Products made in the millions set unrealistic consumer expectations for complex products made in the hundreds operating in wet environments." His point was that unknowing boat buyers often expect too much. Knowledgeable boatowners make maintenance their highest priority because it can drastically reduce the need for warranty claims. (It can't eliminate them, however; some things will break down no matter what you do.) This is another area in which having a good dealer can help; the better ones remind their new customers to bring their boats in for a routine 20-hour checkup (or its equivalent; the exact period varies) to discover potential or developing problems before they become more serious.

It's Getting Better

One bright note in all this is that many within the boating community are clamoring for better and longer warranties, and, in general, manufacturers are responding. Several engine makers now offer warranties good for 5 years, and there are now hull warranties good for 10. The divergence among warranties is still large, and while many now cover

Typical Dealer's Warranty Terms for Preowned Boats

AGE	MOTOR	ACCESSORIES	MISCELLANEOUS
Current to 5 model years	Balance of manufacturer's warranty	60 days on all	Balance of any factory warranties where applicable
6 to 9 model years	30 days	30 days	Balance of any factory warranties
10 model years and older	"As is"—no warranty unless otherwise specified	Extended warranties available on some models	Written list with details of condition of boat, motor, trailer, and accessories

Quick Tips

If you're buying a used boat, the warranty you get usually depends on the boat's age and from whom you buy it. Most manufacturers' warranties carry forward for their entire duration, even through a change in ownership. This means that if you buy a 3-year-old boat that originally carried a 5-year warranty on major components, you still benefit for 2 more years. Many quality dealers also issue a warranty of their own on boats they've taken in trade, selling them as certified preowned boats. The basis for this is that they'll only take in a boat that's essentially sound and then their service department goes over it thoroughly to correct any minor problems. They have to be satisfied that the boat is worthy of their faith—and yours. But a used boat you buy from a private seller most probably has no warranty at all, unless a portion of the original remains.

boats and engines for longer periods than before, in nearly every case it is still shorter than the average 15 years new boat buyers have to repay their loan (see Chapter 5). But since statistics show that most boat loans are paid in full after just 3½ years, even a 5-year warranty can look pretty good.

Whatever the state of boat warranties may be as you read this, all trends suggest that it most certainly will be improved, at least somewhat, by next year and even more the year after that. I'm quite sure this statement will be true for several years to come. Boats will probably never become as reliable as cars, and warranties will continue to reflect this reality. But the future looks very bright.

WHAT ISN'T COVERED

The specifics will be stated in the written warranty you receive and will vary in detail from manufacturer to manufacturer and also with the particular component involved. But in general, warranties cover only normal use of the product, which, in the case of pleasure boats, usually means the boat must be used strictly for pleasure, or what would be considered recreation under the requirements for federal documentation (see Chapter 5).

Chartering, or other commercial uses of the boat, will often void the warranties.

For many components, engines in particular, proper maintenance is also a prime requirement to keep a warranty in effect. If you fail to follow the break-in routine outlined in the manual, or don't change the oil and filters as scheduled, or fail to follow any of the other recommended routine maintenance procedures, you will often be more or less on your own if the engines happen to quit or act up.

With many components, if you allow anyone but an authorized service technician to do so much as even peek inside, you may discover that the warranty has become as inoperative as the equipment itself. When things are still under warranty, authorized service is really your only option. If you take any other route, in many cases you'll void the warranty. Always resist the temptation to do something, even if it appears to be expedient at the moment.

Warranty Cards

Your owner's manual package—with many builders these days, a thick loose-leaf binder enclosed in a vinyl or canvas pouch—will usually contain separate, individual manuals for each of the many mechanical and electronic systems aboard. If you look within these manuals, you'll often find warranty cards that must be filled in and mailed to the manufacturer of each individual piece of equipment. These cards are merely to register you as an owner of the product and keep you current on recalls and updates; they aren't essential to the warranty process. But it never hurts to fill them out and mail them.

Extended Warranties

Let's get one thing straight: an extended warranty really isn't a warranty at all; it's an insurance policy. In fact, many dealers now refer to them as extended service plans. A true warranty is a guarantee—the manufacturer's assurance that "We expect our product to work, totally trouble free, for [a stated length of time]. During this period, if it fails to work properly, for any legitimate reason, we will repair or replace it at no cost to you." After the warranty period, the manufacturer acknowledges that whether the product continues to work trouble free is essentially an element of fate (it *should* work, but there's no guarantee that it will!) and simply washes its hands of the entire matter. Because we normally expect to use products and have them work properly for longer than the manufacturer guarantees performance, we have two options: we can either then pay for the repairs ourselves, or buy insurance to pay the bills for us if and when repairs become necessary. Some extended warranties are backed by the original manufacturer, but most are issued by a third-party insurer. Extended service plans are usually paid for up front, when you purchase the product. A onetime charge that means having repairs covered this way is not without cost; the repairs are not free as they usually are with a true warranty. Whether this added cost is justified is a subject of debate. "To extend or not extend?"—that is the question.

It's Always a Gamble

If you decide to go it on your own, you're taking a chance. If you don't have any problems, you're ahead of the game; you've saved a few bucks. But need just one repair and you may have to spend more than the extended warranty would have cost. So what to do? First, consider your plans. Do you intend to keep the boat longer than the basic warranties cover? If the answer is no, your dilemma is solved. But if it's yes, you may be a candidate for an extension. Your own personality comes into play here. If you're comfortable with risk, you can pass up the option to buy the extension. But if facing any unexpected expense is going to throw you, the cost of extended coverage can be money well spent, especially if you can include the cost of the extended warranties in the boat's total purchase price and finance it along with the boat itself.

Forget about buying extended warranties on electronics. When they are being candid, electronics dealers will admit that they make nearly as much from selling extended warranties as they do from selling product. Thanks to the nature of solid-state circuitry, today's electronics tend to either fail very quickly, while still under the manufacturer's initial warranty, or much later—or not at all. And, given the rapid advances in technology, you may want a new and updated widget long before the old one quits. So buying an extended warranty can be a waste. But even well-made mechanical gear can fail at any time, which means that extended warranties on mechanical devices and systems can be a good idea. Whether they're necessary is a decision you have to base on the way you'll feel if you don't have a warranty but do have a breakdown.

Quick Tips

If you decide to go for an extended warranty, be sure to negotiate its cost as you did for everything else. Dealers usually have a lot of leeway when it comes to pricing accessories and add-ons, and extended warranties are no different. Chances are that the first offer will be higher than the dealer has to charge. As with anything else in the marketplace, there's always a rock-bottom price that's often considerably lower than the initial offer. Always strive to pay rock bottom. Also make sure the warranty is backed by a reliable company that will be in business long enough to pay off if and when it ever becomes necessary.

WRAP

✔ *All* warranties are limited.

✔ The warranties you receive are a very good reason for buying a brand-new boat.

✔ New boat warranties are neither as comprehensive nor as lengthy as most new car warranties, but they are getting better.

✔ The dealer who sold you the boat remains your best source of warranty satisfaction.

✔ Most warranties demand certain actions on your part, such as using your boat only for recreation.

✔ Extended warranties aren't really warranties, they are insurance.

CHAPTER 14

EDUCATION

Do I Need to Read This Chapter?

You should read this chapter if you want to discover

- ✔ Why boating education may be a legal requirement.
- ✔ The four basic types of boating education.
- ✔ The relative merits of each type.
- ✔ Other benefits to a proper boating education.

Do I Need to Read This Chapter?

WHAT KIND OF EDUCATION?

Education is like maintenance in that you totally need it. The difference is that it is for you personally rather than for your boat. Proper education is fully as important as proper maintenance, and though it usually won't have a high cost when measured in dollars, you will have to invest time. Since you may not be able to operate your boat until you've obtained the requisite education (depending on where you do your boating), it's a good idea to get started early, possibly even before you complete all the details of your purchase.

Why is education so important? In many states, you can't operate a boat legally without it; laws prohibit the operation of a powerboat by anyone who has not successfully completed a NASBLA-approved boating course. To whom this requirement applies varies by state and covers the gamut from everyone operating a powerboat to only

those born after a certain date. Before you hit the water, be sure you know the laws for your boating area.

Even if your state doesn't currently mandate education, you should still consider taking a safe boating course. No one is born knowing how to operate a powerboat; it's something we have to learn. Sure, there's a steering wheel and throttle, but operating a boat is different from driving a car in many, many ways—certainly no harder but different nonetheless. First, there are no brakes! And then, steering action is different, being in the stern rather than up front. Add to this that there are no streets or highways with neatly lined travel lanes (though in many places there will be channels to follow and markers to show where they are) and no traffic lights or signs to tell you who can go and who should stop or yield when the waters become congested. Compound all this with rules of the road, which, though

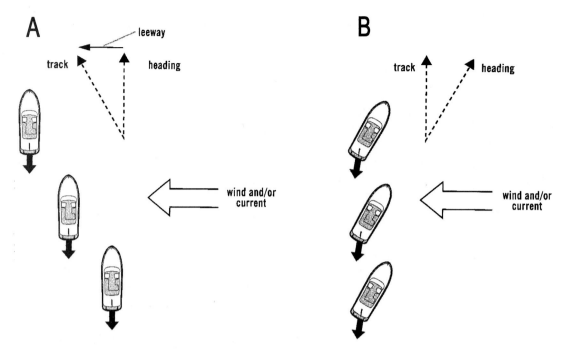

Figure 14-1. Wind and current tend to push boats off course. In (A), the boat is pointed straight ahead but is actually moving to the left. This offsetting effect is called *leeway*, and as the illustration shows, if you don't allow for it, as in (B), you can get into trouble by not actually going in the direction you think you're going. Imagine what would happen if the channel straight ahead is clear but there are some nasty rocks over to the left. *(Joseph Comeau)*

similar to highway rules, are also different., and finally, add that boats rarely travel exactly the way they're pointed, and you can see that there are many new concepts to grasp.

NASBLA Approval

NASBLA has set the standards for approved courses, and if mandatory education is the law in your state, you can satisfy the requirement only by taking and passing an approved course. In my opinion, this approval is a double-edged sword. On the plus side, it does guarantee that minimum standards are met. But I believe that in being geared to meeting these minimums, most approved courses fall way short of covering all you should know before you hit the water. I look at NASBLA approval as the lowest common denominator. And while a course that merely meets the NASBLA standards must be considered better than no education at all, it is far from what's really necessary.

I have to admit—even if begrudgingly—that mandatory education has helped the powerboat industry accept the need for education. For reasons I've never been able to understand, the industry has generally been anti-education for years. Too many powers that be within the powerboat industry have long felt that anything that might be construed as a hindrance to just climbing into a boat and immediately getting to use it is a deterrent to sales. They believe (falsely, in my opinion) that potential boat buyers will consider education to be that kind of hindrance. And yet, other leisure-time industries—music, tennis, golf, and skiing, to name just a few—have long used the offer of free lessons with the purchase of equipment as an incentive to buy. Their opinion seems to be that education isn't a deterrent to sales but, rather, is an inducement. And I've seen people buy very nice boats only to turn around and sell them shortly thereafter because their lack of knowledge prevented them from enjoying the sport. They never discovered the potential fun their boat could have provided because they were too busy trying to stay out of trouble. You can't have fun if you are constantly scared or even just perpetually worried that you might do something wrong. So in addition to fulfilling a need, getting a sound boating education can also add to your enjoyment of the sport. And like a lot of things you may learn, the basics are simple enough that you can grasp them quickly and get started on the water without extensive preparation, and yet, becoming truly proficient can take a lifetime. So there's always something new to learn; it never becomes boring.

Oh, yes, there's another benefit: passing an approved course will usually earn you a discount (normally about 10%) on your boat insurance premiums.

COURSE OPTIONS

There are essentially four ways to acquire this education: (1) independent classroom study, (2) home study, (3) dealer-sponsored classroom study, and (4) private lessons. We'll look at each.

Independent Classroom Study

Among the best known—and, in my opinion, the very best, period—are the basic boating courses offered by the U.S. Coast Guard Auxiliary (Boating Skills and Seamanship) and the U.S. Power Squadrons (the Squadron Boating Course). Both organizations operate on a not-for-profit basis

and are independent of any boat or engine manufacturers or dealers. Their curriculums are different, yet similar, and they have some very solid upsides:

- **They are NASBLA-approved, and then some.** They cover far more than the minimum required for NASBLA approval, and in greater depth and detail.
- **They are free.** There is usually a nominal charge for the text, workbook, and other course-related materials, however.
- **They are taught by local volunteers.** Locals will know the local waters. In addition to teaching the basics, these folks can also offer valuable insights about such things as good waterfront restaurants and other interesting places to visit as well as good local anchorages. Perhaps more important, they can warn you about any sneaky local hazards that are out there just waiting to ambush the unaware. This sort of info is a definite bonus, and much of it will be unavailable elsewhere.
- **They are the first step toward joining either organization.** Membership is never a requirement for taking a basic course, however. Both groups offer advanced education programs for their members along with other opportunities for the betterment of their membership and boating as a whole.
- **The social aspect.** These classes offer the opportunity to meet and mingle with other new boaters in your area.

With all that going for them, it might be hard to believe there could possibly be any downsides. But there are:

- **Time.** Because of the extensive material these courses cover, there are many classroom sessions involved, which are

Figure 14-2. Offering partly multimedia-enhanced lectures (top) and partly hands-on practice sessions, including elementary chart work (bottom), an eight- to twelve-session classroom course has the breadth and depth of content to provide you with the best possible basic boating education. *(First Lt. Ronald Bloom, Seaman, and Past Commander Ronald Gensemer, Senior Navigator, courtesy United States Power Squadrons)*

usually spread over several weeks, one or two nights per week. This is definitely not the quickest way to learn, even if it is the most thorough.

- **Travel.** The distance is rarely great (there are usually a number of class locations in areas that offer good boating—at least one should be close to where you live), but you do have to leave the comfort of home and drive to the school, yacht club, or other place where classes are held.

- **Limited hands-on opportunities.** They exist in such elements as *marlin-spike seamanship* [learning about lines (ropes), knots, and such], navigation techniques, and a few other topics, but you don't get to take the helm of a boat on the water. This essential aspect is covered in theory only.

- **The instructors are volunteers.** They will vary not only in the extent of their knowledge but also in their ability to teach. Obviously, some are better than others, but you have to accept what you get.

Home Study

Studying on your own has always been possible; the lack of formal programs just made the process more difficult. Now, home study is easy; you can even do it online. The are several upsides to home study:

- **You proceed at your own pace.** You can cover the total gamut of material as quickly or as slowly as suits your schedule and ability to learn.

- **You don't have to get dressed up.** You do everything in the privacy of your own home.

- **Most home study courses are NASBLA approved.** They will satisfy the mandatory education requirement in many states.

Get Started

If you can find the time, taking a basic boating course from either the Coast Guard Auxiliary or the United States Power Squadrons is the best way to learn the bulk of what you need to know. Between the greater scope of subject matter and the comforting reality that you can always ask the instructor to clarify any points that seem problematic, classroom study is so far superior to home study that there's really no contest. The benefits to be gained are well worth finding the time to take one of these courses, no matter how busy you may be.

There are downsides, too:

- **There's no instructor.** You are entirely on your own; there is no one to help clarify troublesome concepts.

- **There's no interaction with other students.** Learning with others often helps make the process easier and more pleasant.

- **You have to master everything by reading or viewing an on-screen demo.** This can complicate such hands-on subjects as knot tying or navigation. There's no in-person instruction, no one to personally show you the shortcuts.

- **Home study may not satisfy your mandatory education requirements.** Some states demand a proctored exam

Quick Tips

Home study isn't always the best choice. Some of us need an instructor to prod us. And if you live where passing a proctored exam is required for certification, it doesn't matter how much you learn from the course; you still won't satisfy mandatory education requirements if you answer the questions in the privacy of your home without a proctor to oversee the exam and attest to the validity of its results. It is sometimes possible to arrange for someone to monitor your exam after taking a home-study course, so don't rule it out completely if you live in a proctored exam state.

and others also call for a minimum amount of classroom time. If you opt for home study, be sure it counts in the state where you live and/or do most of your boating.

Dealer-Sponsored Classroom Study

This is also a fairly new development, although the better dealers have been offering some form of instruction to boat buyers for years. Formerly, there was no structure to the lessons. Usually, an experienced staff member would come aboard on delivery to go over the boat's features and, if the buyer was a first timer, also cover some of the aspects that make operating a boat so different from driving a car. But the session was usually

brief, and rarely covered much of the material that NASBLA considers necessary for course approval, such as the all-important Rules of the Road. It was better than nothing, but far from being true boater education.

Now, many dealers are offering structured classes with a NASBLA-approved curriculum. Principal among them is Boater101, the offshoot of an in-school multimedia instruction program that was developed for the water-oriented youth of Broward County, Florida. The program was successful and later, with help from the OMC Foundation and the Brunswick Public Foundation, Inc., it was expanded into the program now available through dealerships all over the country. (Boater101 is also an online course; see the Resources section.)

One main advantage of taking a structured course at a dealership is that the curriculum will cover all of the basics and relate them in an easy-to-comprehend format. Another is that the instructor(s) will be certified, trained professionals.

Many dealerships will combine this structured classroom instruction with some hands-on training when they deliver the boat. Whether this is handled by an experienced staff member or subcontracted to a professional captain/instructor depends on both the attitude of the dealership and the availability of outside help. The overall situation seems to be improving on both counts, and many dealerships now subcontract delivery and new owner instruction to professionals.

Private Lessons

This is a great way to learn: actual hands-on, on-the-water instruction, often on your own boat and always at your own pace. What could be better? But there are drawbacks. For one, a lot of private instructors don't use a NASBLA-approved curriculum, though

When you enroll in a classroom course, you are but one of many. If you don't have an empathy with the instructor, too bad. But with private instruction, there's only one student to please: you. If it doesn't seem to be working, change instructors. Considering that interpersonal chemistry is crucial in one-on-one learning situations, you not only have the right to switch if things aren't going well but have an obligation to yourself to make the change ASAP. You need a teacher who will show you what you need to know in a way you can grasp easily. Anything less is unacceptable.

A good way to kill several proverbial birds with one very practical stone is to hire a professional captain on a part-time basis to (1) oversee your boat's maintenance, thus ensuring it will be properly taken care of despite your busy schedule; (2) operate the boat for you on long trips or any other time you might be over your head in terms of knowledge and experience— or whenever you simply want to enjoy your boat without the work; and (3) gradually show you how to do things by yourself, effectively working himself out of a job. If you choose the right captain, you can find yourself flying solo in rather short order.

the mandatory education requirements now in effect in many states seem to be motivating more and more instructor/captains to include an approved text and test as part of their program. If you want to combine your mandatory education with the practical, you'll need to shop around until you find a teaching captain who also offers a NASBLA-approved curriculum that meets your state's requirements for certification. In many areas, you won't be able to.

Another potential problem is quality of instruction. As music students have sadly learned over the years, being good at something doesn't necessarily provide a person with the ability to pass their skills on to others. Even virtuoso performers sometimes disappoint as teachers. And talented, skillful captains are not always equally gifted as instructors. Here, too, you may have to shop around.

Adding the Hands-On Component

Since few classroom-based programs (and, naturally, none of the online courses) include the on-water aspect, I recommend hiring an instructor/captain for the hands-on instruction I firmly believe everyone requires. But there are two advantages to taking one of the better classroom courses first:

1. You no longer have to be concerned about the on-water training being NASBLA approved; you will already have covered that requirement with your classroom study.

2. By getting a thorough grounding in the theoretical before you take to the water, the hands-on sessions should progress more smoothly—you'll have a better understanding of the whys before your instructor shows you the hows, which helps to make the on-water training more efficient.

If you read this as a put-down of the shorter programs, you are somewhat correct. I applaud them for what they do, and if you don't have the time for a longer one, they are much better than nothing, especially if your state has mandatory education and a shorter program will meet your state's requirements. If that's the case, take it, by all means; you'll benefit from doing so. But having sat through a number of shorter courses (out of curiosity and also to see what I might learn from them) and also having been involved in the development of yet other short programs that worked despite their brevity, I still firmly believe that none of them, including the ones I was involved with, was either broad enough or deep enough to provide the type of education that's truly necessary. One online course (see www.boatsafe.com) even offers this caveat: "This Basic Boating Safety Course gives only the minimum requirements for safety equipment and general information. To obtain a greater knowledge of boating skills and seamanship we encourage you to attend more in-depth boating courses."

I was once involved with a NASBLA-approved program that included hands-on training, and it took basic boating education to a higher level despite its brevity. I wish that the sponsoring company's lack of capital hadn't doomed the program to an early demise. But because so few current programs are both NASBLA approved and also contain the hands-on element, I recommend that you explore both avenues, even if you think it would be unnecessary duplication. It won't be. A proper education includes both the theoretical and the practical. And in boating, there currently aren't many programs that offer both. If one is available near you, consider yourself lucky and take it. Look around in your boating neighborhood; you just may discover an all-inclusive education program that doesn't yet exist as I write this. I wish you well.

WRAP

✔ A growing number of states have mandatory boating education requirements.

✔ Only NASBLA-approved courses satisfy these state requirements.

✔ You need some training even if you don't live in a mandatory education state; no one is born knowing how to operate a boat.

✔ The USCG Auxiliary and the U.S. Power Squadrons offer the most thorough classroom education.

✔ Home-study programs are the most convenient.

✔ Dealer-sponsored classroom study is also an option in many areas.

✔ Private lessons are currently the best (and, often, the only) way to get hands-on training.

CHAPTER 15

WHEN IT'S TIME TO SELL

Do I Need to Read This Chapter?

You should read this chapter if you want to discover

- ✔ What you need to do before you sell your boat.
- ✔ How to price your boat to sell.
- ✔ Where to advertise your boat for sale.
- ✔ The advantages of working with a dealer or a broker.
- ✔ What you gain (and lose) by selling a boat by yourself.
- ✔ What paperwork is required when you sell a boat.

PARTING IS SUCH SWEET SORROW

If you followed the advice in this book before buying your boat, I bet that your decision to sell is based not on dissatisfaction but, rather, on that your needs (or desires) have changed and it's time to move on. If this is the case, whatever sadness you may feel at the thought of losing an old friend will be tempered with anticipation of what's to come. Owning two boats can more than double the inevitable headaches, so I suggest that you sell your present boat before you take on the challenges of a new one.

Get Your Boat Ready to Sell
Clean Up the Junk

This is an easily overlooked but terribly important part of the process. You have to start by getting rid of things. When we have a property that is in any way "home," we forget just how much all the good stuff that makes us feel comfortable will appear to be junk and clutter to a prospective buyer. Try to make the boat look more as it did when you purchased it. You're going to have to remove these things anyway after you've sold the boat, so why not help make the sale easier by removing them now? Don't strip the boat bare; you will probably continue to use it, and whenever you show it you'll want it to look usable. But clean out your refrigerator, empty the *hanging lockers* [the nautical equivalent of closets], and get rid of all the unnecessary junk in the drawers and other stowage areas. You'll be amazed at how much of it is actually trash. The rest of it can go home or into temporary storage. Just get it off the boat.

Get Started

First, you have to forget all the fun your boat has given you and also discard any "forgiveness" you may have developed for its shortcomings and idiosyncrasies. You have to try to view your baby as if you didn't know it at all. This is the way prospective buyers will see it, and the closer you can come to seeing your boat with fresh, unbiased eyes, the better your chances of making it the most presentable and desirable to others. Don't discard your passion, however; it may help you persuade a potential buyer that you are selling a great boat. But try to be as objective as you possibly can so you will be able to eliminate everything that might stand in the way of a sale.

Clean and Paint the Bottom

This will allow the boat to survey better, in both its on-the-ground inspection and its sea trial. A boat with a clean and freshly painted bottom performs better. It also looks better than a bottom covered with marine growth. To save a few bucks, you can coordinate the haulout and repainting with your own premarket survey, so you won't have to haul the boat twice.

Have Another Survey?

Yes. It is a good idea to invest in a full prepurchase survey, though in this case it will be called a premarket survey, since you, rather than a prospective buyer, will be paying for it. This will cost you. Doing so can pay in the long run because it might save you from being blindsided by unknown defects that a prospective buyer's surveyor would certainly uncover if they exist. This way you can correct any major problems before you put the boat on the market. The good news is that you can more or less disregard the minor problems. By correcting the major ones, you eliminate the key stumbling blocks to a sale, which is your objective. No one has ever refused to buy a boat because it has minor problems as long as the seller is willing to bend on the price to allow for them. I suggest this approach because it will usually be less costly than fixing them. But don't try to hide any problems you know about, even if they are minor; lack of full disclosure can come back to bite you.

If your maintenance program has been up to snuff and you're reasonably sure a surveyor won't find any unpleasant surprises, you can skip the premarket survey. One of my proudest moments as a professional captain came when a surveyor told the buyer of a boat I'd taken care of for years: "I can't say you won't have problems with this boat; I couldn't say that about a new one. But I can tell you that this boat has been maintained very, very well. I saw no signs of jury-rigging or other shortcuts. Everything appears to have always been repaired the way it should have been; and you won't find that on a lot of used boats." Of course, keeping the boat in that condition had cost its owner some money, as I had told him it would when he hired me. But I believe it was money well spent. When he sold the boat, there was nothing in the buyer's survey report to suggest even a slight drop in price and my boss got exactly what he was asking. I tend to harp on this, perhaps even to the point of your saying, "yeah, yeah, yeah, I heard you already," but it's absolutely true: Proper maintenance pays!

Clean the Bilges

If you've been keeping up with routine maintenance, this won't be a huge chore. But even if you have to make up for months (or even years) of neglect, it is important enough to undertake this job in earnest. Steam-clean them if you must, but don't settle for less than totally spotless. Sometimes it's even worthwhile to repaint the bilges, especially in the engine compartment, so they not only look clean but actually shine.

Eliminate Leaks

Whether they are seawater, coolant, fuel, lube oil, or transmission fluid, any leaks in your engine compartment will only spoil your cleanup efforts—often, quickly. Having a competent marine mechanic find and correct any leaks on or around the engines will be money well spent. After this is done, you might even have the engines thoroughly steam-cleaned and repainted with heat-resistant engine paint. If you paint them white, new leaks will be easier to spot and thus nip in the bud. And shiny white engines look better than dirty ones any day. Potential buyers can't help but be impressed.

It's also worthwhile to repair any leaks around ports, hatches, or windows because most buyers will want to keep all water on the outside of the boat regardless of its source.

Add Some Spit and Polish

A wise advertising executive many years ago advised, "Don't sell the steak; sell the sizzle!" As it applies to your boat, this means you can temporarily forget about such meaningful matters as performance and concentrate on the boat's appearance. Another wise person once stated the obvious, but we must remember it nonetheless: "You never get a second chance to make a first impression." If your boat is absolutely dazzling when prospective buyers first view it, you face a greater probability of their being interested in buying it. They will still have to like the layout and other physical aspects, and the boat will ultimately have to perform well in a sea trial, but the deal won't get anywhere near the sea trial stage if you don't first get the prospects interested.

Detail, Detail, Detail

This makes it absolutely essential to invest in hiring a professional detailing service. These people will go over every inch of every visible surface to make sure that shiny objects really shine, that clear ones are truly clear, and that painted ones are waxed and polished to their absolute sparkling best. Boats these days don't usually have much *brightwork*

Quick Tips

Detailing can be a do-it-yourself project. But there are two good reasons it shouldn't be. One, it takes a lot of time to do the job correctly, and chances are you can earn more than what the detailers will charge by doing your normal work while they detail your boat. Two, there are trade secrets to detailing that you probably don't know. To put it bluntly, professional detailers will probably do a much better job.

[varnished wood], but if yours has any, even just a tiny amount, make sure it is all smooth, bright, and shiny before you try to sell the boat. Nothing can be a quicker turnoff than varnish that needs work. The correlation isn't necessarily valid, but obviously neglected brightwork often suggests overall neglect, which makes many people question the condition of the boat as a whole.

Don't Do the Unnecessary

If the exterior has become too dull for waxing and buffing to help much or if the interior is getting worn and shabby, you'll generally be better off reducing the sale price than you would be refinishing or redecorating. So I suggest you get estimates but do nothing.

You could have the exterior refinished; there are several very good paint systems designed to go over old gelcoat and the results can be amazing—like new, in most cases. But this means using professional painters, which will cost you plenty—probably more than the refinishing adds to the value of your boat. Plus, making the outside look brand-new has the possible unwanted outcome of making the inside look shabbier by comparison. So I'd suggest refinishing the exterior only if the interior isn't too bad and everything else is near perfect. As for redoing the interior, you stand a better chance of selling a boat that "needs some cosmetic work" than you'd probably have trying to sell one that's obviously just been redone (and, hence, would be a poor candidate for having the work done again anytime soon) in colors or patterns the prospective buyer absolutely hates. If the boat performs well, you can tell the potential buyer: "I know the boat needs new upholstery, so I'm knocking X dollars off my asking price to allow for it, which means you can have the work done to your liking and still get a very good deal

Quick Tips

One exception to the above advice can be carpeting. If the coverings on the cockpit or interior soles are terribly worn or badly stained, they can make the whole boat look worse than it really is. If you have any really bad sections, replace all the boat's carpets (so everything will match) with inexpensive new ones. Don't get the cheapest grade available; it can reflect badly on the entire boat. But don't spend too much, either. For one thing, you're probably going to have to eat the cost regardless—new carpet doesn't really add to the boat's value but merely makes it show better. The less you spend, the better your bottom line. You also don't want anything that looks too good because it might make worn upholstery or other interior finishes seem even worse. Also, an obviously expensive new carpet yells out, "You can't replace me! I'm brand-new and still worth a lot of money." And yet, even if you've selected something comfortably neutral, it might not go with your buyer's idea of perfect decor. Your new carpet should look like it doesn't need to be replaced but could be, with no regrets, to complement a new decor. It's a bit of a tightrope to walk, but a good carpet dealer should be able to help you pick the right product.

in the process. You won't find a better price on a boat like this anywhere, and you will have exactly the interior you want."

How to Set an Attractive Price

This is the easy part. All you have to do is review some used boat ads and listings to see what similar boats are going for and then set your price a shade lower. But don't set your asking price any lower than true market value. In fact, you actually need some bargaining room, so you should start a little higher than market value (but no more than 10%), unless you are in a real hurry to sell and can stand to eat the difference.

Your premarket survey report will contain an estimate of fair market value, and you can also search for the book value of your make and model online (see the Resources section). If you're working with a lender on purchasing a new boat, you can also ask him or her for advice on pricing your old one. You have several avenues available from which to draw a consensus. Never set your price too low. This can scare buyers, who may wonder, "What's the catch?" But always remember that the lower the price of your boat in relation to comparable models, the more attractive it can be. Everyone likes a bargain!

Finding Ready and Willing Buyers

With a Little Help from a Broker or Dealer

The easiest way to get rid of your old boat is to trade it in with the dealer that's selling you your new one—if you chose correctly for the old boat, it will be the same dealer. You'll perhaps net a little less, but when you factor all the headaches you eliminate, the slightly lower gain will undoubtedly balance out.

Of course, this only works when you are buying a new boat from a dealer. When you're buying a larger vessel, particularly a previously owned yacht, chances are you are working with a broker and a trade-in is probably out of the question. But because you don't want to own more than one vessel, you can list your old boat with the same broker and make it clear that you will not be ready to buy a new one until the old one goes. You can also offer a commission that's a couple of points over standard if the boat is sold by a certain date. Either of these can be effective motivation for the broker to move your boat quickly.

Going It Alone

This is doing it the hard way. But the option does have an upside: you don't have to share the proceeds with anyone (except the lender, of course, if you still owe on the principal). The downside is considerable, however. And though you won't have any sales commission to pay, you will have expenses, so your net will always be less than your gross.

Make Like Madison Avenue One main expense will be advertising. If people don't know your boat is for sale, they can't even begin to think about buying it. Publications such as *Soundings* and *Boat Trader* are relatively inexpensive to advertise in, and they have many readers who are primarily looking for one thing: used boats. Local newspaper classifieds are also a possibility, though how good depends on where you live. I've had luck in selling upscale boats with ads in the *Wall Street Journal*, though I can only guess as to whether this would be a good route for smaller vessels. One thing I do know is that the more exposure you buy, the better your chances of finding an interested buyer. You want to be economical and efficient and not waste money advertising to those who aren't interested in buying a boat. So while greater exposure is good, targeted exposure is better, which is why I suggest the two boating publications mentioned above. Also consider that when you choose to sell the boat by yourself, you miss out on being included in the multiple listing services to which most brokers and dealers subscribe. So your advertising takes on greater importance; it's the only exposure you have.

It's important for your ads to have good pictures and enticing, but definitely not overblown, copy. In short, merely advertising a boat for sale is generally not enough. You need strong ads that will attract prospective buyers. Creating them is rarely a do-it-yourself project unless you happen to work in advertising.

Keep in mind that publications have lead time. That is, you must submit (and often pay for) your ad weeks before it will actually appear in print. Fortunately, there are Internet boat-selling services that have a much shorter lead time. I can't vouch for any of them (I have no firsthand experience with them), but given the general overall effectiveness of the Internet in selling things, I have to believe it should be good for boats as well. I've listed some possibilities in the Resources section. As a bonus, some of them are even free.

If your marina or storage facility allows it, be sure to display a "For Sale" sign on your boat. There's no telling when a passerby might find your boat attractive, and if it isn't obviously for sale, you could miss many a prime prospect. The drawback here is that while lots of facilities have no objection to such signs, others consider them to be visual blight and forbid them on any boat anywhere on the premises. By the way, if you have listed the boat with a broker, s/he will most probably want to hang a "For Sale by . . ." sign, so this advice isn't strictly for when you are selling the boat yourself.

Show and Sell   Finally, if you opt for selling your boat by yourself, you have to allow time for showing it to prospective buyers—*a lot* of time, if your ads are good. You also have to be ready to put up with tire kickers (as the auto industry calls them), people who aren't really looking to buy but are just looking. You also have to develop a thick skin when prospective buyers start talking about everything that's wrong with the boat—this is your baby they're putting down. You can correct them if they've obviously missed an important detail, but for the most part you can only grin and bear it—and also ignore it. Some of the negative talk will be serious objection, but the bulk of it will be aimed at making you believe they think your boat is worth much less than you are asking.

It's only my opinion, but for what it's worth, the time you have to spend in showing your boat to every single prospect can be very expensive when you consider what you could be earning if you were practicing your own profession or trade instead of acting as a boat salesperson. When you do the math, I would bet you'll conclude that the cost of having professionals handle the sale of your boat is actually money in the bank. Think of all the headaches you'll save as well.

Passing the Papers

Among the things you'll normally need to provide to your buyer(s) are:

- proof of ownership; preferably, a bill of sale
- a title you've signed off as the current owner (if possible; remember, some states don't issue titles)
- the original registration if it's a numbered boat

A proper bill of sale will include:

- the buyer's name and address
- your name, address, and signature
- the length of the craft
- the year it was built
- its brand, or the name of the manufacturer
- its hull identification number (HIN)
- the previous registration number, if applicable
- the date of purchase
- the purchase price and, where applicable, proof that the sales tax has been paid (if it has)

Not all states require it, but having your (seller's) signature notarized isn't a bad idea for every bill of sale. Fortunately, if you've chosen to have the sale handled by a dealer, the paperwork will all be taken care of, even to having a notary public on staff.

As noted in Chapter 5, the Coast Guard bill of sale form (CG-1340) *must* be used in the sale of a documented vessel or the new owner won't be able to get a new document. These bills of sale must be notarized and submitted in duplicate. They must be error free, also; the Coast Guard is notoriously finicky about perfection on the forms required for documentation and will reject paperwork for even the smallest discrepancy.

Since a broker will most often handle the sale of vessels large enough to be documented, the brokerage office will probably prepare all requisite paperwork so the buyer and seller don't have to give it a thought. But a little awareness never hurts.

It's a Wrap

WRAP

✔ Trading your old boat in is often the easiest and simplest way to get rid of it if you are also buying a new one.

✔ Listing your boat with a broker will also get it exposure through brokerage multiple listing services.

✔ You can learn your boat's true value from a premarket survey, which can also alert you to any major problems you should correct before selling it.

✔ You should set an asking price no higher than 10% over the boat's true market value and be prepared to ultimately accept less.

✔ Don't waste money in redecorating; it won't add enough to the boat's value to make it anywhere near worthwhile.

✔ But definitely have your boat in its most showable condition at all times, and hire professional detailers to get (and keep) it that way.

GALLERY OF POWERBOATS

When shopping for a boat, you'll see descriptions that may be puzzling because they are unfamiliar. Here are some photos to help you recognize various types. Please understand that this gallery is by no means all inclusive; it does not represent every builder or model, though I did strive for a reasonably representative balance.

BOWRIDERS

Bowriders are a type of runabout, but they have seats up forward while runabout bows are enclosed with a foredeck. The Regal 1900 Bowrider keeps the traditional pointed bow, while the Four Winns 244FS displays a common trend in the type and is broader. Both boats are sterndrives, while the Sea-Doo 230 Challenger is a jet. This photo also shows that the open bow can be multipurpose.

REGAL 1900 BOWRIDER
(Regal Marine Industries)

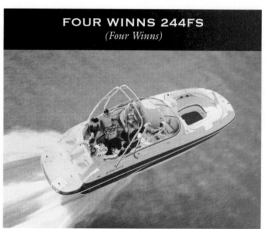

FOUR WINNS 244FS
(Four Winns)

SEA-DOO 230 CHALLENGER
(Bombardier Recreational Products)

CENTER CONSOLES

Logically named for their freestanding helm, these boats also usually have an open bow. We see the most basic form in the Boston Whaler 180 Dauntless. The Cobia 314 swaps the pilot seat for a leaning post, though it has other seats, and is totally rigged for fishing. The Regulator 29 Classic takes "for fishing" to the extreme by eschewing seats completely.

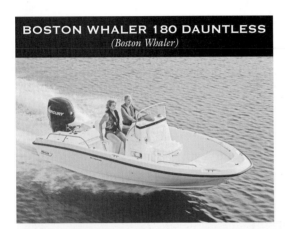

BOSTON WHALER 180 DAUNTLESS
(Boston Whaler)

COBIA 314
(Cobia)

REGULATOR 29 CLASSIC
(Tom Reid, courtesy Regulator Marine)

CONVERTIBLES/SEDANS/SPORTFISHERMEN

What's the difference? These boats all feature a flying bridge and a cockpit, and their designation can be more about their rigging than their design. But not always. There's no doubt that the as-yet-unrigged Cavileer 53 is as much a fishing boat as the Luhrs 35 beside it. And while this Regal 4080 has a functional flying bridge, we'd still call it a sedan even if it had outriggers—the bridge lacks the view of the cockpit that's needed in a convertible, which is a more family-friendly name for "sportfisherman."

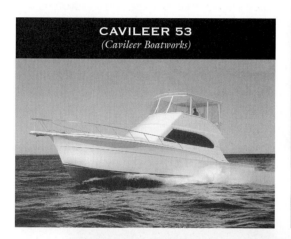

CAVILEER 53
(Cavileer Boatworks)

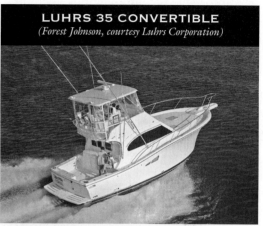

LUHRS 35 CONVERTIBLE
(Forest Johnson, courtesy Luhrs Corporation)

REGAL 4080 FLYBRIDGE SEDAN
(Regal Marine Industries)

CUDDY CABINS

Cuddy is an old seafaring word that means small cabin, so the term "cuddy cabin" is as redundant as it is common. Cuddies appear when designers don't want to sacrifice a boat's open space or when it's too small to have anything bigger. The cabins are often minimal, like the one on this Boston Whaler 320 Outrage, which, though small, offers shelter and protection that's lacking in the bow of the open center-console version of the boat (builders often offer several models based on the same hull). The Larson Cabrio 240 is a smaller boat, but more of it is cabin, so the cuddy is larger and has everything you expect in comfortable accommodations, including a galley with a dual-voltage refrigerator, stove, microwave, and sink, and an enclosed head with a shower.

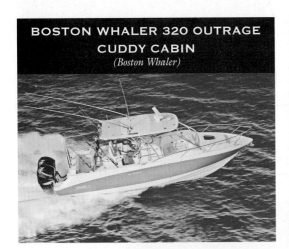

BOSTON WHALER 320 OUTRAGE
CUDDY CABIN
(Boston Whaler)

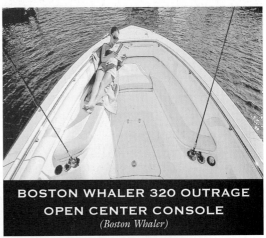

BOSTON WHALER 320 OUTRAGE
OPEN CENTER CONSOLE
(Boston Whaler)

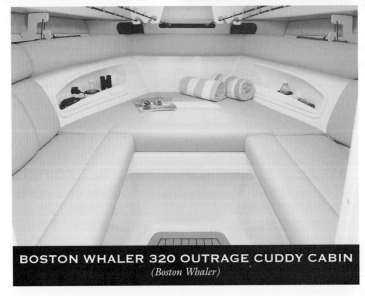

BOSTON WHALER 320 OUTRAGE CUDDY CABIN
(Boston Whaler)

LARSON CABRIO 240
(Larson Boats)

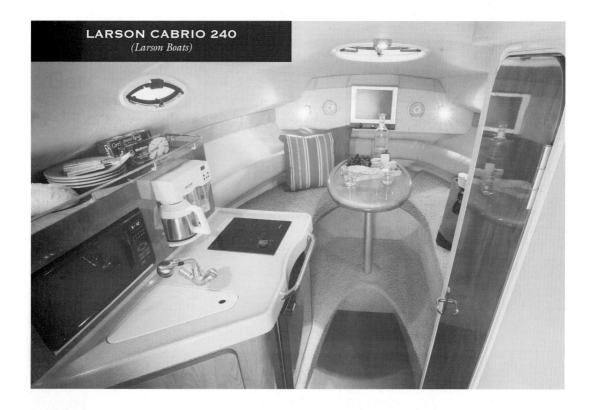

LARSON CABRIO 240
(Larson Boats)

DECK BOATS

These are another variation on the runabout, an expansion of the bowrider concept. And "expansion" is an apt description: deck boats are usually even broader in the bow, often nearly rectangular. Most of them also have a boarding ladder in the bow, which is appropriate since the entire boat is cockpit. The Four Winns 224FS is typical of the type. The Glastron DX 235 expands on the concept even further by adding a table to the forward section. Deck boats offer many advantages of a pontoon boat while retaining the performance and handling characteristics that result from having a true hull.

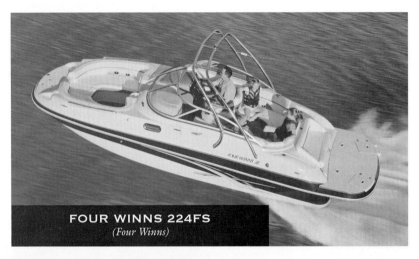

FOUR WINNS 224FS
(Four Winns)

GLASTRON DX 235
(Glastron)

EXPRESS CRUISERS

These boats have a large, often two-level, cockpit with a raised portion forward for the helm. Many of them feature an added "guest room" (or at least an expanded saloon) beneath the forward area; in others, it is engine room. The cockpit can be totally open (and enclosed, when needed, by canvas and plastic), as in the Regal 4060, or it can have a hardtop (and maybe a half-tower), as on the Wellcraft 330 Coastal. All express cruisers have a cabin down and forward, and some also have a permanent enclosure on the cockpit level that may be either modern in styling, as in the Riviera 4700 Sport Yacht, or more traditional, as in the Grand Banks 49 Eastbay SX. Express cruisers are great for most activities, including fishing, though they lack the visibility of a flying bridge.

REGAL 4060 COMMODORE
(Regal Marine Industries)

WELLCRAFT 330 COASTAL
(Wellcraft Boats)

RIVIERA 4700 SPORT YACHT
(Riviera)

GRAND BANKS 49 EASTBAY SX
(Grand Banks Yachts)

HOUSEBOATS

Once more "house" than "boat," these spacious craft still boast a huge interior and are ideal for inland cruising. Houseboats are typically more seaworthy than they used to be, and many are now NMMA certified, but they are still better suited to lakes, rivers, and other protected waters. Houseboats come in all sizes, from the 8-by31-foot (and thus trailerable) Catamaran Cruisers Lil Hobo to the massive 20-by-119-foot custom-built Sumerset, with an amazing variety in between.

CATAMARAN CRUISERS LIL HOBO
(Catamaran Cruisers)

SUMERSET CUSTOM-BUILT HOUSEBOAT
(Sumerset Houseboats)

MOTORYACHTS

These craft have accommodations that are similar to those of a houseboat (albeit less spacious) but they also have a greater ability to venture far and wide. Ranging from the Cruisers 385 to the Grand Banks 72 Aleutian and even larger, motoryachts offer superb cruising and also make great liveaboard boats.

CRUISERS 385 MOTORYACHT
(Cruisers Yachts)

GRAND BANKS 72 ALEUTIAN RP
(Grand Banks Yachts)

PERFORMANCE BOATS

Some are center consoles, and a few are even powered by outboards, but most needle-nosed "zoomies" are inboard cuddies on steroids (though there are performance cruisers, which have an amazingly spacious cabin for their size and shape, far more than a mere cuddy). Many people call every boat of this type a "cigarette boat," but Cigarette is just one brand among many. And the builder of this 35 ICBM/Lightning would be quick to point out that it's not a Cigarette, it's a Fountain.

FOUNTAIN 35 ICBM/LIGHTNING
(Fountain Powerboats)

RIBS

"RIB" stands for rigid inflatable boat. These craft have a hard bottom (usually fiberglass, but occasionally aluminum) combined with a soft inflated collar that forms the topsides. This type is used for everything from tenders, like this Novurania Williams Turbojet, to the multipassenger Ribcraft 9.0.

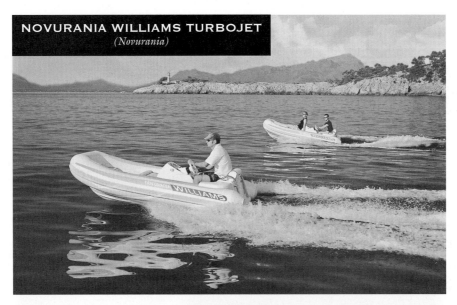

NOVURANIA WILLIAMS TURBOJET
(Novurania)

RIBCRAFT 9.0 OFFSHORE
(Ribcraft)

RUNABOUTS

The quintessential motorboat, these are available in lengths from the low teens to over 30 feet (though most are between 18 and 24 feet). Whether powered by outboard, stern-drive, inboard, or jet, they usually have a relatively shallow draft and a spacious open cockpit with plentiful seating.

The Four Winns 258V and the Glastron 209 are just two examples of the nearly infinite variety of cockpit seating/sunpad arrangements these boats may have. For the most part, runabouts are fun with a capital F!

FOUR WINNS 258V
(Four Winns)

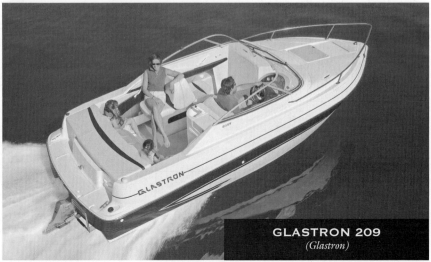

GLASTRON 209
(Glastron)

SKI BOATS

Ski boats are also a variation of the runabout, yet they have their own special attributes. They throw a very slight wake and are highly maneuverable, especially for single-screw inboards, as many of them are—note the engine boxes. The MasterCraft Prostar 190 has a pylon to attach the towrope just forward of the engine box. Correct Craft's Ski Nautique 206 has its attachment forward of the transom also, but not on a pylon and mounted farther aft. Given that they are meant for use on waters flat enough for skiing, really good ski boats are often not that comfortable when the seas kick up.

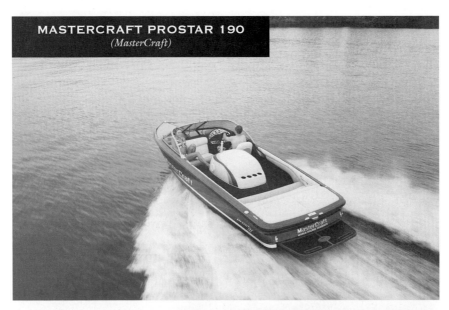

MASTERCRAFT PROSTAR 190
(MasterCraft)

CORRECT CRAFT SKI NAUTIQUE 206
(Correct Craft)

TRAWLER YACHTS

With lines based on the North Sea fishing vessels from which these boats derive their name, trawler yachts are usually as seaworthy as they look. Some models, like the Krogen 48 North Sea, are pure displacement and relatively slow (as was the entire genre in the early years), but many, like the Nordhavn 62, now have a semidisplacement hull that allows more speed while retaining the overall seakeeping qualities and salty appearance that draw people to this style in the first place.

KROGEN 48 NORTH SEA
(Kadey-Krogen Yachts)

NORDHAVN 62
(Pacific Asian Enterprises)

WAKEBOARD BOATS

These are also a specialized form of runabout. While many are made by builders who also produce ski boats, and despite the obvious similarities (both types are designed to pull people on the water), there is one huge difference: good ski boats throw a small, flat wake, while wakeboarders want a large one. There are some ski boats that can be ballasted down in the stern to produce a bigger wake, but dedicated wakeboarders often prefer a dedicated wakeboard boat. And given the aerial acrobatics a good wakeboarder will want to perform, the best towboat for this sport pulls from a higher point than most skiers would want or need—note the arch on the models shown.

The Four Winns 180H is a good example of a boat made by a builder who has not been especially noted for ski boats. But many, such as the MasterCraft MariStar 200, are still produced by well-known ski-boat companies. In both, the arch provides not only a high point for pulling the wakeboarder but also a place to stow the boards when they're not being used. Note that the MasterCraft is also a bowrider!

FOUR WINNS 180H
(Four Winns)

MASTERCRAFT MARISTAR 200
(MasterCraft)

WALKAROUNDS

A variation on the basic cuddy, these boats are also intended to resemble center consoles in that an angler can work a fish from any part of the boat, walking around the entire perimeter if need be. They are designed to permit this while still including a fairly comfortable, albeit compact, cabin. The Hydra-Sports 230WA shows the typical layout; the Seaswirl 1851WA shows how functional the design can be.

HYDRA-SPORTS 230WA
(Hydra-Sports Boats)

SEASWIRL 1851WA
(Seaswirl Boats)

RESOURCES

The following pages contain contact information for firms or organizations either specifically mentioned in the text or whose principal activity is strongly related to the subject matter.

1. DO YOU REALLY NEED TO BUY A BOAT?

Boat Clubs

While most boat clubs are local organizations, a number of them of them are growing beyond their local boundaries and are either franchising or licensing their program on a wider basis. The locations vary considerably in their geography, but the expanding nature of the concept suggests that there will be more of them by the time you read this than there are as I write it.

All Points Boating Club,
   www.allpointsboatingclub.com
Boat Fleet,
   www.theboatfleet.com
Freedom Boat Club,
   www.freedomboatclub.com
Nautical Toys Boat Clubs,
   www.nauticaltoysboats.com

Fractional Ownership

SailTime Licensing Group,
   www.sailtime.com/powerboating

SeaNet,
   www.seanetco.com
Voyage Yacht Share,
   www.voyageyachtshare.com
Yachtlease,
   www.yachtlease.com

Leasing (Outright)

ING Private Banking,
   www.ingprivatebanking.com/
   yachtleasing.html
YachtLease International,
   www.yachtvantage.com

Rentals

Because most rental operations are small and local I've made no attempt to list them here; you'll do better with your local Yellow Pages or searching online by locale if you plan to travel. Boatrenting.com, however, is a clearinghouse for rentable boats located all over the world and allows you to book rentals online.

2. CHOOSING THE RIGHT BOAT

Books

To expand on information that was highlighted in this chapter, you might also be interested in reading the following, which are available at major bookstores.

Getting Started in Powerboating. *3rd ed. Bob Armstrong. Camden, Maine: International Marine, 2005.*

Sorensen's Guide to Powerboats: How to Evaluate Design, Construction, and Performance. *2nd ed. Eric Sorensen. Camden, Maine: International Marine, 2008.*

Magazines

Your search for the right boat should include reading magazines devoted to the sport; almost all of them feature reviews and/or tests of different boats and reading them is a great way to become familiar with new models. The following list may not be complete, but it's reasonably so and a good place to start. Several also have online boat listings.

Boating,
   www.boatingmag.com
Boating Life,
   www.boatinglife.com
Boating World,
   www.boatingworldonline.com
Go Boating,
   www.goboatingmag.com
Lakeland Boating,
   www.lakelandboating.com
MotorBoating,
   www.motorboating.com
Northeast Boating (formerly Offshore),
   www.offshoremag.net
Power & Motoryacht,
   www.powerandmotoryacht.com
Powerboat,
   www.powerboatmag.com
Power Cruising,
   www.powercruisingmag.com
Sea,
   www.seamagazine.com

Soundings,
   www.soundingspub.com
Yachting,
   www.yachtingmagazine.com

3. NEW OR USED?

Blue Books

ABOS Marine Blue Book,
   www.pricedigests.com
BUC Used Boat Price Guide,
   www.bucvalue.com
NADA Marine Appraisal Guide,
   www.nada.com/b2b/ products/print_products. asp?s=focD886-95427616-7532

Online Boat Listings

The following sites all pride themselves on having a huge number of listings (and, often, links to other sources and other information as well). Any of them would be a likely place to start looking for a boat, either new or used.

www.boat-finder.com
www.boats.com
www.boattest.com
www.boattrader.com
www.everyboat.com
www.iboats.com
www.newboats.com
www.soundingspub.com
www.usedboats.com
www.yachtaccess.com

Repo Sales

www.americanyachtsales.com
www.boatbankrepo.com
www.yachtauctions.com

4. PACKAGE DEALS

Accessories, Equipment, and Supplies

Even if you're able to get the most complete package deal ever, you'll still need other equipment and supplies eventually. Here are some good sources.

> www.boatersworld.com
> www.defender.com
> www.discountmarinesupplies.com
> www.go2marine.com
> www.marineengine.com
> www.myboatsgear.com
> www.overtons.com
> www.westmarine.com

Survival Gear

This will rarely be a part of any package deal. Survival equipment, such as a life raft or EPIRB, is really only necessary on boats that venture far from safe ports either via long open-water passages or simply by cruising to more remote regions where neither assistance nor ports of refuge are conveniently close. But since this equipment should be considered along with the purchase of many boat types, I'm including some sources here.

> www.lrse.com
> www.reveresupply.com
> www.winslowliferaft.com

5. FINANCING

Associations

The National Marine Bankers Association (www.marinebankers.org) is an organization of lenders that specialize in boat loans. Any NMBA member (www.marinebankers.org/links/memberlist.asp) will be able to provide more than just the money to buy a boat.

Banks

Always look first to the bank you normally do business with; you know them and they probably know you. But to broaden your horizons, keep in mind that the following organizations actively seek boat loan business from nearly everywhere; they may have an office near you.

> www.bankofamerica.com
> www.key.com

Credit Reports/Scores

Reports from all three credit reporting agencies are available for free once a year (once every 12 months). For simplicity's sake, you can get these reports from the Annual Credit Report Request Service, www.annualcreditreport.com.

For individual reports, or to dispute an entry on a report, you must contact each reporting agency directly: www.equifax.com, www.experian.com, www.transunion.com.

For information on credit scores, contact Fair Isaac Corporation, www.myfico.com.

Credit Unions

Because credit unions are usually highly localized institutions, I've made no attempt to list any here, other than for Digital Federal Credit Union (www.dcu.org), a "sort of" national organization that operates extensively online. Chances are that if you are eligible for membership in local credit union, which is a requirement for getting a loan, you will already know how and where to contact it.

Documentation

Federal documentation is managed by the Coast Guard National Vessel Documentation Center. For more information, go to www.uscg.mil/hq/g-m/vdoc/faq.htm. There are also agencies you can hire to assist you with all the paperwork involved in documenting a vessel. You'll find them advertised in the classified sections of most boating magazines.

Financial Service Companies

www.beaconcredit.com/boat-loans.htm
www.boatfinance.com/boat/index.cfm
www.boatloans.net
www.eboatloans.com
www.essexcredit.com/boat.shtml
www.excelcredit.com

6. WHERE WILL YOU KEEP IT?

Finding Available Space

www.discoverboating.com/boating/marinas.aspx
www.marinas.com

7. THE JOYS OF TRAILERING

Magazines

Trailer Boats,
www.trailerboats.com

Trailer Manufacturers

www.discoverboating.com/buying/certified/trailers.aspx

8. CHOOSING THE RIGHT DEALER

www.discoverboating.com/buying/certified/dealers.aspx

9. BE YOUR OWN SURVEYOR

Online Value Guides

BoatU.S. valuation service,
www.boatus.com/buyer/valueform.asp
www.bucvalue.com

10. BUT YOU'LL NEED A PROFESSIONAL SURVEY, TOO

Professional Organizations

National Association of Marine Surveyors,
www.nams-cms.org
Society of Accredited Marine Surveyors,
www.marinesurvey.org

Referral Service

BoatU.S. surveyor referral,
www.boatus.com/insurance/survey.asp

11. INSURANCE: ANOTHER WAY BOATS ARE DIFFERENT

Before you agree to a policy, it is wise to check the financial stability of the insurer you'll be depending on. A.M. Best Company has been rating insurers since 1899 and now offers online rating information at www3.ambest.com/ratings.

Agencies/Programs/Providers

Allstate,
www.allstate.com/boat-insurance.aspx
Atlass Insurance Group,
www.atlassinsurance.com/boat_yacht_insurance
INAMAR Marine Insurance,
www.inamarmarine.com
Old United Insurance Companies,
www.oldunited.com

Sea Insure,
　　www.seainsure.com
State Farm,
　　www.statefarm.com/insurance/
　　boat/boat.asp
United Marine Underwriters,
　　www.unitedmarine.net
Voyager Marine Insurance,
　　www.voyagermarine.com
Worldwide Marine Underwriters,
　　www.worldwidemarineins.com

Associations with Insurance Programs

BoatU.S.,
　　www.boatus.com/insurance
National Boat Owner's Association,
　　www.nboat.com

Towing Services with Membership Plans

BoatU.S.,
　　www.boatus.com/towing
Sea Tow,
　　www.seatow.com

12. MAINTENANCE

Engines

Each of the following websites is a good place to start when looking for authorized parts and/or service for most of the currently popular makes of engine or genset.

Inboards

　　www.crusaderengines.com
　　www.cumminsonan.com/marine
　　www.cmdmarine.com
　　www.cummins.com
　　www.detroitdiesel.com/Off-Highway/
　　　MtuDetroitDiesel

www.indmar.com
www.kohlerpower.com/marine
www.perkins-sabre.com
www.volvo.com/volvopenta
www.westerbeke.com
www.yanmarmarine.com

Outboards

　　www.evinrude.com
　　www.honda-marine.com
　　www.mercurymarine.com
　　www.suzukimarine.com
　　www.tohatsu.com
　　www.yamaha-motor.com

Manuals and Parts

　　www.marineengine.com
　　www.marinepartsexpress.com
　　www.repairmanual.com

13. WARRANTIES

Basic warranties are provided by boatbuilders and/or their suppliers. Extended warranties are provided by third-party insurers. I've listed some of the leading suppliers of extended warranties for watercraft and other recreational products. There are others, but they all work only through established dealerships.

　　www.excelcredit.com/boat_yacht_
　　　service_contract.aspx
　　www.oldunited.com
　　www.warrantyservicescompany.com

14. EDUCATION

Basic Requirements

Boater education is mandatory in many states but not in all. Even among the states where education is mandatory there is considerable divergence as to exactly who must meet the requirements.

> BoatU.S. Foundation State Educational
> Requirements,
>   www.boatus.org/onlinecourse/
>   edrequirements.htm
> National Association of State Boating Law
> Administrators,
>   www.nasbla.org

Classroom Instruction

> BoatU.S. Foundation,
>   www.boatus.com/courseline
> Marine University's Boat Dealer Academy,
>   www.boatdealeracademy.com
> USCG Auxiliary,
>   www.cgaux.org (click on Boating Education)
> USCG Local Notice to Mariners,
>   www.navcen.uscg.gov/lnm (lists current
>   and upcoming boating safety classes)
> United States Power Squadrons,
>   www.usps.org (click on Take a Boating
>   Course)

Hands-On

While hands-on instruction tends to be localized, this type of training is so valuable that it can be worth traveling to find it, and many captain/instructors will also fly to you if you pay their expenses. So I am including a number of sources here despite their essentially limited geographical coverage at the present time.

> Captain Bob Armstrong,
>   www.captainbobarmstrong.com
> Boatboy Marine Training,
>   www.boatboymarinetraining.com
> Chapman School of Seamanship,
>   www.chapman.org

> Captain Fred Christian,
>   www.captainfred.com
> Confident Captain/Ocean Pros,
>   www.confidentcaptain.com
> Captain Phil Cusumano,
>   www.onthewatertraining.com
> Captain Shar Fillingham,
>   www.powerboatsos.com
> Tres Martin's Performance Boat
>   School,
>   www.performanceboatschool.com
> Captain Ron Morin,
>   www.serviceafloat.com
> Offshore Marine,
>   www.yachtdeliveryusa.com
> San Juan Yachting,
>   www.sanjuanyachting.com/
>   instruction.htm
> Sea Safety Marine Service,
>   www.handsonboating.com
> Southwest Florida Yachts,
>   www.flsailandcruiseschool.com

Home Study

Home study courses do not meet the mandatory education requirements of all the states that have them. And while no form of boating education is a waste of time, it would be disappointing to take a course with the expectation of satisfying your state's education requirements only to learn that it didn't. Always check first!

> America's Boating Course,
>   www.americasboatingcourse.com.
> Boat Ed,
>   www.boat-ed.com
> Boater101,
>   www.boater101.com
> BoatU.S. Foundation,
>   www.boatus.org
> Basic Boating Safety Certification Course,
>   www.boatsafe.com

15. WHEN IT'S TIME TO SELL

Online Listing Services
The following websites are all good possibilities for listing boats for sale. Some are purely online, others also offer links to their in-print partners.

www.boat-finder.com
www.boattrader.com

www.sellaboat.com
www.soundingspub.com
www.thelog.com
www.usedboats.com
www.waterskiboat.com

Online Value Guides

www.bucvalue.com
www.boatus.com/buyer/valueform.asp

INDEX

Numbers in *italic* indicate pages with illustrations.